# AN
# ANTHOLOGY
## OF
# JEWISH HUMOR
## AND
# MAXIMS

◆

A Compilation of Anecdotes, Parables,
Fables and Proverbs

With Illustrations, Biographies
and Portraits

◆

**PARDES PUBLISHING HOUSE, Inc.**

New York 10, N. Y.

5705-1945

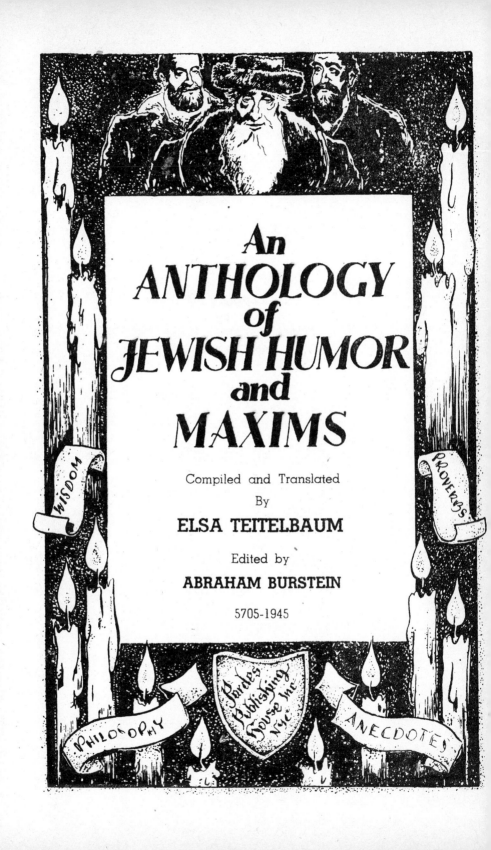

# An
# ANTHOLOGY
## of
# JEWISH HUMOR
## and
# MAXIMS

WISDOM

PROVERBS

Compiled and Translated
By
**ELSA TEITELBAUM**

Edited by
**ABRAHAM BURSTEIN**

5705-1945

Pardes Publishing House Inc. Nyc

PHILOSOPHY

ANECDOTES

DEDICATED TO
THE SACRED MEMORY OF MY
BELOVED SISTER

## SYLVIA

*"O my dove, that art in the clefts of the rock, in the covert of the steep place, let me see thy countenance, let me hear thy voice; for sweet is thy voice, and thy countenance is comely."*

*Song of Songs,* II, 14

## PUBLISHER'S NOTE

The material for this anthology was collected by the Pardes Publishing House, Inc. from various sources, for a number of years.

The major part of this collection consists of stories, which have been told, and retold through the ages, in many variations. Therefore, it was difficult to establish their origins.

We gratefully acknowledge the efforts of the author and editor, whose craftsmanship made this publication possible.

U. Z. BOOKBINDER

# EDITOR'S PREFACE

I was pleased to have been requested to assist in preparing this compilation for publication, for Jewish humor has always been a major tangential interest of mine. In jokes, anecdotes, and Sprichwörter of Jewish import one discovers more of a people's character than is true of any other racial or national form of humor. For one thing, only the Jew appears able to evolve laughter out of his own perennial disabilities; he is the only kind of person who always seems to be laughing with tears in his eyes. For another, the Jew is intensely ethical even when funny —he speaks so extensively about miserly, irreligious, and self-hating brethren because while telling the story he wants you not only to laugh but to take heed.

However, much that is called authentic Jewish humor could readily be transmuted into jokes of general interest. The man who captured an enemy soldier in order to fill out a minyan, could just as properly seize a captive to serve as a fourth at bridge. The Jewish highwayman who could not stab a victim when he discovered his knife was *milchig*, might have been equally frustrated by finding his weapon a vegetable knife, unsuited for meat. A young man wired that he was broke, and was asked whether he had used his tefillin; when he returned, his father showed him the hundred dollar bill secreted in the sack. The money

9

might as readily have been concealed in the folds of the extra shirt the traveler had neglected to don. The vaudeville "switch" can be used with most "Jewish" jokes.

But there still remains a residue that is essentially Jewish. The stories about rabbis and maggidim and sextons with which this volume abounds are in their essence tales to be told of Jews alone. Even the short quotations from Shakespeare, Rousseau, and other non-Jews, sprinkled among talmudic and midrashic citations, were included by the compiler because they so closely approach the realism of the Jewish proverb. Which is by way of saying that this book seems, above all its class (at least in the English language) a true picture of the Jew and his lighter thought processes. It reminds American Jews of the old country, the old man, and the old synagogue. It is Israel's spirit of comicality, actual and potential.

And that is why I say I was pleased to have been given a hand, howbeit late, in editing the volume. I enjoyed reading it the several times the task entailed, and I shall feel a kinship toward it during the many rereadings I have promised myself. It has interest, variety, and authenticity.

ABRAHAM BURSTEIN

# AUTHOR'S PREFACE

Through nineteen centuries of exile and persecution, Jews have never failed to extract humor out of any situation, however oppressive. They have laughed both at their foibles and their misfortune, and their animadversions on the world without have been at the same time lightsome and profound.

There are pleasant moments in the Bible and in the great literature of ancient medieval Jewry, such as the Talmud and Midrash, are not without their incisive humor.

Strangely enough, the talmudic period provided not alone a corps of professional mourners, but also a succession of funmakers who earned their livelihood after the manner of today's Cantors and Jolsons.

Jewish literature, of course, abounds in gnomic material. Proverbs, maxims, bon mots, are to be found on almost every page of the early and later Jewish writings.

The use of parables, begun in the Bible, was continued in the Talmud, and brought to its full flower in recent centuries. Itinerant preachers—*maggidim*—who could be relied on to begin their discourses with novel illustrative and didactic anecdotes achieved a tremendous popularity.

The full development of modern Jewish humor was to be found in East Europe of a century or more ago. Such names as Motke Chabad of Vilna, Mordecai Rakover of Plotzk, Ephraim Greidinger of Pinchev and Hershel of

Astropol, bring reminiscent smiles to many a countenance of present day Yiddish readers. The subjects of their barbs were plutocrats, misers, scheming paupers, ignorant pietists, inflated personalities, and similar folk to be met on these pages.

Many of the best of the Jewish tales have been forgotten or neglected with forgetfulness of their subjects. There is much work still to be done in unearthing pleasant bits of humor from crumbling Jewish documents, or, after the maner of modern folklorists, of taking down the stories of talkative old timers.

I have also included some stories, jokes and maxims by non-Jews as they seemed to fit the general collection.

I wish to proffer my thanks to Mr. U. Z. Bookbinder of the Pardes Publishing House, Inc., for his encouragement and aid through the time this work was in the making; and to Rabbi Abraham Burstein for preparing the manuscript for final publication.

E. T.

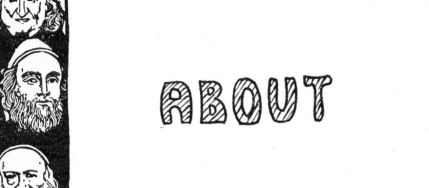

ABOUT

RABBIS

# SAGE ENTRAPMENT

A Jewish merchant came to Reb Eliah Chaim Lodzer, and confided the following story to him:

*     *     *

I am not a native of this city. Originally I come from Lomza, where you were once rabbi, but I came to Lodz to buy merchandise. I stayed at a hotel overnight, and this morning, when I was prepared to leave, settled my bill with the hotel keeper, and started out to my train. When I wanted to pay for my ticket, I realized that my wallet with a large number of bills, and my gold watch, were missing. I then remembered that I had left them on the dressing table in my room, and quickly ran back to the hotel.

"What is the meaning of this?" the owner greeted me. "Aren't you leaving?"

"No," I replied, "I've forgotten my wallet and watch."

"Really!" he exclaimed, pretending surprise. "I wouldn't know, because I haven't been in your room yet. Let us go up, and we shall see."

Before we went in, I had an intuition that I would not find anything there. As soon as we entered I sensed that someone had already visited the room, and that my belongings were gone. My heart sank with fear, because I had a large amount of money in my wallet.

"I suppose it was taken out of your pocket, while you were in the street," the hotelkeeper suggested. "You just can't trust those Lodzer thieves."

"What are you talking about!" I retorted angrily. "I distinctly remember that I put my watch and wallet on the dressing table last night, and forgot to take them this morning!"

"Nothing was ever lost in my hotel!" he shouted furiously.

Seeing that I would get nowhere with him, and realizing that he might also dispose of my belongings, I nodded, "Yes, you are right. Perhaps someone did take the things out of my pocket while I was in the street. It is just my misfortune."

With those words I left, and went directly to you. Rabbi, in our city Lomza people still speak of your great mind and sharp wit. What advice can you suggest, so that I may be able to save my money? I am certain that the hotelkeeper took it.

*   *   *

Reb Eliah Chaim knew the type of individual the hotel owner was, because he had appeared before him several days before with reference to another case, and it was obvious that the man was dishonest. After listening to the merchant's story, Reb Eliah Chaim asked him to walk into another room, and meanwhile sent the sexton to call the hotelkeeper. The other came quickly, thinking that the call was with reference to his other trial. Reb Eliah Chaim deliberately began to discuss the previous case, and the man became flustered, insisting that he had done nothing wrong. While speaking, he had a habit of holding his silver snuffbox in his hand.

"Let me have a little snuff," Reb Eliah Chaim asked, reaching for the silver case. He took a few sniffs, and then walked out of the room.

"Run quickly to the hotel," he said to the sexton, "and tell the owner's wife that her husband, who is with the rabbi now, said that she should give you the watch and the wallet that the Lomza merchant forgot." As a warrant for his request, he sent along the silver snuff case.

In a short while, the sexton returned with the watch and the wallet. Reb Eliah Chaim returned the case to the hotelkeeper, spoke with him for a while, dismissed him, and then called in the merchant, who, after giving the rabbi a description of his belongings, received his wallet and gold watch.

## PROGRESSIVE REIMBURSEMENT

A Jew dashed into the house of the Warsaw Rabbi, Reb Berish Meisels, screaming frantically, "Rabbi, save me! I've had a great misfortune!"

"Tell me what has happened, my friend," the rabbi spoke.

"I am a merchant," the Jew began, "and I came to Warsaw to buy merchandise. I arrived here on Friday afternoon and had 5000 rubles with me. Since I was afraid to stay at a hotel, I stopped at a friend's house, who is also a prominent merchant in Warsaw. Friday

17

evening, before the services, I gave him my money to hold till Sunday morning. I then asked him to return it. 'I don't remember you giving it to me, he said. 'What do you mean?' Regardless of whatever proof I presented, he continued to say that he knew nothing. Now, rabbi, what shall I do? The money was not mine. I borrowed it."

"Calm yourself," the rabbi reassured him. "You will have your money. Go into the other room, and I will send for your friend. When you hear me raise my voice, walk in."

The rabbi sent for the Warsaw merchant, and said that he wanted to discuss a certain problem with him. As soon as the rabbi began to speak loudly the other Jew walked in. When he saw the Warsaw merchant he be-gan to shout, "Rabbi, here he is! Make him return my money!"

"Do you know this man?" the rabbi asked.

"Yes, rabbi," was the reply. "He stayed at my house Saturday. I gave him food and drink, and now he says that I took his 5000 rubles. He must be insane."

The Jew gave him a piercing glance. "You yourself accepted the money and counted it before my very eyes. How can a Jew tell such a falsehood, and make such de-nials!"

"You can see that you will not get rid of this man," the rabbi intervened. "Give him a few rubles, and be done with it."

"All right, rabbi, if you say so," the Warsaw merchant agreed, "I am willing to give him twenty-five rubles, so that he will not bother me."

The Jew refused to hear of the compromise. "What is he giving me?" he shouted.

"Give him another few rubles," the ecclesiastic suggested.

"All right, rabbi, I'll give him fifty rubles, and let us finish the whole thing."

The other, hearing this, began to sob wildly, crying that if he did not regain his 5000 rubles, he would kill himself.

Turning to the Warsaw merchant, the rabbi again addressed him, "You can see that you've fallen into trouble. You will not dispose of this man so easily. Take my advice and give him a hundred."

"I am only doing this for your sake, rabbi," the merchant replied. "I'll give the nuisance a hundred, and now let us be through with it."

"I don't want charity," the poor Jew wailed. "I want my money."

"Try again," the sage pleaded. "Give him five hundred."

"As you say, rabbi," the Warsaw merchant consented.

"You are a liar and a scoundrel," the rabbi suddenly called out. "Give the Jew back his 5000 rubles immediately! Now I can clearly see that you took the money from him. I know you. You are not such a liberal individual. Some time ago I asked you for a donation, and you refused me. Now you give five hundred rubles away so freely. Unless you return the money you will not leave this place, for I will call the police."

19

The Warsaw merchant became ghastly pale, confessed, and shortly afterwards returned the entire 5000 rubles.


## PRAISE THE DEAD

When Reb Mordecai Aaron Ginsberg of Vilna died, several modern scholars of the Haskalah movement asked Reb Velvele to deliver a eulogy over the deceased. Reb Velvele, who was a strong opponent of their movement, did not relish the idea, but agreed to their request since he did not care to antagonize these scholars of Vilna. It happened that two rabbis of small cities near Vilna also died during the same period. Reb Velvele devoted the entire oration to praise of these two sages, stressing their sincerity, work, and ability. Only toward the end of the eulogy did he offer a few insignificant words about Reb Mordecai Aaron Ginsberg. The members of the Haskalah movement were greatly disappointed and grieved. Adam Hakohen approached Reb Velvele and reprimanded him.

"I'll tell you a story," Reb Velvele said. "A prominent merchant of Vilna married off his youngest daughter. He made an elaborate wedding and invited all his friends, among them a wealthy merchant of Koenigsberg. The entertainer at the affair was Isaac Smargoner, who was famous for his rhymes based on the names of the bride and groom. The merchant of Koenigsberg greatly admired the entertainer's talent, and afterwards invited him to participate at his own daughter's wedding. At this affair Isaac Smargoner greeted his German guests and hosts, but his rhymes were not as witty and humorous as always. The merchant of Koenigsberg was astonished.

" 'Herr Smargoner,' he said, 'Was ist mit Ihnen geschehen?'

" 'I am sorry,' Isaac apologized, 'but I have always been accustomed to attend weddings where the groom's name is Abraham, Jacob, or Moses, and the bride's name is Esther, Miriam, or Sarah. Today is the first time I am at an affair where the groom's name is Fritz, the bride is called Elsa, and the in-laws are Ignatz, Ernest, and Berta. I haven't the slightest idea of how to rhyme or fit these names in appropriately. If I should attend weddings like these more frequently, I would become accustomed to the German names and it would be easier for me to utilize my talent.'

"The same is true in my case," Reb Velvele explained. "I am accustomed to deliver eulogies for sincere rabbis and religious Jews, for those are the only people with whom I am acquainted. Therefore I never lack material. Today, however, was the first time I had to deliver a eulogy for a member of the Haskalah movement. It is hardly a wonder that it was not very good. But if I could deliver such eulogies more often, I would acquire the art and really excel in them."

## DEBATABLE PHILANTHROPY

Rabbi Mohilever arrived at a city to collect money for Palestine. The sage delivered a sermon before the distinguished personalities of the city and stressed the importance of Palestine. Rabbi Mohilever urged them to contribute all they could to aid in building up the Holy Land. At the end of the sermon a wealthy, pious man arose and declared that he would not spare money for that cause, since the scholars of that generation believed that in restoring the Jews to their Holy Land, the coming of the Messiah and the ultimate release of the Jews from bondage would be delayed.

Rabbi Mohilever listened to the man's explanation and said, "My good people, there was a young lad of another town, who studied in the yeshivah of my city. He received money regularly from his parents, which was sent in care of the sexton.

"One day he received a letter from his father which said that he had sent twenty-five rubles, and that he was worried because he had not heard from him. The boy ran to the sexton with the letter but the man knew nothing about it, for he had not received the money. Again the lad received a letter from his father wherein he explained in detail the money he had sent. The sexton was then summoned to appear before the ecclesiastic magistrate, who decided that the man would have to take an oath. When the sexton heard this, he handed twenty-five rubles to the rabbi and told him to give it to the plaintiff. After that was done, he swore that he had never received any money. Those present were baffled at the procedure. 'Since you paid the money, why did you take the oath?' they asked in amazement. 'If I had taken the oath,' the sexton explained, 'and in such a manner cleared myself of paying,

I'd be suspected of perjury. On the other hand, if I had paid and not taken the oath, people would say I had taken the money, but because I was frightened of the oath I had returned it. ·That is why I paid the sum and them swore that I did not receive it. Now is it clear to everyone that I did not take the money and swore truthfully?'

"The same is true in this instance,'" Rabbi Mohilever continued. "When a Jew argues that he does not want to give money, we become suspicious that his religious argument and fear of sin are merely a camouflage not to give. My dear fellowmen, first you should give and then debate your point. In such a manner we will know that you are honest men."

## LOW FINANCE

A gentile came to Eliah Chaim Lodzer and said that he would like to speak to the rabbi confidentially.

"I was connected with a liberal movement in Lodz," the gentile began, "where I was in charge of the treasury. When the movement was abolished, I remained with the sum of 8000 rubles, which I buried in the cellar of my house. From time to time I would go down, count the money, add my own savings to it, and put it back in the hiding place. This went on for a long time. Several days ago I realized that all the money was gone."

"Do you suspect anyone?" Reb Eliah Chaim asked.

"There is a carpenter living in my house, who was al-was very poor. Suddenly he became wealthy and began to live in a grand fashion."

23

"Did anyone question the carpenter about his riches?"

"Yes," the gentile replied. "Several neighbors asked him, and he said that his wife's uncle had died in London, leaving them his fortune."

"Come in tomorrow. I will see what I can do," Reb Eliah Chaim suggested.

After the gentile departed, Reb Eliah Chaim summoned the carpenter.

"I've heard that you've inherited a great deal of money," he began. "Why didn't you give some for charity?"

The carpenter, taken aback by such a direct question, soon composed himself and said, "Rabbi, you are right. It escaped my mind, but it still isn't too late."

"Was your uncle very wealthy?"

"Yes, very wealthy indeed."

"Did he leave any other heirs?" the rabbi probed further.

"Er—yes," the carpenter stammered.

Reb Chaim realized that the story about the inheritance was not legitimate.

"Listen to me," he whispered to the carpenter. "I want to help you. Someone told me that you are using counterfeit money. Do you realize what that means?"

The carpenter turned ghastly pale. Now he understood. His neighbor had been engaged in making counterfeit money!

"Run home quickly and bring whatever money you still have," the rabbi instructed him. Soon the carpenter returned with a package of bills.

24

"Let this be a lesson to you," the rabbi rebuked him, "never to take that which does not belong to you. This money is genuine, but it is not yours."

The following day the gentile received his money.

## LEARNING WILL OUT

When Reb Laib, the Shaagas Arieh (so named after his book), was in banishment, he wandered into Koenigsberg. He entered the home of the rabbi, Reb Laibele Epstein, and said to the rebbitzin: "Here is some barley in a pot; cook it for me."

The rebbitzin looked at the peculiar intruder, went to the rabbi, and told him that there was a poor Jew in the house, no doubt a scoundrel, who wanted to have something cooked for him, in his own pot. Reb Laibele understood that the man was not an ordinary Jew, and advised the rebbitzin to fulfill his request.

Reb Laibele then went out to greet the guest and invite him into his private study. The rabbi of Koenigsberg through force of habit started to discuss the Torah. Now the Shaagas Arieh was able to show his genius, and began to shower the rabbi with questions. Reb Laibele, who also was a gaon, attempted to answer them, but the Shaagas Arieh disagreed, and so the two wise men argued for quite a while. In order to substantiate his statements Reb Laibele Epstein said, "The Shaagas Arieh also is of the same opinion."

The other, a temperamental individual, angrily called out, "When the Shaagas Arieh stands in the bookcase he

25

is a Shaagas Arieh, but when he stands on his feet he is not a Shaagas Arieh!"

When Reb Laibele Epstein heard this he became panicky. Jumping from his chair, he grasped his guest's hand, saying, "Shalom alechem, rabbi!" and immediately ushered him into the best room of his house.

A few days later, several distinguished men of Metz came to Reb Laibele's house with a contract. During those years Metz was considered the oldest and most outstanding of Jewish communities, always engaging the greatest rabbinical genius of the time. After Reb Laibele listened to the messengers of Metz, he rose and called out, "We have in our midst the greatest genius of our generation, the Shaagas Arieh. He is more entitled than I to preside as Rabbi of Metz." That is how the Shaagas Arieh became Rabbi of Metz.

## PROFESSIONAL DEVOTION

The Jews of Vilna asked Rabbi Israel Salanter to become head of their Reform Seminary. At that time Rabbi Salanter was Chief Rabbi of Vilna. He refused to listen to such a suggestion. Since the people were greatly interested in the Seminary, they sought the aid of the government to influence Rabbi Salanter to accept the place. Rabbi Salanter became aware of their intentions and left Vilna.

Years later Dr. Schaffer of Kovno met him. "Rabbi, why didn't you want to take the position in the Reform Seminary?" Schaffer asked. "If the Seminary had been conducted under your supervision, it would have possessed a more Jewish spirit, and produced great rabbis, with both religious and secular knowledge."

"I want to ask you something," Rabbi Salanter replied. "When a poor man comes to a rabbi with a problem, the rabbi will put his food aside and answer him immediately. If it is a difficult question, he will delve into large tomes, struggle and search, until he has found an answer satis-factory to the poor man, so that he will not have to suffer a loss. On the other hand, when a rich man comes to him with a question, the rabbi is in no great hurry to declare the matter kosher for him. With a doctor, it is just the contrary. When a wealthy man calls him, he will run breathlessly, even in the middle of the night; but when he is called by a poor man he will give all sorts of excuses so as not to go. When he runs short of alibis, he goes without enthusiasm. Why is it that rabbis love the poor and doctors love the rich? The answer is very simple. A rabbi doesn't study to become a rabbi. He merely studies because he wants to study. Thus he learns and imbibes the ethics of the Torah, whose foundation is righteousness and justice, and which teaches us to help the poor and the oppressed. Incidentally he becomes a rabbi, following the footsteps of his teacher. A doctor deliberately studies to become a doctor. He doesn't enter the university for humane or sympathetic reasons. He studies medicine be-cause it is a good profession. There are money and respect in it. That is why he will attend the rich more readily than the poor. They give him more.

"The Reform Seminary came about in this identical manner. They want to produce rabbis for a professional purpose, where young men should prepare for the rabbinic profession. And so they will cater to the rich, and shun the poor. That is why I did not want to take part in it. I do not belong in that group."

## IT HAPPENED ONE NIGHT

While the Vilner Gaon was in exile, he wandered from city to city. One day he met a Jewish coachman on the road. The coachman, noticing a Jew wearily trudging along with a sack on his back, stopped him and asked, "Where are you going, my friend?"

"To the city," replied the traveler.

"Get into my wagon," the coachman suggested, "and I will take you there."

The Gaon got in, and the two started off. While they were traveling it became quite warm, so the Gaon discarded his top coat. He remained sitting in his tallis and tefillin, and peered into a book of the Torah, as was his custom. In the middle of the journey, the coachman said to him, "My friend, I am sleepy. Will you please take my seat on the coach box, and lead the horses to the city? Take the whip and reins in hand, and you will not have much difficulty, because the horses know the road very clearly. One does not have to be particularly clever for that."

The Gaon said nothing, did as he was told, and in this fashion drove into the city.

28

A Jew, who had once been in Vilna, passed by and recognized the Gaon. When he saw him in the place of a coachman, and driving another man, he ran into the market place and shouted very loudly, "My friends, the Messiah has come, the Messiah has come!"

All the people of the city assembled and queried, "What are you talking about? Have you lost your mind?"

"I swear to you that I saw with my own eyes a wagon enter the city, and the Vilner Gaon himself was the driver. Now who is the man he was driving, if not the Messiah?"

As they were standing and talking, the wagon rode into the market place, and the Jews were astonished to see the Gaon, in his tallis and tefillin, indeed leading the horse and wagon. Quickly they ran over, looked in, and saw the city's coachman snoring and fast asleep.

## DEMANDING

Reb Eliah Baruch was in dire need when he first came to Karelitsh. The prominent Jews of the community in conference decided to sell a part of the land they owned in the market-place and give the money to the rabbi. Several days later, one of them called out, "Rabbi, how did you like our gift?"

"A king once had a good friend, whom he loved very dearly," Reb Eliah Baruch began. "He appointed him treasurer, so that he could be near him constantly. No day passed wherein the king did not enjoy his friend's company. Then for one week the friend did not appear.

The king sent for him. When the friend arrived, he looked pale and fatigued.

" 'What has happened to you?' the king asked. 'Are you ill?'

" 'No, I am rather well,' the man replied, 'but I am tortured by morbid and painful thoughts which give me no peace.'

."The king understood that there must be money missing in the treasury and he ventured, 'I possess a fine book that will alleviate your misery and make you a happy man. I will send you the book; it will make you feel like a new person.' The king ordered one of his cabinet members to paste the pages of part of a book with ten thousand dollar bills and deliver it to his friend. The following day the treasurer arrived, his face wreathed in smiles.

" 'How do you like my book?' the king asked.

" 'I am much obliged for your gift,' the friend replied. 'I appreciate it to such an extent that I would want the other part.'

"And so," Reb Eliah Baruch smiled, "I also ask, 'Have you another part?' "

## ENFORCED CANNIBALISM

Nicholas II called Minister Von Plehve to attend a rabbinical conference in St. Petersburg concerning the condition of the Jews in Russia. Among the rabbis were Isaac Elchanan, Chaim Brisker, and Eliah Chaim Lodzer. Von Plehve, who was an anti-Semite, attempted to show that the Jews were an inferior race and had inferior ethics.

"You will notice," Von Plehve remarked, "that Russia is composed of many nationalities, such as Poles, Russians, Jews, and many others. Yet in no nationality will one snatch the piece of bread away from the other. Tailors, shoemakers, storekeepers, all live at peace with one another, and all make a living. Not so with the Jews. One will do his utmost to destroy the other fellow as soon as he has the opportunity. When one Jew opens a bakery, the next fellow will open one directly across the street. Should one Jew open a restaurant, others will open restaurants in the same neighborhood, and they will become bitter enemies."

"Please allow me to say something, Your Honor," Reb Eliah Chaim requested. "It is the nature of animals not to devour one of their own kind. A lion will not devour a lion, a wolf will not eat a wolf ; only fish swallow one another. Why is that so? It is because all animals have access to the entire world, and they can use all avenues to obtain their food, to satisfy their wants, and to secure their other necessities. Fish, on the other hand, are imprisoned in their waters. They dare not attempt to leave their element for fear of death. What then is left for them to do? They must swallow one another, or else perish from hunger. The same is true of the Jews. For the gentiles all places are open, and they can go everywhere to earn their living. The Jews, unfortunately, cannot do that. The government has imprisoned them in a ghetto. They are not permitted to live, nor to conduct business elsewhere. What can the poor souls do? They must devour one another."

31

## TWO WORLDS

The butchers of the city came to Abraham Zhetler with a difficult ritual question. It was shortly before Passover, and since the butchers were very poor people, they had borrowed the money with which to purchase the slaughtered ox. Rabbi Abraham wanted to help them, but according to the interpretation of the Rema, it was difficult to declare the doubtful animal kosher. Rabbi Abraham delved among his books, and finally discovered an elastic clause in a later edition of the law.

"Let us both take it upon ourselves to make the carcass kosher," Rabbi Abraham said.

"God forbid!" cried the butchers, trembling. "How can we stand up against the laws of Rema?"

Rabbi Abraham took it upon himself to decide that the ox was kosher.

"Are you really strong enough to shoulder this responsibility against the decision of Rema?" they asked.

"If I had declared the animal not kosher," Rabbi Abraham explained, "I would have had to deal with the butchers when I came to the other world. They would then drag me to the Supreme Justice, and state that I had ruined them, for it was borrowed money with which they bought the ox, and they would have had to sell it at a loss. You know how impossible it is to deal with simple people. Now that I've made it kosher, I will only have to confront the Rema, and I am certain that I will be able to manage somehow with so great a scholar!"

## HANDS ACROSS THE GRAVE

A wealthy Jew died in a Warsaw hospital. His heirs knew that he had a great deal of money with him at the time, but it was nowhere to be found. They became suspicious of the attendant. When they brought him before Reb Berish Meisels, the Warsaw Rabbi, he denied being guilty of such an act.

"Then you didn't take the money?" Reb Berish asked.

"No, rabbi," he staunchly replied.

"In that event," the rabbi said, "you will have to clasp the dead man's hand and take an oath to substantiate that which you say."

The attendant seemed to shrink for a moment, but summoning up courage he said, "All right, rabbi, I'll do it."

Reb Berish called several of his people into his study and said: "One of you will go to the hospital, and pretend that he is the dead man. When the attendant gives you his hand, hold it fast for a few minutes, without releasing it."

The rabbi's plan was accepted, and one of the men was placed on the floor, covered with a sheet, and his body surrounded by candles. The attendant was brought in, and was told to go over to the corpse and take an oath. He did as he was told. He walked over to the dead man, grasped his hand, but when he wanted to let go found he could not. The corpse held him tightly.

The poor attendant turned pale, and in a wild voice shrieked, "Please have mercy! Let me go! I'll return the money!"

## GIVE AND TAKE

A hassidic rabbi, who was to leave on a journey to a distant city, was followed by a large group of his hassidim. A modern young man asked one of them, "Who is that man whom all the people are crowding around?" "Don't you know?" the hassid replied. "He is a great zaddik."

The young man then asked the sexton for permission to see the great rabbi. When he met the rabbi, he clasped his hand and gave him five dollars.

"Did you want something, young fellow?" the rabbi asked.

"No," the man replied, and handed him another five dollars, which the zaddik put into his pocket, saying, "Perhaps your wife is ill and you would want me to bless her?" "No, dear rabbi, I am a bachelor," and again he gave the rabbi a five dollar bill, which he did not refuse.

"You certainly must have something to ask, my good man," the zaddik insisted. "Maybe your business is not very good, or you have some sins to atone for."

"On the contrary, rabbi, my business is exceptionally fine this year and I have committed no sins," and thus speaking he handed over another five dollars.

"Young man, there must be something that you definitely want. You certainly have a purpose in all this."

"Yes, rabbi, I'll be frank with you," the young man finally spoke up, "I have a reason. I wanted to see how long a man can stand and accept money for nothing."

## REVERSING THE COIN

When Reb Heshel was Rabbi of Krakow, two wealthy men appeared before him with a dispute. It was difficult to come to a decision immediately, and Reb Heshel postponed the case. A few days later one of the men came to him and said, "Rabbi, please see that I am not treated unjustly," and thereupon handed him 100 gold coins.

Reb Heshel took the money and told the man to come the next day. He then called in his wife and asked her to prepare a fine supper and invite all their children. That evening, when everyone was seated around the table, the rabbi took out the money and began to count the coins. His children sat and looked on respectfully, thinking that their father would divide the money among them, for that must have been his purpose in gathering them together. But after counting the money several times, the rabbi put it back into his pocket and spoke.

"My children, I want you to know that this money is a bribe. It is definitely stated in the Torah that one must not take a bribe. That is my reason for calling you here. I wanted you to see such money with your own eyes, and to know that you must always stay away from it. Run as soon as you see it."

The very next day Reb Heshel returned the coins to the merchant, and sharply reprimanded him.

"Not only must a bribe not be taken," he said; "it must also not be given."

## HAIL AND FAREWELL

During the days of Rabbi Nachum Grodner an anti-Semitic governor oppressed and persecuted the Jews of Grodno. However, he greatly admired and respected Rabbi Nachum, who was regarded as a venerable and sincere saint.

On New Year's Day the overseers of the community together with the rabbi paid their respects to the governor and greeted him according to custom. "A new year, noble sir, and new luck!"

The governor asked Rabbi Nachum to remain after the others had left. "Do you regard me as a fool?" he addressed the venerable sage. "I am well aware that the Jews do not relish me too much, because I have never done anything for them. I know that while they wished me well, they merely did it out of fear and in order to please my vanity. I am sure that deep in their hearts they cursed me. However, I am not surprised at their hypocrisy. But how can you, who are reputed to be the shining example of honesty and sincerity, utter such deceitful words?"

"Heaven forbid, your excellency!" said Rabbi Nachum. "That which we wished you we all meant sincerely without pretense. We wished you a new year and new luck. No doubt, you would like to know our interpretation of 'new luck' for you. That, noble sir, means you should be elevated to the position of state governor, minister, or prime-minister, and then you will leave Grodno. I swear to you that this is heartily wished by all the Jews of the city."

## TWO WORLDS

A Polish Jew came to Germany and on a Sabbath attended a synagogue and heard a sermon on morale. The rabbi explained that this world was meaningless. The other world only was important. He who is poor here will be rich in the world to come.

The following day the Jew came to the rabbi and said, "Rabbi, is it true what you said yesterday, that he who is poor in this world, will be wealthy in the world to come?"

"Definitely," the rabbi replied. "There is no doubt about it."

"Then will you please loan me a thousand marks!" the Jew asked. "I will pay it back to you in the next world."

"Yes," the rabbi agreed. "Here you have it," and he immediately handed the money to the Jew, who stared at him unbelievingly.

As he was about to pocket the money, the rabbi confronted him: "What do you intend to do with the money?"

"I expect to go into business."

"Do you think that you will make money?"

"If luck is with me, I expect to."

"In that case I cannot give you the thousand marks!" and with these words the rabbi took the money back and put it into his pocket.

"Why do you do that, rabbi?" the Jew asked, in confusion.

"Since you are going to become rich in this world," the rabbi replied, "you will be poor in the world to come, and then you will not be able to return my money."

## THE PALESTINE CURE

An orthodox American Jew, who had migrated with his family to Palestine, visited Rabbi Cook and told him he had decided to return to America. He explained that Palestine did not suit his purpose.

"Why?" asked Rabbi Cook.

"I came to Palestine," the man elucidated, "because I intended to raise my children in a religious atmosphere and a Jewish spirit. This land is filled with heretics and free thinkers."

Rabbi Cook thoughtfully observed the speaker. "Tell me," he asked, "what place in America would you consider the finest health resort for people afflicted with tuberculosis?"

The Jew mentioned a popular resort famous for its salubrious fresh air.

"While I was in America," Rabbi Cook replied, "I visited that place, and wherever I turned I met individuals suffering with that dreadful disease. Their systems were torn with racking coughs. Now tell me, my good man, what purpose does the pure air of this resort serve?"

"That is just it," the American Jew said. "Because the air is healthful the people come there to cure themselves."

"Very well, then," Rabbi Cook agreed; "the same is true of Palestine. That is why you see so many sick Jews here who are suffering from a religious ailment. Their souls are sick, and because the air here is beneficial for all such distressed individuals, people of the entire world come to Palestine to get well."

## ON THE FRINGE OF JUDAISM

During the reign of Nicholas I a conference of rabbis was held, of which Reb Itzele Woloziner was chairman. Avarov, the minister of education, wanted to enforce a new law among the Jewish people, that they cast off their customs of wearing long garments and beards. Their example was to be Dr. Lillienthal, a modern rabbi, who played an important part in those days. He traveled about the Jewish cities, preaching that the people heed and practice what the government proposed. They were to dress in modern fashion and send their children to modern schools.

At one of the conferences Minister Avarov said to Reb Itzele, "Why do you wear such a long tallis and tsitzis that show from underneath your clothes? Can't you be a religious Jew and wear a smaller one? Look at Dr. Lillienthal, also a rabbi and a pious Jew. His tsitzis do not show."

"Your honor," Reb Itzele replied, "we Jews wear tsitzis that we may remember God's commandments. Dr. Lillienthal is a young, educated man, with an excellent memory, and a small tallis suffices for him to remember the commandments. But I am an old-fashioned rabbi and a much older man. My memory doesn't serve me very well. I must have a large tallis, with long tsitzis, so that I will remember our commandments."

39

## NEW GENERATION

Reb Israel Rezhiner lived in a very comfortable fashion. A modernized Jew once visited the rabbi and was amazed at his luxurious surroundings.

"This is quite a contrast from the way the rabbis lived in past years," he remarked. "Then they resided in wooden houses, dressed in plain linen, and traveled on foot, whereas the rabbis of today dwell in palaces, garb themselves in velvet and satin, and travel about in beautiful coaches."

"There are three classes of people who come to a rabbi," Reb Israel Rezhiner replied, "hassidim, ordinary people, and frivolous men. All three give the rabbi contributions. These monies the rabbi spends according to the donors. The money that the hassidim give him, the rabbi spends for mitzvoth and for charity. The money that ordinary people give, he spends for sustenance of himself and his family. But the money he obtains from frivolous men, the rabbi spends on luxuries. Years ago there were no frivolous people, therefore the rabbi was not able to indulge in anything too costly. Nowadays the frivolous have multiplied to such an extent that he can afford to travel about in a coach and live in comfort."

## STEALING THE SPOTLIGHT

Reb Abraham Shmuel delivered a learned discourse in the Volkovisker Synagogue. In the audience there was a learned Jew, Reb Abraham Aaron, who always insisted on showing up the rabbis. All the rabbis of Volkovisk had been greatly annoyed by this man. He stopped Reb Abraham Shmuel in the middle of a sentence, and directed a question at him.

Reb Shmuel was not irritated; instead he smiled and calmly replied, "You do not ask like a learned man at all," and with these words he continued his sermon.

The sharp reply hurt Reb Abraham Aaron's pride, and he would not visit the rabbi's house any longer. Reb Shmuel understood Reb Aaron's anger, so he went to visit him. As was the custom, they first discussed and interpreted various passages of the Torah.

Then Reb Shmuel said, "I notice that you have a grudge against me."

"Yes, it is true. Why should I deny it?" the other replied. "You embarrassed me when you said that I did not ask a question like a scholar."

"You certainly didn't," Reb Shmuel agreed. "When you halted me point blank, in the middle of my sermon, then you did not act like a scholar, but like a thief."

## NO REBATE

In Yosla there lived a miserly Jew who never gave a penny for charity, and who would take high rates of interest for his loans. When he died, the officials of the synagogue decided that they must get some money from the inheritance. They approached the heirs and asked 2000 crowns for the burial ground. The family was enraged. They called the rabbi, Reb. Pinchus Yosler.

"How do you allow yourself to ask three or four times the price of a grave for this body, than for any other?" the family demanded.

"For this body," Reb Pinchus explained, "you must pay more than for others, because we believe in resurrection. When a Jew dies, he merely leases the grave for a short while, hence it is cheap. This Jew, on the other hand, was an extremely mercenary person, who demanded exorbitant rates of interest, and hence according to the Jewish religion will never be resurrected. His burial ground is sold to him in perpetuity. That is why it is so expensive."

## COMPARATIVE AGONY

In his youth, Reb Isaac Vorker and a friend rode with a coachman to a nearby city. They had a miserable and uncomfortable journey. Several times the coachman asked them to get out and walk. At other times he stood still and refused to go any further. When the men paused to say their evening prayers, the coachman showed his comtempt and threatened to leave them on the road. Reb Isaac's friend argued with the driver during the entire trip, but Reb Isaac remained silent.

"How could you have been so calm during such a nerve racking journey?" his friend asked.

"You have never traveled with coachmen before," Reb Isaac replied, "and that is why you did not anticipate such difficulties. I, however, have made such trips dozens of times, and am well acquainted with their behavior. Before

I leave the house I usually prepare myself to endure a great deal more misery than may actually confront me. Therefore, regardless of whatever I may have to suffer, or how coarsely the coachman treats me, I still owe him something."

## UP-SIDE-DOWN PIETY

A Jew remarked to a rabbi that the Jewish religion was like a business nowadays. As proof he mentioned the fact that the overseer of the synagogue always honored the sinners, those who did not keep the Sabbath, because they paid well for it. The rabbi listened thoughtfully and then replied: "A candle made of tallow is definitely not kosher. Yet we use it in all synagogues. When you light the candle and keep it pointing upwards, the light it throws off brightens the entire room and makes everything appear cheerful. If you hold the candle pointing downwards, it will melt, spread stench throughout the room, and be extinguished. The same is true when one honors a man who sins. It is not done because a paltry few dollars are involved, but because of the man. As long as he comes to the synagogue and keeps in contact with his people and his faith, he should be paid the necessary respect. If not, he may turn completely over and become entirely extinguished."

## THE GREAT PRESENCE

The Austrian emperor, Francis Joseph, was a liberal man, friendly to the Jews. Whenever he came to Cracow he would visit a synagogue wherein his portrait was displayed. One day, when the king was to visit the synagogue, with all the people waiting to greet him, the portrait disappeared. When this was discovered, it was too late, for the king had already arrived. Francis Joseph asked Reb Simeon Soifer for an explanation.

"Jews pray daily with tefillin. That is a symbol of their belief," the rabbi spoke. "On the Sabbath, however, they are not allowed to use tefillin, because the Sabbath is so holy, that they must not substitute any smaller symbol for it. The same it true of your picture, Your Majesty. While you are not with us we have your picture, which reminds us of you; but when we have the honor of seeing you in person we do not need it. It is only a copy of you, and does not compare with your great personality."

## SEASONAL LAW

One snowy wintry morning a merchant hired a coachman to deliver some glassware for him. The roads were slippery and several articles were broken on the way. The merchant summoned the coachman before the rabbi. The rabbi decided that according to Jewish law, the coachman had to pay for the damage.

"Rabbi," the coachman naively asked, "when was the Torah written?"

"At the time when the Jews were released from bondage in Egypt," replied the rabbi.

"No," the coachman insisted, "I mean during which part of the year?"

"On Shavuoth," the rabbi answered.

"Aha!" the coachman smiled. "That means the Torah was written in the summer, when the roads are dry and smooth. Now, rabbi, do you understand why the decision of the Torah is that I must pay? If it had been written during the winter, when the roads are wet and covered with ice, the law would have been entirely different."

## FOOD FOR THOUGHT

A hassid confided to Reb Bunim that he had been fasting for a long time and exposing himself to self-torture in order to be elevated to a higher spiritual station, but with no success. Reb Bunim listened and said, "One day the Baal Shem Tov had his horses harnessed, and departed on an urgent mission. Since he had to make good time, the Baal Shem Tov set out at a galloping pace. The horses ran past various inns, where they were accustomed to stop for food and water. 'Maybe we have changed into human beings and are no longer horses,' they said to one another. 'In that event we will not be fed until we reach the city.' But soon they passed one city after another without pausing for food. The horses then began to consider themselves greater than human beings. Perhaps even angels! Angels never eat. Finally, when they reached the designated spot, the horses were led to a stable and they immediately began to eat ferociously, like horses!

"So, my good friend," Reb Bunim concluded his story, "fasting alone does not raise an individual to a high spiritual standard. The point is, how one conducts himself after the fast."

45

## INTERVENTIONIST

Reb Lipele Byalistoker, renowned genius and brilliant personality, could solve the most difficult problems. Great merchants, who were in trouble, would come to him for advice.

"There is something I would like to have clarified," said Dr. Silberberg, a friend of Reb Lipele. "A man studies many years until he becomes a doctor, then he struggles before he gets a practice, and when he is called to treat a patient, what does he get? Half a ruble. I, who am a widely-known doctor, get one ruble. Now let us take the rabbi. He gets sometimes as much as one hundred rubles for one hour of consultation. Why is it so?"

"You must understand that there is a great difference in the treatment administered by the doctor and that by the rabbi," Reb Lipele explained. "When two men have a litigation, they begin suffering from headaches, heart-aches, and insomnia. Whom do they come to? The rabbi, and he takes over all their worries. Immediately they are relieved of their difficulties, and they sleep and live comfortably. For this the rabbi is surely worth a liberal reward. Now, when a doctor visits a patient, he merely gives him a prescription. If the doctor were to take over the aches and pains of his patient, then he too would deserve a large fee."

## CALCULATING

The Belzer Rabbi, Reb Sholom, rebuked a farmer for working on Saturdays. The farmer promised to keep the Sabbath holy all year round, except during harvest time.

"You remind me of a story," the rabbi smiled. "A wealthy poritz invited his friends to supper. Each one praised the Jew who worked for him. The host said that there was no one more devoted than his Moshke. He would even convert himself if he asked him to. 'Really, that is incredible!' the poritz's friend exclaimed. Moshke was then called in. 'Moshke, are you faithful to me?' the poritz asked. 'There is nothing that I wouldn't do for you,' Moshke obediently bowed his head. 'I want you to renounce your religion and take on mine,' the poritz demanded. 'All right,' lisped Moshke in a trembling voice, and he was converted. After a few months the poritz sent for Moshke and said, 'You may now become a Jew again.' 'Please, Sir, can you wait until I discuss this with my wife?" Moshke pleaded. The following day Moshke appeared and said, 'My wife is heartbroken. Passover is almost here, and we will have large expenses, such as wine, matzoh, and new dishes. She begs you to allow us to remain gentiles until after the holiday.' "

## AX-IOM

Reb Zanvel Klepfish, Chief Rabbi of Warsaw, regularly gave a contract of sale of unleavened food before Passover, to a wealthy liquor manufacturer. One Passover the rich man sent a messenger to the rabbi, desiring him to come to his home to write out the contract, otherwise he would consult another rabbi. Reb Zanvel refused, and the owner of the factory took someone else.

After Passover Reb Zanvel met the other rabbi. "I owe you much gratitude, and thanks," Reb Zanvel said. "It is through you that a certain part of the Mishnah was clarified for me. The learned men are warned not to use the Torah as an ax. So I asked myself, why don't they say as a needle, or a hammer? Well, the answer is that tailors or carpenters can take their work to their homes, and do it there, but a woodcutter cannot bring the trees to his home. He must take his ax to them. Therefore, a learned man who respects the Torah, must understand that for a few dollars he must not go to a home because the man is rich. He should not use the Torah as an ax."

## OTHER WORLDS

The gaon Rabbi Moishe Teitelbaum of Hungary, who was most insistent on praying on time, discovered that his son-in-law, Rabbi Laibish Wishnitzer, was always late in reciting his daily prayers. He wrote his son-in-law a long reprimand, pointing out that he who disobeys even one law of the Jewish code, will go to gehenna after death. Upon which Rabbi Laibish replied:

Dear father-in-law:

I have been thinking how punctually you adhere to your morning prayers every sunrise. I know that after death you will be in paradise, and I who do not follow that tradition will be in gehenna. No doubt you will meet in paradise men like yourself, such as Berel the butcher, Zalmen the cobbler, Getzel the coachman, and Yankel the tailor. I, however, will meet in gehenna all those who have not adhered to the Jewish code in the matter of praying on time, like the Rabbi of Lublin, the Rabbi of Koshenitz, the Rabbi of Ropshitz, and his brother. Therefore I have decided it would be more gratifying for me to be with those men in gehenna than with your people in paradise.

## THICKER THAN WATER

The Amshinover Rabbi, Menachem David, asked a wealthy man to give financial aid to a poor relative. The rich man attempted to dismiss the subject, by saying that the relative was distant, and so deserved no help.

"Do you pray every day?" the Amshinover Rabbi asked.

"What a question, rabbi! Do you suspect me of not praying?"

"If you do pray, how does the first prayer of Shemoneh Esre begin?"

"Everyone knows that," the other impatiently replied. "God of Abraham, Isaac, and Jacob."

"Who were Abraham, Isaac, and Jacob?"

"Our forefathers, of course!"

"How long ago did they live?"

"A few thousand years."

"You are correct," the rabbi agreed. "They did live a few thousand years ago, and still you mention them in your prayers three times a day. You feel that through the virtues of these distant relatives you will be helped. Yet when I ask you to aid a living relative of your family, you say he is too distant."

## THE FAULTY POT

Whenever Reb Eliah Chaim Lodzer came to Marien-bad many people visited him to discuss social and Jewish problems. During the course of conversation one man spoke highly of Chwolson, who had taken on the Christian faith, but had made many sacrifices for the Jews. Reb Eliah patiently listened, but remained silent. The people, anxious to hear his opinion, kept looking at him intensely, waiting for him to speak.

"I have a story for you," Reb Eliah finally said. "A Jew who lived in Lithuania came to a very small town, in a distant part of Russia, where no Jews resided. He was a very religious man and had no place to eat. Since he was familiar with the procedure of slaughtering and ko-shering meat, he decided to buy a chicken and prepare a meal. When he was through, he realized that he had cooked the chicken in a pot that was not kosher. 'Alas,' sighed the poor man, 'of what consequence is the entire work, when the pot is not kosher!' "

## DEBT PROGRESSIVE

Rabbi Eliah Chaim Lodzer gave a great deal of charity. He donated more than his salary warranted, and so was always in debt. While he was in Lodz, the community of Warsaw offered him a contract. Reb Eliah Chaim refused their offer.

"Rabbi," he was asked, "why do you turn down the position of rabbi in Warsaw?"

"As you all know," Reb Eliah Chaim replied, "I spend much more than I earn, and am always in debt. The only thing that I can depend on is that when a larger community takes me as rabbi, they will pay my debts. That is the way I have always conducted myself. When I was in Dretchin, I borrowed money on the account of Pruzen. When I was in Pruzen I borrowed on the account of Lodz. Now that I am in Lodz, I can borrow money on the account of Warsaw; but what will I do when I leave Warsaw? What greater account is there for me to borrow on?"

## MAN WANTS BUT LITTLE

"This is a story," the Gerer Rabbi began, "of a rich man's son who had chosen the wrong path in life. The father, in order to chastise the lad, sent him to live among beggars, so that he would acquaint himself with poverty. The son became so absorbed in the beggars' mode of living that he completely forgot his previous life. Finally the father had mercy upon him and sent to ask what he would most desire. The son joyfully replied that he would appreciate a new beggar's sack, because his old one was torn.

51

"The same is true of the Jews," the Gerer Rabbi continued. "We are so immersed in suffering and slavery, that often our desires do not extend further than to pray for a new sack. When we are redeemed, we will realize that man has greater aspirations in life, which were lacking in our dark days, than a beggar's sack."

## UNWITTING INVESTMENT

Reb Isaiah Zhuchovitzer was a great zaddik and a very hospitable individual. A traveler who had spent the Sabbath at his house forgot his fur cap when he departed. Reb Isaiah waited for his guest to return and claim the article; and when he did not Reb Isaiah attempted to trace the man, but to no avail. He could not be found. The venerable zaddik then sold the fur cap for ten gulden, with which he purchased a small plot of land. The soil was cultivated and Reb Isaiah sold the produce in the market place. This went on year after year.

Several years passed and the same guest again visited the sage. Reb Isaiah immediately recognized him. "Do you recall forgetting something at my house a long time ago?" he asked.

"Yes, I forgot my fur cap," the guest replied, "but that was ages ago."

"How much was it worth?" the zaddik probed.

"About ten gulden."

Reb Isaiah Zhuchovitzer then opened his safe, took out 200 rubles, and handed it to his guest. "Take this money, my friends, for it is yours," he said. "This is what your fur cap brought."

## NO PARDON

Rabbi David Leliner and the Holy Jew from Psycha together collected contributions for a worthy cause. One afternoon they entered the home of a wealthy miser, who did not recognize the distinguished personalities and furiously berated them when he learned what they wanted.

"Men like you," he raged, "should be ashamed to go around panhandling. Why don't you go out and work for a living?" The men left quietly.

Soon afterwards the skinflint realized who the two Jews were he had so crudely insulted, and he frantically ran in search of them. He tearfully apologized and pleaded to be forgiven.

"I have made a grave error," he wailed. "I mistook you for two ordinary beggars."

"We can only forgive you for belittling our honor," the reverend sages replied, "because you insulted us unwittingly. But we cannot forgive you for slurring the character of some unknown man whose personality you slandered. That is not within our power."

## SPUR TO WICKEDNESS

Rabbi Hirsch Levine, who was rabbi in Halberstadt, then in London, and later in Berlin, once remarked, "On three different occasions I met a certain person. The first time I saw him, he was sad and depressed. The second time, he was dashing wildly through the streets, and had no time to spare. The third time I saw him peacefully strolling about without worries or cares. He had no more tasks to perform, for his job was done. I refer to the *Yezer Hara* (evil inclination). While I was rabbi in Halberstadt I saw him sad and lonely, because only fine Jews dwelt in that city, and he met with no success there. Later, when I was rabbi in London, I saw him running around, because he had a great deal of work to accomplish. Here in Berlin, I meet him walking about contentedly, with his hands in his pockets. He does not have to work hard any longer, or chase after the people. Here the people run after him."

## IGNORANCE AND BLISS

A rich Jewish farmer came to the Chernobiler Rabbi and complained that he was in fear of losing his estate. He had leased it for a number of years, but now a goy was willing to pay a higher rental.

"What do you want me to do?" the rabbi asked.

"Rabbi, I want you to advise me," the rich man pleaded.

"Has a poor man ever derived any benefits from your estate?" the rabbi inquired.

"What a question! Dozens of men have received bread from my estate."

"Then be good enough to go to the Strikover Rabbi and present your request. He will be able to aid you," the Chernobiler Rabbi replied.

"Why do you send me to him?" the farmer asked, under the rabbi's sharp glance. "Can't you tell me what I want to know?"

"When you tell me that poor men were fed from your estate, I know that it is a lie," the rabbi rejoined. "The Strikover Rabbi doesn't know that and it will be easier for you to fool him."

## FEATURE STORY

A woman rushed into a rabbi's house and pleaded for his help. Her husband had deserted her two months before, and she did not know where he was. The sexton took the piece of paper on which she had written her request, and brought it to the rabbi. Soon he came back, and said, "Go home, my dear woman. The rabbi says your husband will return very shortly."

The woman was overjoyed, thanked him profusely, blessed both the sexton and the rabbi, and left. When she was gone, the sexton said to the people present, "Her joy is worthless, because her husband will never return."

"Why," they all queried, "don't you believe that the rabbi can perform miracles?"

"Of course, I believe in the rabbi's capabilities," replied the sexton, "but the rabbi only saw her note. I saw her face."

## DESCENDING DESCENDANT

An atheist visited Reb Israel Rezhiner and told him that inasmuch as he came from a fine ancestry, he would like a favor from the rabbi.

"There was once a king," Reb Israel replied, "who built a beautiful palace. He hired four of the world's most

55

prominent artists and asked each one to paint a wall of his reception room. One artist was very clever. He waited until the others were finished with their work. Then he mixed some paint that is used on mirrors and with it painted the fourth wall. The color schemes of the other three walls cast an unusual, beautiful reflection on the surface of the fourth. The king was delighted with the unique idea of the artist and gave him a grand prize. The same is true of you," the Rezhiner Rabbi added, turning to the young man. "When the son of a great man distinguishes himself with noble deeds and is a good Jew, then the magnificent, colorful reflection of his parents and grandparents is seen. Only in such an event, can he be proud and boastful of his heritage."

## PROPHECY

A gentile came to the house of Reb Itzikel Kalisher and asked for bread. The rabbi's wife had several whole loaves, but did not relish the idea of cutting one up. Reb Itzikel called out, "Cut! No blood will flow." She cut off a slice and gave it to the gentile.

One day while the rabbi was traveling through the woods on the way to another city, a band of thieves attacked him, robbed him of all his belongings, and were ready to kill him. Suddenly one of the bandits recognized the rabbi as the Jew who had given him bread. He commanded the others to return the loot they had taken from him, and free him.

When he returned home he related the incident to his wife and added, "Now, do you understand what I meant when I said, cut—no blood will flow? As a result my blood did not flow."

## CLERICAL APPEARANCES

In a small town there lived a wealthy rabbi who always had dealings and disputes with landowners. Sometimes he was the plaintiff, at other times the defendant. Very frequently he would come to the city of Volozhin, where he tried litigation with landowners before Reb Hirsch Leib. One day Reb Hirsch Leib had a confidential talk with him, and pointed out that it did not befit a rabbi to go about arguing over money matters and suing people.

"It is a shame before God and the Torah," Reb Leib exclaimed.

"But, rabbi," the other protested, "You know that nowadays a rabbi cannot get along without money. He certainly can't make a living on his salary alone and marry off his children."

"You are right," Reb Hirsch Leib agreed. "One can't get along without a needle, either. The wealthiest and the wisest must have one. Yet to wear a needle stuck in the lapel, for everyone to see, makes one look like an ordinary tailor."

## COMPENSATION

In olden times it was customary for the slaughterers of small Jewish communities to show hospitality to all travelers. They would give them a night's lodging, food, and drink. On one occasion, however, a guest complained to Rabbi Israel Rezhiner that one slaughterer had refused to accept travelers and slammed his door on them. The rabbi investigated and when he discovered the charge true, he forbade the slaughterer to continue at his profession. Soon the man came weeping to the rabbi.

"Rabbi," he wailed, "there are so many wealthy Jews in the community, who have much more than I. Why must I be more generous than they in receiving and entertaining visitors?"

"The work of a slaughterer consists of shedding blood," Rabbi Israel Rezhiner explained, "and in order that his heart should not become calloused and cruel it is required that he perform good deeds and be more charitable and hospitable than the others."

## HOLIDAY ORIGINS

A priest in conversation with a rabbi said, "In celebrating holidays, the Jews always consider the evening part of the approaching day, and therefore their celebration starts the previous evening. But why is Purim different, and does your feast take place the evening after Purim?"

The rabbi smiled. "The gentiles act quite to the contrary, for in their holidays they regard the evening part of the day that has passed; yet why do they celebrate Christmas on the eve of the approaching day? I will attempt to answer that myself. We Jews are thankful to a goy named Haman for the festival of Purim, and so we celebrate it according to the gentile fashion. On the other hand, the gentiles owe their Christmas holiday to a Jew, and there-fore observe it according to the Jewish fashion."

## MUTUAL UNDERSTANDING

Moishe Laib Sosover repeated a conversation he over-heard between two peasants, while they were drinking.

"Do you love me?" one asked.

"I love you very much," the other replied.

"If you love me," the first one continued, "do you know my needs or my wants?"

"How should I know?" was the answer.

"Since you don't know my needs," the first peasant retorted, "how can you say that you love me?"

"From this conversation you can learn," the Sosover Rabbi said, "that to love one's fellowman means to know what he is lacking, and to share his needs and sufferings.

## CLOTHES OF HONOR

Rabbi Chaim Sandzer was known to be very charitable. He would give away his last penny, and live in poverty. When his daughter was to marry the son of the Hornos-topolir Rabbi, his wife prepared a handsome wardrobe for her.

A few days prior to the wedding, a widow came cry-ing to Reb Chaim. "Rabbi, I am a poor widow. My daughter is to be wed, and I have nothing to give her."

The rabbi lost no time, and gave her his daughter's complete trousseau.

When the bride saw what her father had done, she began to cry bitterly. "Father, how will I go to the wedding now?"

"Don't worry, my child," the rabbi consoled her. "You will say that you are my daughter."

## MONEY FOR THE MAIMED

A few years before Reb Chaim Sandzer passed away, he ordered that his youngest son Reb Aaron become his successor. The people were amazed that he had not chosen his older son instead.

"I will relate a story to you," Reb Chaim explained. "There lived a blind beggar in a small city, who sat in the marketplace and begged for alms. Everyone who passed felt sorry for him and gave as much as he could. Some made large donations. In this manner the beggar collected huge sums of money, bought much property, and became notably wealthy. He had several children, all healthy, except one who was blind. Before the beggar died, he willed his entire fortune to his healthy children, but nothing to his blind son. 'Why have you neglected your blind son?' he was asked. 'You should be more concerned about his welfare than that of the others.' 'Don't worry,' the beggar replied. 'My blind son will be as wealthy as I. The people will sympathize with him, but who will take notice of or care about my healthy children?' "

## KOSHER LAWS

Reb Moishe Joseph Teitelbaum, rabbi of the Hungarian city, Uhel, was in charge of a large yeshivah, and taught the boys who studied there. The lads ate at various homes, but only such as were orthodox. From the others, who were not orthodox, they accepted weekly or monthly sums of money, but they would never eat with them. A few of the non-orthodox men went to the rabbi with a complaint.

"Why don't you permit the boys to eat at our homes?" they protested. "You only allow them to take money from us. If we are not kosher, then our money, too, is not kosher."

The rabbi listened and answered smilingly. "Did you ever observe what happens when you ask a ritual question about a goose, and the rabbi says that it is trefah? In that case you know that you are not allowed to eat the meat, but you certainly may use the feathers. That means that in spite of the fact that the goose is not kosher, you may pluck the feathers of it."

### "REFORM"

The Zhitomer Rabbi Zev Hirsch Segal, had a "reformed" son who changed his name to Dr. Gregory Petrovitch. One Saturday he stayed at his father's house. He refused to go to the synagogue, but immensely enjoyed the Sabbath meal, which consisted of gefillte fish and potato kugel. Afterwards he smoked a cigar, and discussed the advantages of Reform with his father.

"It is quite strange," his father said. "For me the Jewish religion is not difficult to cope with. You who have disregarded the Torah completely, call yourself Gregory

Petrovitch, smoke on the Sabbath, enjoy all gentile and Jewish conveniences, eat both pork and Sabbath kugel— for people like you the Jewish religion is difficult, and you only seek reforms."

## THE TOO WISE

Rabbi Malbim was in Yekaterinoslaw, and everyone came to greet him. Some of the city's wise men were also present. The rabbi gave them a hearty welcome.

"Who are you?" he asked.

"We are the wise men of the city," they replied.

"That means that you are Men Who Know," the rabbi remarked.

"Men Who Know?" they repeated. "Which man can say he knows?"

"Let me interpret the expression for you," Rabbi Malbim suggested. "If you are wise men, then you know that which a Jew who adheres to the Jewish religion does not. For instance, when I get up in the morning, I don't know what I can eat before I say my prayers. After I wash myself, I don't know what I can eat before I say a blessing. Wise men, on the other hand, know all that!"

## NO WEALTH OF BRAINS

An important conference was being held at the home of the Sandzer Zaddik. Suddenly a well-known wealthy woman entered, shouting very loudly that she must speak to the rabbi. The people tried to calm her, explaining that the rabbi was busy, but the woman pleaded that it was a matter of life and death. The Sandzer Zaddik begged to be excused by the other rabbis and walked out. After a short while he returned, his face wreathed in smiles. The rabbis were curious to know what had happened.

"The women wanted me to interpret a dream," he said. "She dreamt that her son had become crazy."

"How did you explain her dream?" they inquired.

"I told her," the zaddik replied, "that it was a sign he would become a very wealthy man."

## THE OLD AND THE NEW

A Reform rabbi met an orthodox rabbi and the two started a conversation.

"How much do you earn a week?" the Reform rabbi asked.

"Twelve dollars," was the reply.

"So little!" the Reform rabbi cried in amazement. "The sexton of our temple gets five times as much as you, and I get ten times as much, yet your religious people boast that they love the Torah."

"The principal of the matter is this," the orthodox rabbi explained. "The Reform Torah is brand new and it is easy to find many customers for new merchandise. I teach the old Torah to my people. For old merchandise you need people who can appreciate value. Such people are scarce, therefore I get paid little."

## RITUAL OF DRESS

A rabbi spent the Sabbath at a farmer's house. Friday evening, when the farmer came home from his work in the field, he greeted the rabbi warmly. The sage, noticing that the farmer wore his shirt on the outside, over his trousers, remarked, "It is no shame to work in the field. Our forefathers were also farmers, but it is not proper to wear the shirt over the trousers."

On Yom Kippur the farmer came to the synagogue. The rabbi recognized him and gave him a *kittel*. The farmer put it on, and stuffed it into his trousers. The rabbi observed and told him that the kittel should be worn on the outside.

"But, rabbi," the farmer protested, "on the farm where there are no people and no one sees, you instructed me to wear my shirt inside. Here, in the presence of all the people, you tell me to wear it on the outside?"

## DO IT YOURSELF

The overseers of the Brisker Synagogue decided to discharge the sexton. They asked the rabbi, Reb Yoshe Ber, to break the news to him. Reb Ber refused.

"Why don't you want to do it?" the overseers questioned. "You are the rabbi, and he is your sexton."

Reb Yoshe Ber replied, "You recite every morning the passage where God ordered Abraham to bring his son Isaac to the altar as a sacrifice. That command God gave himself. But when He told him to hold back his hand and not strike his son, God spoke through an angel. Why

64

didn't God send an angel to speak at the beginning? Because the angel would have said. 'If you want to kill a Jew, do it yourself.' "

## THE BARGAIN

Slonim had a notorious informer. Whenever there was an important community matter, which the government was not to know about, the people had to bribe him to keep quiet. It happened that something of importance occurred, and the informer demanded 300 rubles. The inhabitants held a meeting with the rabbi, Reb Eisel Chariff, to decide what to do. The informer was called, and they began to bargain with him. He insisted he must get 300 rubles, and not a penny less; otherwise he would speak.

"You are a low-down, good for nothing!" Reb Eisel cried furiously. "If you take fifty rubles, we'll agree. Otherwise the community will get itself another informer who will do it for twenty-five rubles!"

## RULES FOR LIVING

Reb Ber, from Mezeritch, said that man should learn three things from a child, and seven things from a thief.

From a child: 1) He is always happy. 2) He never sits empty-handed for a second. 3) He cries for everything that he wants.

From a thief: 1) He works even at night. 2) What he can't accomplish in one night, he will try again the second. 3) All thieves love one another. 4) He will sacrifice his life for a trivial thing. 5) No object has a specific value attached to it, and he will sell the most valuable thing for an insignificant price. 6) A thief will take a severe beating for what he has stolen, but will insist that he knows nothing about it. 7) He will not change his business for anything else in the world.

## WORDLESS

When Reb Heshel Lubliner was very young people began to talk of marriage to him. A rabbi and a shadchan went to see how much of an education the youth had.

"Is it true what people say about you," the rabbi asked, "that whatever book you are shown, you can read and interpret it?"

"Try me out," the little fellow challenged them.

The rabbi took a Talmud, turned to a blank page, and told him to read.

The little boy began to mumble aloud, but uttered not one distinct word.

"Why can't we hear a word?" the rabbi demanded.

"Because," the lad smiled, "I do not see a word."

## DE CUSTIBUS

A poor woman came to Rabbi Yehoshele Kutner, with a vital query about a chicken. She had found no gall in the chicken when she kashered it. As is the custom in deciding such questions, the rabbi tasted the liver of the chicken, and it was not bitter.

"You taste it," he said, turning to the woman. "Is it bitter?"

66

"Oh, rabbi," the woman wailed, "it is as bitter as death itself! I am a poor widow, with two small orphans. My older child is ill, and the doctor suggested that he eat some chicken broth. I scraped together my last few pennies and bought a chicken, and now to my misfortune there is a vital doubt. Holy rabbi, it is so bitter!"

"If it is bitter," Rabbi Yehoshele said, "it is kosher."

## SARTOR RESARTUS

Rabbi Samuel Mohilever and his friend, a hassidic rabbi, visited a large city.

"Let us go to a theatre, for I am curious to see what it is like," the hassidic rabbi suggested. "In our small city we can't do it, because we are well known."

"How can we appear in our clergyman's clothes?" Rabbi Samuel asked.

"I will take care of the situation," the other replied. "I will secure some modern garments for both of us."

"You are a hassidic rabbi," Reb Samuel smilingly returned, "and as soon as you discard your fur cap and your satin frock, you are a rabbi no longer. Then you may do whatever your heart desires. But I am a regular rabbi among ordinary Jews, and regardless of what clothes I wear, I'll always be a rabbi."

## POMP AND CIRCUMSTANCE

Rabbi Elimelech and his brother were traveling refugees. When in Ludmir they stayed at the home of Reb Aaron, who was a hassid. Several years passed, and the rabbi and his brother were recognized by the government and reinstated to their original rank. This time when they visited Ludmir, they did not come as previously. Instead they arrived in a magnificent coach, drawn by two stately horses. A landlord of Ludmir asked if they would honor him by staying at his house. The brothers immediately refused the invitation and said, "We are the same people that we were before. At that time you never thought of inviting us. Now that we come with coach and horses, you wish to honor us. Then here, take the horses; let them stay at your house."

## RITUAL REFORM

A woman came to a Reform rabbi with a ritual question. While she was boiling a pot of milk, some of the milk had overflowed onto a pot of meat nearby. What was she to do? The rabbi decided that the pot of milk was trefah and the pot of meat kosher. The woman looked puzzled and repeated her problem.

"But, rabbi," she explained, "the pot of milk did not turn over. The milk only overflowed onto the pot of meat."

"Yes, I heard you the first time," the rabbi replied. "That is just the point. From your story I can readily see that it was the fault of the pot of milk. He started the entire thing and he must suffer."

## COMING CLEAN

A rabbi, after writing at an erudite work all day long, went to the synagogue, leaving his manuscripts on his desk. When he returned there was not a trace of his written work.

"Who was in the house?" he shouted. "Who took my papers?"

"I asked the servant to clean your room," his wife explained.

"What have you done with the papers?" he raved at the servant.

"Be calm, rabbi," the servant nonchalantly replied. "You can trust me. I only destroyed all the papers that were written up. The clean sheets I left."

## THORNS AND FLOWERS

A rabbi and priest were discussing religion, while strolling in a garden filled with flowers.

"Do you see these flowers?" the priest said. "They are the different races that compose the Christian religion. Where is your race?"

The rabbi clasped the priest's hand, led him to a fence where briars grew, and said, "See, this is our race."

The priest wrinkled his brow and inquired whether he was in earnest.

"Of course I am," the rabbi replied. "With your flowers anyone can do whatever he desires, but with our briars? Just try and touch them!"

## ISRAEL IS ABUSED

A maggid came to Reb Levi Isaac Berditchev, and told him that his daughter was about to be married, but since he was poor, he wanted the rabbi to allow him to deliver a sermon in the synagogue in order to collect some money. Reb Levi made him promise that he would not reprimand the Jews, as is the custom with all preachers. The maggid consented, but in the middle of his sermon he forgot and began to attack the congregation, pointing out their extreme sinfulness.

Reb Levi Isaac ran over to the Holy Ark, and called out, "Almighty God, don't believe the preacher! Your Jews are the noblest of people. Help the preacher marry off his daughter, then he will not scold your children!"

## FRIEND OF THE COURT

The wife of a rabbi sharply rebuked her servant for breaking several dishes. She dragged the servant to trial before the rabbinic magistrate. On the way the rabbi's wife noticed her husband following them.

"Why are you coming along?" she demanded. "I am capable of defending myself. It does not befit a man of your position to interfere because of an argument with a servant."

"You are mistaken, my wife," the rabbi replied. "I am not going along to help you. I want to defend the servant, who is a poor orphan, and will not know what to say before the venerable judge."

## EDUCATIONAL PROGRESS

A rabbi made a desperate attempt to teach a young American boy how to pray, but all his efforts were in vain. Realizing that the lad would never know how to pray correctly, he began to teach him the kaddish.

When the lad's mother found out what her son was learning, she was filled with fear and ran to the rabbi, crying, "Rabbi, what are you doing? Why are you teaching him the kaddish? My husband and I are young people and expect to live for a long time."

"Please be calm, my good woman," the rabbi consoled her. "You can live for another hundred years, and your son still will not know how to say the kaddish."

## CONVERTING THE TEMPLE

During the great controversy about Reform, the Hasam Sofer ostracized all Reform rabbis. Reb Israel Salanter would not agree to this procedure.

"If I were he, I wouldn't ostracize the Reformers," he said. "For example, in the case of Geiger, I would reason with him and try to explain and enlighten his errors. If I did not prevail and he still desired to build a temple and have an organ, I would agree. Only I would place a minyan of learned men, to sit and study Talmud constantly in the temple, and in that manner the temple would automatically become a *beth midrash* (house of study)."

## COMPARATIVE GREATNESS

Rabbi Solomon Kluger of Brod wrote a letter to a farmer, who lived on the outskirts of the city. He addressed him as "The Grand Rabbi, Gaon." The farmer was amazed at the title given him. He knew that the rabbi did not even address prominent sages in that manner. When he visited Brod he asked Rabbi Kluger why he had called him by this honorable title.

"I called you Grand Rabbi, Gaon," the rabbi replied, "because in the vicinity of your small farm, among so many ignorant people, you are indeed a gaon!"

## SUPERIOR RACE

The Shaagas Arieh, while Rabbi of Volozhin, discussed a difficult philosophical thought in his sermon one Saturday afternoon. The entire audience, including the intellectuals, lost track of the discussion and could not follow. After the sermon the preacher addressed his listeners, "Do you know, my good people, that you are greater than the angels?"

They gaped in surprise.

"The prophet Ezekiel tells us that angels have calves' feet," the Shaagas Arieh smiled, "and you have calves' heads!"

## CAUSE FOR FEAR

Among the hassidim of the Chortkover Rabbi there was one who had a habit of stealing the hats of the Jews. This would occur frequently and the rabbi suspected the guilty person. One day the same hassid visited the rabbi and asked for his blessing. The rabbi, deeply absorbed in the Talmud, and not noticing his visitor, wished him luck in all his undertakings. But soon the rabbi discovered whom he had blessed, and anxiously said to the sexton, "Watch that hassid closely, because I am afraid that the blessing I gave him will fall on my head first."

## PROFESSIONAL

The famous Reb Chaim Brisker was a devoted believer in the Zionist movement, but did not particularly care for the type of people who were leading it. He felt that they were neither capable nor suitable for the effort. "Why don't you take an active interest in the work?" the people asked Reb Chaim. "Why do you let others do it, while you stand apart?"

"It is a world-wide custom," Reb Chaim replied, "that at a wedding the children go first, then follow the musicians, and at the end come the bride and groom."

## COMMUNAL TEARS

During the reign of the Austrian Queen Maria Theresa, a proclamation was issued to drive the Jews out of Bohemia. The Jews sent Rabbi Zalman Krub, of Prague, to the minister to plead that the order be rescinded. Reb Zalman began to sob loudly in the presence of the minister.

"Why do you make so much noise?" the latter asked.

"Because it isn't I alone who am crying," Reb Zalman moaned; "the voices of thousands of Jews are crying out of me."

## GOOD AFTER DEATH

A rabbi had an ill-tempered wife who made life miserable for him. One afternoon she served him some meat from a very lean rooster, which was anything but tasty. The following day she boiled a fat, juicy hen, and the rabbi enjoyed it immensely.

"Now you can see for yourself," she called out with confidence, "a female is better than a male!"

"Yes, it is true," the sage agreed, "but only after death."

## DOUBLE DUTY

The Brisker Rabbi, Reb Yoshe Ber, looked out the window and noticed three wagons filled with hay drawn by three horses, one directly behind the other. Two horses ate the hay from the wagons in front of their own. The Brisker Rabbi turned to a man alongside him and asked, "Which horse do you think is more fortunate than the others?"

The man looked puzzled and did not know what to say.

"The center one," the rabbi replied. "Not only does he eat, but his load also become lighter."

## STRAIGHT TALK

After a rabbi of a small town would end his sermons, his students often discovered the same material in various books. They became suspicious and felt that the rabbi was stealing his matter from other sources.

One day the rabbi enlightened them.

"When you walk along a road," he said, "you are bound to meet other people; but when you lose your path and wander through fields and meadows, then you are alone. Since my thoughts are logical and follow a straight course, they must meet up with other people."

## NINE PLUS NAUGHT

A rabbi discovered at the minchah service that he was short one man to complete the minyan. He looked out the window and noticed a known atheist standing nearby.

"Call him in," the rabbi ordered the sexton.

"Him! an atheist, a good for nothing?" the sexton asked, amazed.

"In order to increase the number to ten," the rabbi answered with a smile, "we don't need more than a zero."

## TEAR BARREL

Reb Jacob David Slutzker was not only a gaon, but also an artist in delivering a discourse. His audiences were always intensely moved by his sermons. On one occasion, however, his listeners did not respond at all. Not one tear did they shed!

That same evening a friend of Reb Jacob David asked him, "Rabbi, why didn't your sermon tug at the heart-strings of the people today?"

"My profession," the rabbi replied, "is only to turn open the spigot. When the barrel is empty, it is no fault of mine."

## COOK'S TOUR

A servant girl came to Reb Abe Pasviler, the Vilner Rabbi, with a question.

75

"Rabbi, what shall I cook for supper?"

"Go home and prepare noodles," the rabbi advised.

The people present were amazed at the peculiar question and the strange reply.

"Why are you so flabbergasted?" the rabbi asked. "What is there to understand? the servant girl probably asked her mistress what she should prepare for supper, and the mistress I suppose, angrily replied, 'Go ask the rabbi!' The maid, not knowing any better, did as she was told."

## UNDER COVER

A yeshivah boy in Wolozin began to dress in modern fashion. The news reached the Chief Rabbi, who regarded the matter as insignificant.

"What is it if one wears *goyishe* clothes?" he asked.

The yeshivah boys were amazed at the Chief Rabbi's words.

"When a clock stops running," he explained, "it is not the fault of the face of the clock, but there is something wrong with the inner mechanism. The same is true of goyishe clothes. They are only a symbol that there is something wrong inside."

## NUISANCE VALUE

The people of a small town in Lithuania, having a dispute with their rabbi, brought in Reb Isaac Jacob Reines to act as judge. They had decided to give their rabbi a certain amount of money, and have him leave the com-

munity. A heated discussion arose, because the rabbi refused to accept anything less than 300 rubles.

"The rabbi is right," Reb Isaac Jacob said to the people.
"Give him 300 rubles."

"What do you mean?" they argued. "Why should
he get 300? Isn't 100 enough?"

"Your rabbi knows," Reb Isaac replied, "that to get
rid of him is worth all of 300 rubles."

## THE DEVIL'S THIEVES

The Sadigurer Rabbi, Reb Abraham Jacob, married off
a daughter. On the way to the wedding his hat, which
had cost him three hundred rubles, was stolen. The rabbi
sent for the King of the Thieves, and asked him to guess
where his hat could be.

"Find my hat for me," the rabbi pleaded, "and I will
give you whatever you ask for. I am ashamed for my
in-laws to find out."

"Rabbi," the King of the Thieves replied, "if one of
my hassidim stole your hat, I still have hopes of finding
it. But if one of your hassidim stole it, then the hat is
lost forever."

## ALL-SEEING EYE

Rabbi Zundel Salanter, while riding with a Jewish
driver, passed a field of hay. The driver was tempted to
take some for his horse. He asked the rabbi to be his
lookout.

When the driver started to gather the hay, Reb Zundel began to shout, "Some one is looking, some one is looking!"

The driver quickly left everything behind, jumped into the wagon, and started to ride. After a while he turned around, but saw no one.

"Rabbi," he asked, "who was it?"

"He who is in heaven," the rabbi explained, "He was looking!"

## DOMESTIC LIFE

Reb Shmuel, who was a neighbor of the rabbi, visited him very often, and would sit for hours at his home. One day he arrived just when the rabbi had finished his meal, and was preparing to take a nap. Reb Shmuel filled his pipe leisurely and asked, "Rabbi, may I smoke?"

"Yes, you may," the rabbi replied, "but smoke the way I do."

"How do you smoke?" Reb Shmuel asked.

"I," answered the rabbi, "I smoke at home."

## ENFORCED TEMPERANCE

The Pitever Rabbi, Reb Israel, always took a drink of liquor together with his people. One day the rabbi doffed his tefillin before the conclusion of the prayers and went over to drink by himself. The people stared at his strange behavior. Later a friend asked the rabbi why he took a drink before his prayers were over.

"For the simple reason," the rabbi smiled, "that yesterday I waited until after the prayers and by then there wasn't a drop of liquor left."

## THE LIVING DEAD

A poor man visited Reb Joseph Saul Lemberger and asked for a donation. Reb Joseph Saul, not having any money with him, left his gold watch on the table and walked into the other room. When he came back he saw that the watch was gone.

"Now I understand what the rabbis meant when they said, 'A poor man is equivalent to a dead man.' As one is not permitted to leave a corpse alone in the house, so is one not allowed to leave a poor man alone."

## MURDER OR PROFIT

A rabbi asked a wealthy Jew for a loan of a few dollars. The Jew looked up innocently and asked, "Rabbi, didn't you say yesterday in your sermon that to loan money on interest is the same as killing a person?"

"What?" the rabbi asked in surprise. "I do not intend to borrow on interest. I merely want a loan."

"Oh, is that it?" the rich Jew retorted. "Then the case is even worse, for in that event I would be killing myself."

## STOLEN WATER IS SWEET

A servant abstracted a bottle of wine that the rabbi had left on his table. The rabbi saw him carrying the bottle and asked him what it contained.

"It is a bottle of water," the servant replied.

"Give me a little to drink," the rabbi asked, then turning to the servant he said, "Now I understand what King Solomon meant when he said, 'Stolen water is sweet.'"

## WHAT FOOLS THESE MORTALS BE

When the Baal Hamoar was a child, he was already teaching older men. One day he saw a goat, and was tempted to take a ride. This annoyed his students, for they felt ashamed of his behavior.

"Every person when young," the Baal Hamoar explained, "must satisfy his eccentric desires. If he doesn't do so when he is young he is bound to do it at an older age. I'd rather act foolishly now, than when I am old."

## HAPPY REASONING

The "Baal Takse" dashed into the house of Reb Yoshe Ber, Rabbi of Slutsk, shouting wildly, "Rabbi, meat is being brought into our city from the outside!"

"What about it?" Reb Ber calmly asked.

"What about it?" the "Baal Takse" exclaimed. "The meat comes from another city, and we don't even know who the slaughterers are."

"That does not worry me," Reb Yoshe Ber smiled. "If we eat the meat of the Slutzker slaughterers, whom we do know, we certainly may eat the meat of those slaughterers whom we don't know."

## MISDEMEANOR

A notorious liar from Radomsk invited the author of Tifereth Shlomo to act as godfather at a circumcision.

"You commit numerous sins, but me you honor with good deeds," the rabbi remarked.

"If the rabbi is not present I will be greatly embarrassed and the rabbi will then have a sin," the other replied.

"You are a strange fellow," the rabbi said. "You allow yourself to commit great sins, but me you begrudge even a little one."

## LITERARY SALTATION

Several rabbis wanted to publish a book with commentaries on the Torah. They asked all the rabbis to contribute to the work. Reb Eisel Chariff refused.

"Why do you decline, rabbi?" they questioned him. "Many other rabbis have already agreed."

Reb Eisel laughed. "Great dancers," he said, "dance alone. Those who cannot dance, gather together in a circle and jump around."

## MAN AND THE EARTH

Mendele Kossiver said that the man possessing a great knowledge of the Torah is noble only when he conducts himself in the same manner as the earth. The earth yields all her valuable products to humanity, and never says, "If I give you all that I possess, why do you step over me? Why do you dig me up, and make dust out of me?" So must a learned man be. In spite of the fact that all people reap knowledge from him, he should not be proud, and give what he has freely to everyone, just as the earth does.

## RETORT

Reb Chaim Jacob Vidrevitz, Rabbi of Moscow, had a speech defect. One day he had to solve a difficult business problem for an ignorant farmer. The other became furious over the rabbi's decision and indignantly called out, "You are a liar, a hypocrite, and a fool!"

"A-a-nd y-you," Reb Chaim Jacob stuttered, "are a s-st-stammerer."

"I, a stammerer?" the farmer laughed.

"Well," Reb Chaim Jacob explained, "since you tell me what you are, I tell you what I am."

## UNFAIR EXCHANGE

Reb Chaim Woloziner's brother Reb Zalmele was a great scholar and a genius. Friday afternoon, while he was in the bath-house, someone stole his shirt. Reb Zal-mele murmured not one word about it, dressed, and went home.

"Where is your shirt?" his wife asked in surprise.

"Oh, someone just made an exchange with me," Reb Zalmele replied.

"Then where is the other man's shirt?" she demanded.

"The other person," Reb Zalmele smiled, "forgot to leave his."

## HEAVENLY BURGLARS

Rabbi Laib, the Shpaler Zaydeh, was a philanthropist, who divided all his money among the poor. He never questioned who the needy person was, and so even gave money to thieves. The people of the city disapproved of Rabbi Laib's actions, and reprimanded him, "Rabbi, who ever heard of supporting thieves?"

82

"It happens very frequently," the Shpaler Zaydeh replied, "that the 'doors of mercy' are locked. Then I send my thieves, and they break them open!"

## THE LEFTIST

The prominent Warsaw rabbi, Reb David Brisk Meisler, was one of the select few permitted to attend city committee meetings. Whenever he attended a conference he always seated himself on the left side of the room.

One of the members of the committee approached him and said, "Rabbi, it is not becoming for a personality like you to sit on the left."

"I sit there," Reb Meisler retorted, "because the Jews have no rights."

## CONFESSIONAL

A sinner came to Reb Naftali Rapshizer to beg repentance. Since the man was ashamed to admit that he was the sinner, he told the rabbi that a friend of his who had committed sins, but was too embarrassed to appear personally, had sent him in his stead. He then gave the rabbi a list of the sins his friend had supposedly committed.

"What a fool the other man is," the rabbi smiled. "He could have come himself and said that his friend sent him."

## PULPITEERS

A rabbi of a small town disliked sermons and preachers. One day a relative of his, a preacher, came to the town, and the rabbi not only had to give him permission to preach, but was also compelled to listen.

When the sermon was over, the preacher asked the rabbi, "What is your opinion of my sermon? I've preached well, haven't I?"

"Yes," replied the rabbi, "you spoke well, but if you had not spoken at all it would have been just as well."

## THE LONG ROAD

A Polish Jew asked the author of Tifereth Shlomo for his opinion concerning a match proposed to him with a girl from Russia. The famous rabbi would not give his assent.

"Perhaps the match was made in heaven," the young man suggested.

"How could the angels arrange anything like that," the rabbi replied, "when they know that you haven't even train fare!"

## THE FIRST WILL BE REWARDED

Reb Moishe Itzel Paniveshner had a peculiar trial. Two Jews were disputing about cemetery plots they had bought. Each claimed the better plot of ground. They argued the question constantly, and finally decided to ask the rabbi for his decision. Reb Moishe Itzel listened carefully to their arguement, and then gave his verdict: "He who dies first will get the better grave." From then on their dispute ceased.

## SELF-SERVICE

A hassidic rabbi, when he wanted a smoke, would go into the kitchen, strike a match, and light his pipe. He never would have anyone cater to him.

One day a hassid sought to help the rabbi light his pipe, and thus show respect to a great scholar.

"I, too," the rabbi replied, "enjoy catering to a great scholar."

## ON THE OTHER FOOT

Rabbi Shloime Pfeffermintz, the famed gaon, did not live at peace with his wife, and decided to divorce her. His friends reprimanded him, saying it was not proper to divorce a woman beloved and respected by all. Reb Shloime pulled off his shoe, lifted it high before the eyes of his friends, and said, "See how good-looking this shoe is, how well it is made; yet no one knows where this shoe is pinching me."

## HIERACHY

A priest attempted to pursuade a rabbi to give up his religion. He explained how high a Jew could rise if he would convert himself into a Catholic.

"You will have the opportunity to become a bishop, then a cardinal, and if you are clever enough you can even become a pope."

The rabbi remained calm and refused to be tempted. Finally the priest called out, "You cannot become a God!"

"Why not?" the rabbi innocently demanded. "It happened once before that a Jew became God."

## DOUBLE-TAKE

A coachman of a small town asked the rabbi, "Rabbi, I am a kohen, may I take a divorcee?"

"You may," the rabbi replied.

The people present were amazed. When the coachman left they said, "Rabbi, what is the idea of permitting a kohen to take a divorcee?"

"There is nothing wrong about that," the rabbi answered. "The man is a coachman, and he wanted to know whether he could take a divorcee on his wagon and bring her to the market."

## DISADVANTAGE

Reb Berish Meisels, Rabbi of Warsaw, while traveling on a train, sat opposite a Russian lieutenant, an anti-Semite who had a dog he called "Yankel."

"I feel sorry for the dog," Reb Berish remarked. "The poor creature has a Jewish name."

"So what?" the lieutenant asked.

"If it were not for that," the rabbi returned, "he could become a lieutenant."

## NEXT GENERATION

The Holy Jew from Psychah would say, "When a man is asked 'For whom are you working and toiling?' he usually replies, 'Personally I am content with little, but I must consider the welfare of the children.' When the child grows up, he also begins to toil for the same purpose, namely 'the children.' I would like to see," the Holy Jew from Psycha then said, "the ideal child for whom all generations work and slave."

## DEVOTIONS

Reb Zelmele, while sitting with his hassidim, jokingly said, "When a Jew has finished saying his prayers, one should greet him and say Shalom Alechem."

Why?" the hassidim asked.

"Because I'm sure there isn't a spot on earth to which he did not wander, while standing in prayer!"

## SPIRITUAL FOOD

A rabbi, seated at the table one Friday night, asked a hassid, his guest, whether he had already eaten.

"I didn't come here to eat," the hassid replied.

"Man's soul also doesn't come into this world to eat," the sage smilingly remarked, "but if it isn't fed, it runs away."

## LEARNED RABBI

A rabbi was given a position in a small town. One day the butcher came to him with a ritual question about a cow.

Butcher: Where is the rabbi?

Sexton: The rabbi is studying.

Butcher: I can't understand this. Couldn't they hire a graduate rabbi, not one who first has to learn?

87

## THEE AND ME

Rabbi Jehuda Satmarer would always ridicule his audience. During one sermon, when he realized what he had done, he paused and said, "My friends, don't think for a moment that I intended all those harsh words only for you. In reality I meant myself. But since I am aware that you are no better than I am, I spoke a little louder so that you too should hear."

## THE WINE-BIBBER

Reb David Diniver visited Reb Chaim Sandzer, and while at the table the host poured a glass of wine for his guest.

"I am not permitted to drink wine," Reb David said. "The doctor forbade it."

"It's all right; you may drink," Reb Chaim smiled. "The doctor who forbade it is sleeping now."

## CANING THE RABBI

When the Lubliner Rabbi was in America, he prayed one Yom Kippur in the synagogue of a small city. He was requested to chant Neilah. After the service, a committee presented him with a golden cane.

"It seems," the rabbi joked, "that I am not worth more than a stick for my performance."

## CONCEALED VIRTUE

A rabbi urged a wealthy man of his city to donate some money for a worthy cause. The man refused by saying that he gave enough money in secret.

"Why is it," the rabbi asked, "that when you sin in secret the entire city knows about it, but that no one ever heard of the charity you give secretly?"

## THE THREE KINDS OF JEWS

A clean-shaven man visited Reb Eisel Slonimer.

"Are you a cohen or a Levite?" the rabbi asked him.

"What makes you believe that I am either a cohen or a Levite?" the man said in astonishment.

"My dear man," replied the rabbi, "you certainly do not look like an Israelite."

## JOY IN FAITH

When asked to interpret the verse, "Let the heart of them rejoice, who seek the Lord," Rabbi Bunim said, "When a person searches for something he has lost, he is usually filled with sorrow while he looks for it. When he finds the lost article, he is happy. But they who seek the Lord are happy during the search."

## ALL ALIKE

A rabbi, whose wife was a hunchback, would always rise when a woman with such a deformity came into his presence.

"Why does the woman deserve so much respect?" a friend once asked him.

"There is no doubt," the rabbi replied, "that she is a rabbi's wife."

## DIRECTIONAL

A rabbi met a young man running rapidly along the street.

"Why do you run?" the rabbi asked.

"I am running after a job," the other panted.

"How do you know that your job is before you and you have to chase after it? Perhaps it is behind you and you are running away from it?"

## ON LEARNING

A hassid asked the Gerer Rabbi for advice. Since he was an expert in writing Torahs, and also a capable teacher, which one of the two professions should he select?

The Gerer Rabbi advised him to choose teaching. "Because," he said, "it may happen that you meet a very clever student, and you will be able to learn something from him."

## RETORT COURTEOUS

A wealthy man said to Reb Eisel Slonimer, "You can see for yourself that a rich man is greater than a rabbi. The rabbi comes to the rich for money, but the rich never go to the rabbi."

"Does the sick man go to the doctor," Reb Eisel asked, "or does the doctor come to the sick?"

## DOUBLE TROUBLE

Reb Yoshe Ber, the Brisker Rabbi, was asked why large cities have only one rabbi and smaller cities have two.

"It's very simple," Reb Yoshe Ber replied. "When a wealthy man buys one fat cow, it supplies him with plenty of milk. A poor man, on the other hand, buys two goats and has nothing from both of them."

## RECIPROCITY

A hassidic young man visited Reb Mendele Kotzker.

"How advanced are you in your studies?" Reb Mendele asked.

"Rabbi, I have learned the whole Talmud," the young man boasted.

"Really?" Reb Mendele asked. "But what has the Talmud taught you?"

## CUMULATIVE

A rabbi said to a sinner, "I envy you. Soon the High Holidays will be here. You will pray, and all your sins will become mitzvoth. You will have more mitzvoth than ten rabbis put together."

"Rabbi," the sinner replied, "wait another year, and you will have much more for which to envy me."

## LET GOD CHOOSE

Reb Hirsh Melech Dinuber placed his festival prayer-book (machzor) on his desk in the synagogue, turned to the front page, and said, "Almighty God, I don't know what prayer to offer You. Here is the whole machzor; select whichever prayer pleases You best."

91

## THE DIFFERENCE

The Kotzker Rabbi was asked what was the difference between a zaddik and an evil man. "Somehow they are both sinful," the rabbi replied, "but the difference is this, that the zaddik while he lives knows that he is sinful, and the wicked man when he sins knows that he lives."

## PARTITION

An atheist had a dispute with Rabbi Jonathan of Prague. A fence stood between them during their conversation.

"Rabbi," said the atheist, "tell me please what is it that keeps a pig at a distance from a Jew?"

"Dear man," replied the rabbi, "a fence."

## NO CHANGE

An ignorant Jew came to a famous rabbi and said, "Rabbi, do you remember the days when we were children, and played a game as horses?"

"I remember that very well," the rabbi replied. "Once you were a horse, but in the end who remained the horse?"

## RARE CATCH

Reb Eisel of Slonim spent months in various cities where he published his books. Whenever he returned to Slonim he would say to his people, "It's no wonder that the town of Slonim does not discharge me. They never find me home."

## THE PURE

A doctor examined a zaddik who was ill, and asked him to show his togue.

"Your tongue is not clean," the doctor remarked.

"Which human being," asked the zaddik, "has a clean tongue nowadays?"

## FOR PROTECTION

A rabbi's daughter married a rich coachman's son. On the day of the wedding the rabbi said to his wife:

"Do you know what I intend to do? I am accustomed to wear shoes and white stockings, but in all respect to our mechutan, who wears high boots, I, too, will buy myself such a pair, so that he will not be shamed."

The coachman, on the other hand, in order to please the rabbi, decided to don shoes and white stockings. At the wedding the people were shocked to see the footwear of the rabbi and the coachman. One of the guests approached the rabbi and asked him to explain this peculiar change.

"What is there to understand?" the rabbi replied. "My mechutan is getting out of a mud puddle, so he can wear shoes and white stockings, but I am getting into one, therefore I must wear high boots."

## AFTER ME THE DELUGE

It happened that in the days of Rabbi Landau of Krakow there was no rain one summer. The people of the town were called upon to gather at the synagogue to pray for rain.

During the service, when the prayer for rain was being said, a sinner entered to say Kaddish. He walked over to the pulpit and began to pray. The crowd demanded that he be thrown out, but Rabbi Landau winked knowingly and said, "Let him stay."

Afterwards the rabbi was asked, "How is it that you allowed such a man to pray?" and Rabbi Landau wisely replied:

"Men like him once brought the flood upon the world. If not a flood, perhaps he will bring a little rain."

## INFECTION

When Reb Chaim Laib, the Sosnitzer Gaon, was rabbi in Smargon, there lived a very wealthy, stingy Jew in the city who never gave a penny for religious purposes. One day, while he was having a chat with the rabbi, he asked:

"Rabbi, how are you getting along financially?"

"Well, if I would have four or five contributors like you, I wouldn't have to worry about making a living," Reb Chaim Laib replied.

"Rabbi, please don't be angry with he," the man pleaded. "Perhaps I do not give, but you know, rabbi, times are bad, expenses high, and people rate me richer than I actually am."

"You misunderstand me," Reb Chaim Laib interrupted. "This is what I meant. If I should have four or five men like you, I would be perfectly contented. The trouble lies in the fact that I have two hundred like you."

94

## COMPARISON

A farmer traveled a long distance to the city to ask the rabbi a ritual question.

There were several pots of milk standing on his threshold, and his dog had drunk from one of them. Therefore, he wanted to know whether the rest of the milk remained kosher.

The rabbi looked at this peculiar Jew and thought he would humor him.

"Tell me, my good man," he smiled, "is he a large dog?"

"How can I describe him to you, rabbi," the farmer replied; "he is quite a large mongrel. When he stands up on his hind legs, I think he is a little taller than you.'"

## DUST TO DUST

Two landlords, neighbors, had a dispute about a piece of land. They came to Reb Liplen for a hearing. The rabbi saw that they would be difficult to deal with, so he decided to look at the plot of land himself. In the midst of their heated argument, Reb Liplen bent down and put his ear to the earth, and said:

"It is quite strange. One says that the plot of earth belongs to him, the other says it is his, and the earth itself says that you both belong to her. Since both your arguments are futile, you should listen to the correct decision and fulfill it!"

## DIVISION OF LABOR

Several Socialists came to the famous Reb Velvele, Preacher of Vilna, and said:

95

"Rabbi, since you have such a great influence on the people, we would like you to preach on Socialism, because it is a very important principle in life. Why should the capitalists seize the entire wealth of the world, and the poor workers suffer and struggle, barely earning a living for their families? A new system must be introduced into the world."

"I will do what I can, and you do what you can," Reb Velvele replied. "You try to see that the capitalists part with their wealth, and I will see to it that the workers ac-cept it."

## TOO LATE

A young man asked Reb Laizer Kelmer to ordain him as rabbi. Reb Laizer spoke to the fellow and found him to be very intelligent.

"What would you do if you were confronted with a case where a man cut his hand on Saturday, and the blood flowed profusely?" Reb Laizer asked.

"Just a moment, rabbi; I will look into the Shulchan Aruch," said the candidate.

"No, my dear man, you cannot be a rabbi. Before you look into the Shulchan Aruch a Jew will bleed to death."

## ZOOLOGICAL NOTE

A coachman came to a rabbi with the complaint that his horse ate so little that there was danger of his collaps-ing.

"Do you pray every day?" the rabbi asked.

Not always," the coachman replied.

"Do you wash your hands and say grace before you eat?"

"No," was the reply.

"Well, then, it all makes sense; since you eat like a horse, your horse eats like a human."

## KINDLY JUDGMENT

Reb Levi Isaac Berditchever met a Jew smoking one Saturday. The man, on seeing Reb Levi Isaac, tried to conceal his cigarette.

"Almighty God'" Reb Levi Isaac exclaimed, turning his eyes upward toward heaven, "see how fine your children are. When they do commit a sin, they are terribly ashamed of themselves!"

## TAKEN FOR A RIDE

A group of writers came to visit Rabbi Samuel Mohilever on Saturday. They drove over to his house in a carriage. As they approached his home they found him sitting on the balcony studying the Talmud. Suddenly they became aware that it was Saturday and turned pale, looking up with shame.

"I see that you people are sick with humiliation," Rabbi Samuel called out. "There is a law which says that those who are sick on the Sabbath may be helped. Pray be seated."

97

## FAR-FETCHED

An author came to Reb Eisele to ask for approval of a book he had written. Reb Eisele agreed and wrote his remarks on the top of a large sheet of paper and affixed his signature at the very bottom.

"Rabbi," the author asked quizzically, "why did you leave so much space between your opinion and your signature?"

"I wanted to fulfill the law, which says to keep at a great distance from a lie."

## FULL HOUSE

A well known hassidic rabbi came to a small town. An insane man, on seeing him, jumped into his carriage and under no condition would he leave.

"Why are you so anxious to want to ride with the rabbi?" a hassid asked him.

"I want the whole world to be with us," the lunatic replied. "Insane people run after the rabbi, and sane people run after me. When we ride together, the whole world will follow us."

## THIS IS THE END

Zalman, a notoriously loose character, once visited the rabbi of his town, who was very ill and whom no one was permitted to see. When the rabbi was told who had come to visit him, he asked that he be admitted immediately.

"Rabbi, I can't understand why you allowed me in, when your other friends are kept outside," the visitor asked.

"Well," the rabbi replied, "my religious friends I will be able to meet in the other world, but you—perhaps I am seeing you now for the last time."

## CONTINUOUS PERFORMANCE

A husband and wife who were constantly cursing each other decided in the presence of the rabbi to change their behavior. They gave their word of honor that such words would never leave their mouths any more.

As they were ready to leave the woman called to the rabbi:

"Rabbi, do you believe that he will keep his word? I should have so many good years and he so many black years, how many curse words he will say to me before we even reach the house."

## JUVENILE ACUITY

The famous gaon, Rabbi Heshele, when a child, was already known for his sharp, keen mind. One day he had a quarrel with another little boy, whom he gave a good beating. His father, on learning what had happened, sharply rebuked the lad. The young Heshele defended himself by saying that the other fellow had started with him and he was forced to strike back.

"Why doesn't he start up with me?" his father asked.

"All right," Heshele agreed, "have it your way. You say I started up with him? Then why don't I start up with you?"

## FAIR EXCHANGE

When the gaon Malbim was rabbi in Mohilev, his students whom he always criticized, sent him a picture of a dog, made of sugar, as a Purim gift. On receiving the present, the rabbi sent them in return a photograph of himself with these words:

"You sent me your picture, so I send you mine."

## STATUS QUO

A man came to a rabbi with the intention of divorcing his wife, but the woman refused to agree. She argued that she wanted to be left as she was at the time he married her. The rabbi did not understand, and asked her to explain.

"Well, when my husband married me, I was a widow. Now he wants to make a divorcee out of me. I don't want that. I want to be left a widow as before."

## ASININE ADVANCEMENT

An anti-Semitic minister asked the gaon Reb Jonah, of Prague:

"Why are you Jews of today so proud? It seems that you will only ride on horses, whereas your ancestors used to ride on donkeys. Even Moses, his wife and his children, rode on donkeys, and your Messiah also will come riding on a donkey."

"It is not because we are proud," the gaon replied, "but because the donkeys think they have made progress and act important, so we have to ride on horses."

## CANDIDATE FOR CONVERSION

A foreign Jew came to Rabbi Nathan Adler, of London, and asked him for money. When the rabbi refused the foreigner threateningly said:

"Rabbi, if you won't help me, I will be compelled to go to the missionaries."

The rabbi extended his hand and said:

"Give me your hand, and promise me that you will be an honest missionary. You were never an honest Jew, at least be an honest missionary."

## RETORT DISCOURTEOUS

The Jews of Prague helped to elect a mayor, not knowing that he was an enemy of the Jews. That evening a dance was given in his honor.

"It is a known fact through the ages, that the Jews like to dance," the mayor remarked. "They danced before the golden calf, too."

"Yes, it is true. They did dance when they made a leader out of the calf," Gaon Noda Biyehudah replied, smiling.

## PHILANTHROPIST

A wealthy man chanted the services in the synagogue one Saturday. He was not an educated man, did not have a voice, nor could he read correctly. When the services were over the rabbi approached him and asked:

"Did you have to say kaddish today?"

101

"No," the Jew replied, "I just donated my services to the synagogue.

"That is, indeed, very kind of you," the rabbi nodded with a grin. "You are an idealist. A person who is not able to, yet donates—that is, indeed, very noble."

## NO PROFIT IN PROPHETS

A rabbi preached a long sermon about the Hebrew prophets—the major prophets and the minor ones. He devoted a great deal of time discussing the genius of Isaiah. After speaking for two and a half hours, he called out enthusiastically:

"Now let us see what place we can give to the prophet Habakkuk."

"I will give him my place," a man in the audience cried out. "I've already had my nap, and I think it is time for me to go home."

## PERFECTLY KILLING

A hassid came to a rabbi and asked him to pray for his wife, who was critically ill.

"Go home, and don't worry," the rabbi consoled him. "I will take care of everything."

A few days later, the same hassid came again to the rabbi, this time crying bitterly.

"Rabbi, my poor wife died."

"That is impossible," the rabbi replied with an air of conviction. "I personally grabbed the knife out of the hands of the Angel of Death."

"But, rabbi, she is dead."

"Well, in that event, the only conclusion that I must come to is that the Angel of Death just went ahead and simply choked her."

## DEFILED

A young man, who had the reputation of being a vulgar person, became engaged to a beautiful young girl. Soon afterwards he decided to break the engagement. The girl's parents went to the rabbi and demanded that the young fellow pay a fine for his actions.

"But, rabbi, what have I done that I must pay for? I was engaged for such a short time. Who ever heard of anything like that?" the man pleaded.

"One hears and sees those things constantly," the rabbi replied. "Let us assume that an apple fell off a tree, was picked up, washed, and eaten by the one who found it. But at the same time if a swine were to take that apple in his mouth, and then spit it out, no one would touch it."

## SEQUITUR

A rabbi was summoned to recite the confession with a wealthy old lady, who was very ill. When she was through, she turned to the rabbi and asked:

"Rabbi, may I have a drink of water, or must I die right now?"

## NO SMOKING

When Reb Shimeon Soifer, the Rabbi of Krakow, sat in the Austrian Parliament, the king invited the members to his palace. It was a Saturday afternoon. The king presented the guests with cigars. Every one began to smoke. Reb Shimeon took his cigar and put it in his pocket.

"Herr Rabbiner," the king demanded, "why don't you smoke?"

"My Lordship," Reb Shimeon humbly replied, "I treasure the king's gift too highly to let it disappear in smoke."

## HI-LO

When Rabbi Landau became the Rabbi of Prague, the people had a new chair made for him, but it was not in proportion to his height. When he sat down for the first time to study with his people, he had to stoop over, because the chair was too high.

"Rabbi," one of his wittiest friends remarked, "it seems that the chair is too high for you?"

"No," laughed the rabbi, "the table is too low."

## CONVERSIVE

A young rabbi, envious of colleagues who were authors, decided to write a book. On the completion of his work he went to see the Brisker Rabbi and ask for an approbation. The Brisker Rabbi looked over his work and said:

"I am sorry, young man, but I cannot endorse your work."

"Why not?"

"It seems that your ideas are contrary to those of the rest of the world."

The young rabbi, believing that he had expressed intricate, philosophical thoughts, pleaded with the Brisker Rabbi to be more explicit.

"The whole world makes paper out of rags," the rabbi eloquently explained, "and here you've made rags out of paper."

## ILLUMINATING

On a very dark night a fire broke out in a small town near Kovna. All the inhabitants of the place ran to the spot, and attempted to put it out. The rabbi too was there. After the fire was extinguished he said to the crowd:

"It was a miracle sent from heaven above!"

The people became curious, and wanted to know his meaning.

"Well," said the rabbi, "if it were not for the bright flame of the fire, how would we have been able to see how to put it out?"

## DIAGNOSIS

During the time when Reb Shneur Zalman, the hassidic rabbi, was imprisoned in St. Petersberg, King Pavel unexpectedly paid him a visit. The king entered disguised in peasants' clothes, but Reb Zalman recognized him immediately. He quietly muttered a prayer, and during the course of conversation addressed him "Noble king." This made the king very angry.

"How do you know that I am the king?" he demanded.

"Because," the rabbi quickly replied, "I became terror stricken as soon as you entered."

## ANGLE IN GIVING

Reb Israel Mayer, the "Hafetz Hayyim," lived in dire need before he became famous. When the people became aware of his poverty, they offered him money, but Reb Israel refused it. One day his mother asked him:

"My son, you see how poor we are. We haven't a piece of bread in the house. When people want to help you, why do you refuse?"

"Mother," Reb Israel Mayer replied, "don't you realize that people want to give only because I refuse? As soon as I accept, they will not want to give."

## RETURN PERFORMANCE

A teacher was explaining to his pupils the part of the Bible where Joseph was sold by his brothers, and the hardships he endured. The teacher's wife sat nearby the entire time and wept bitterly. The following year the rabbi again explained the same portion of the Bible, and again emphasized Joseph's misery. This time the wife went into a fit of laughter.

"Are you insane?" the rabbi rebuked her. "Last year you were crying, and now your sides are splitting with laughter."

"Shouldn't one laugh at such a fool?" the woman chuckled. "After what happened to him last year, why did he go back to them?"

106

## HAM ACTOR

A German Jew came to a rabbi for permission to eat ham. After a few moments' thought the rabbi advised him to say a few psalms after his prayers every day. The Jew accepted the rabbi's advice, and religiously did as he was told. Several months later, while he was praying together with a Litvak, he observed how fervently the Litvak kept repeating psalm after psalm. In great amazement he burst out:

"My God, I would never believe that such a little Jew could eat so much ham."

## UNPREPARED

A wealthy merchant, who had heard a great deal of the Vilner Gaon's sharp wit, decided to have a talk with him. In the middle of their conversation, the merchant asked the gaon,

"Do you think that I will lead a happy life in the next world, rabbi?"

"Have you had happiness in this world, that you are worried about the next one?" the gaon asked.

"What have I here?" the merchant moaned. "I work so hard, and rest so little. I have so many worries and troubles, that I am actually sick. That is all I have."

"Then you can very well understand yourself," said the gaon, "if you have worked, slaved, and suffered for this world, and admit that you've derived nothing, what can you expect in the next world for which you haven't even an inkling of an idea to do anything?"

107

## PROFESSIONS

An argument took place among the people of a small town as to who was more important, a doctor or a lawyer. One group said a doctor was more necessary, because he must treat the sick. The other said that the healthy should be taken care of first. The Jews always lost out with the gentiles because there was no lawyer. The rabbi intervened, and gave his opinion:

"A doctor was essential as soon as man was created, when God cut out Adam's rib. A lawyer came later on, when Cain killed Abel."

## PRAY TELL

The Minsker Rabbi was very angry with his congregation because they always chattered while the prayers were being said. One Saturday after services, he noticed a small group of people standing and talking.

"This is something I can't understand, my good people," the rabbi said.

"During the services you must talk, but why must you talk after the services?"

## LIMITED JURISDICTION

A hassid visited the Kaidonover Rabbi on the eve of Rosh Hashanah.

"How are you, and how is business?" the rabbi inquired.

"Quite well, thank God," the hassid sighed, "but I have continuous disputes with my brother-in-law because

108

of the goy who is working for me. My brother-in-law wants to take him away for himself. Rabbi, a new year is approaching; please pray that this goy meet with misfortune. That will end all my troubles."

"I would gladly do that," the rabbi grinned. "But do you know, God won't pay any attention to me. He is not a hassid of mine."

## DUOLOGUE

A brazen young man came to the famous Rabbi Malbim and laughingly said:

"Rabbi, I have a question to ask you. When one walks on the street and meets a mad dog, the only remedy for him is to sit down, and when one meets a rabbi he must stand up. What happens when one meets both a rabbi and a dog together, what is he to do then?"

"That is a difficult question to answer," the rabbi replied. "The only test would be to see how people will react in such an event. I'll tell you what. Let us both walk along the street together, and we'll see what will happen."

## DOUBLE COVER

A young man asked Reb Chaim Laib, the Sosnitzer Rabbi:

"Rabbi, why do religious people wear both a skull cap and a hat? Isn't a hat alone enough?"

"People in a house have both a ceiling and a roof over their heads, but cows in a stable have only a roof," Reb Chaim Laib explained.

## MOOT

A new rabbi in a small town was anxious to become acquainted with the people. He walked into a house where a heated argument was going on.

"Who is the boss here?" the rabbi inquired.

"Kindly be seated, rabbi. My son and daughter-in-law are busy discussing that question now," the father replied.

## UNIQUE TIE-UP

Reb Eisel was invited to a party. The host, desiring to please the rabbi, placed a book Reb Eisel had written, which was bound together with Reb Isaac Elchanan's book, "Be'er Isaac," on the table. When Reb Eisel noticed that Reb Elchanan's book appeared before his, he called out:

"It is a strange thing. The world says that he is sane, has a brilliant mind, and that I am insane; yet he was tied up before I was."

## SLIMY ERROR

A Jew who had been baptized for the sake of a career attempted to make apologies to his cousin, a rabbi.

"I do not conform," he explained, "with any rules of the other religion; all I do is attend the services where holy water is used. I am still as I was before."

110

"Jews are compared to sand," the rabbi replied. "With sand you can do whatever you wish, and it still remains sand. But once you pour some water upon it, then it becomes mud."

## ON LITERARY GENIUS

An author once brought his book, entitled "The Hands of Moses," to Reb Charif, for his approbation. After reading it through, and not finding anything he liked, Reb Charif returned the book to the author, saying:

"I would suggest that you change the name of the book. Instead of calling it 'The Hands of Moses,' call it 'The Face of Moses,' because it is something one can't look at."

## INVERSION

A non-observant Jew asked the gaon Malbim whether he could legalize his smoking on the Sabbath.

"It may be done, but with a slight change," the gaon replied. "You would have to take the lit side into your mouth."

## UNHAND ME

A wealthy, intelligent young woman visited an orthodox rabbi of Germany, and on leaving extended her hand.

Jestingly, the rabbi remarked:

"A rabbi can be taken at his word, he does not have to give his hand."

111

## THE THOUGHTS OF MAN

A friend of the gaon Reb Chaim Auerbach, of Lunshitz, gossiped about the rabbi, because he had seen him speaking to a woman on the street.

When the rabbi heard this, he said:

"I would rather talk to a woman and think of God than talk to God and think of a woman."

## REASONABLE

A rabbi entered a house and noticed that the owner sat down to eat as soon as he got out of bed.

"How does a Jew dare to eat before he prays?" the rabbi indignantly asked.

"God forbid, rabbi!'" the Jew quickly replied. "I don't pray."

## THE PEOPLE ARE SICK

The well known Reb Hirsch used to say:

"Since the rabbis began to call themselves doctors the Jewish people are sick."

## MAN VS. GOD

One Yom Kippur eve Rabbi Levi Isaac Berditchev stood before the pulpit wrapped in his tallis, prepared to say Kol Nidre. The people were huddled together, anxiously waiting for the venerable rabbi to proceed. Suddenly he turned to the sexton and asked, "Is Jacob the tailor present in the synagogue?"

112

"No, rabbi," the sexton replied.

"Go fetch him," the sage ordered.

Shortly afterward the sexton returned with Jacob, who was dressed in his working clothes.

"Why aren't you at the synagogue on such a holy occasion?" the rabbi asked.

"I deliberately didn't come," Jacob replied, "for I have a complaint against the Lord. If the reverend rabbi is interested I will explain."

"All right, then; proceed," Rabbi Levi Isaac said.

"I had been unemployed a long time," Jacob began, "when one day before the Succoth holidays the poritz sent for me and ordered that I make him a fur coat for the winter. I realized that our merciful God had come to my rescue at last and that the plight of my family would be eased."

"Is it possible that my people were aware of your poverty and did not come to your aid?" the rabbi interposed.

"I did not want the help of man," Jacob answered, "and so I was overjoyed with the opportunity to earn my own livelihood. The poritz supplied me with the finest beaver skins and whatever else was necessary for the coat. As you know, it is a custom that the leftovers belong to the tailor. Since I have a large family to support and am always in dire need, I decided to take the remaining pieces for myself. I could sell them and have something toward my daughter's dowry. When I completed the coat I took the leftover pieces, stuffed them into the hollow of a large

loaf of bread, and set off for my home. After I had gone
a short distance with my prize I heard a galloping of horse's
hoofs. 'Jacob,' the rider called out, 'come back! The
poritz wants you!'

"Paralyzed with fear and thinking that the poritz had
discovered my act, I quickly hurled the bread which contained the leftovers into a clump of bushes nearby. I made
a sign whereby to find it when I returned. Later I learned
that my fright was unwarranted because the servant informed me that I had forgotten to sew buttons on the coat.
The following day, when I went to look for the bread with
the fur, it was gone. It was a desolate spot, and I know
that no man comes there, so it must have been through an
act of God that it disappeared. Therefore if the Lord can
be so inconsiderate I refuse to serve him."

After listening attentively to Jacob's story Rabbi Levi
Isaac raised his eyes toward heaven and fervently called,
"Dear Lord, I, Rabbi Levi Isaac Berditchev, acting as judge
in this case, have decided that Jacob the tailor is justified
in his claim. However, he forgives You for Your act, but
asks that You forgive his sins and the sins of all Israel."

Whereupon the gaon turned his face to the pulpit and
commenced to chant Kol Nidre.

THE
MAGGID

# REGURGITATION

One Friday evening the famous Vilner Maggid arrived in a small town. He went into the synagogue, introduced himself to the sexton, and declared he would like to preach a sermon on Saturday.

"My good man," the sexton said, "you may be a preacher, but the Vilner Maggid came here several weeks ago and he is going to speak at the synagogue this Saturday."

Saturday afternoon the real Vilner Maggid was present in the audience. He was anxious to listen to the man impersonating him. At first the other repeated large portions of the Vilner Maggid's sermons, but towards the end gave some original thoughts which were utter nonsense.

The legitimate preacher could not tolerate this any longer. He jumped to the platform and exclaimed:

"Listen to me, my people. I am the real Vilner Maggid. That man is an imposter. You will ask why I kept silent until now? My answer will be in the form of a story.

"In a small town a rich man's daughter was to be married, and the father decided to hold an elaborate wedding in her honor. In the same town there lived a poor cousin of the wealthy man, who fasted on the day of the wedding in order to have a hearty appetite for the feast that evening.

"As the day drew to a close he sat and waited for the sexton to call for him. It was getting quite late, and still no one came. The poor man was half starved, so he asked his wife to give him some food. There was nothing in the house but a pudding of cold beans, and that she gave him. He ate very rapidly, and as he was finishing the last spoon-ful, he heard a tap on the door. The sexton had come. He got into his best clothes and was off to the wedding.

"When he arrived dinner was being served. First the delicious fish was served, and of that he did not leave a morsel. Then hot, golden soup, which he finished to the last drop. Finally when the roast came the poor man was full, but how could he resist? It would be a sin to pass it up. So, he pulled himself together and ate the entire portion.

"His stomach couldn't hold so much, so he began to bring up all he had consumed. The roast chicken, the fish, the soup, and at last the bean pudding.

"At sight of this the wealthy man became furious: 'When you vomited up my dinner I suffered and kept quiet, but when you begin to spit up your own beans, that I do not have to tolerate. Get out of here!' "

## OCCASIONAL RELIGION

On Rosh Hashanah the Dubner Maggid noticed several men in the synagogue, who never visited the place during the year. He saw them wrapped in their talesim, fervently praying to the Lord for a happy and prosperous new year. That evening, when the maggid delivered his sermon from

118

the pulpit, he said, "My good friends, a merchant who had purchased all his wares on credit lost his entire fortune in a fire. The poor man was in a terrible predicament, for he was now penniless. His friends suggested that he tell the manufacturer of his misfortune and perhaps the other would extend the time of payment or even void the debt. The storekeeper heeded his friend's advice, but when he arrived at his creditor's home he stood on the threshold and had not the courage to enter. 'How can I face that man emptyhanded,' he murmured, 'when I owe him such a tremendous amount of money?' In his great misery he began to sob.

"The creditor, frightened by the loud weeping, ran to the door and called out, 'What has happened? Why are you crying?' 'What else can I do,' the poor man moaned, 'when I owe you so much money and can pay nothing of it?'

"The manufacturer was touched by the honesty of the man. 'I will grant you the few thousand rubles you owe me,' he said, 'and will also give you a new supply of merchandise.' With these words he tore the notes into fragments.

"The merchant, overjoyed, ran home and told everyone of his good fortune. One of his listeners, realizing that here was a chance to make easy money, snatched at the opportunity and ran wailing to the wealthy manufacturer. The other, seeing this man for the first time, asked him what he wanted. 'I am in dire need,' the scoundrel groaned. 'Could you present me with a few thousand rubles?' 'But why should I give you such an amount?' the wealthy man asked in amazement. 'Well, why did you give my friend so much money? Am I worse than he?'

" 'Wretched soul!' the manufacturer shouted, 'how can you compare yourself to the other? I have had business dealings with that man for years, I sold him thousands of rubles worth of merchandise, and now when a misfortune has befallen him and he can not pay his debt I have helped him. But who are you? I never saw you before and never had any business relations with you. How dare you come and ask me for money?'

"When a religious Jew who attends the synagogue all year round," the Dubner Maggid continued, "performs good deeds, and is in contact with the Lord constantly, commits a sin and repents, God will forgive him. Since he has fulfilled his duties to the Lord during the year, if an accident occurs and he sincerely regrets it, he should be treated with compassion. But when a total stranger . who has had no relations with God all year round, and who never enters a synagogue, suddenly appears there dur-ing the High Holidays and appeals to the Lord to grant him long life and happiness, that, my friends, is indeed an outrageous audacity."

## COMIC WAIT

The Kelmer Maggid came to a city where a modern Talmud Torah had been erected. The leaders wanted the new school to receive a certain amount of the charity money that belonged to the old school. A heated argument arose, and the Kelmer Maggid was asked to give his opinion. So he rose and addressed the people in his own inimitable way:

"My good friends, I want to tell you a story. A man arrived at the gates of paradise dressed in modern clothes, with a beard trimmed in the fashion of a Frenchman. He wanted to enter. Father Abraham, who stands near the entrance, approached him and asked, 'Who are you?' 'I am the Vilner Maggid,' the man explained. Abraham stared at the newcomer's attire and repeated, "You are the Vilner Maggid? Tell me, in which synagogue did you preach?' After a few similar questions the man broke down and confessed. 'The truth is that I am a former actor of a Vilna theatre. When I acted on the stage, I impressed my audience to such an extent that they shed many a tear. Tell me, Father Abraham, am I not a preacher who is worthy of being in paradise?' 'Perhaps you are right,' Abraham replied, 'but in the meantime you cannot come in. You will have to wait until one of your listeners whose life has been improved by your moral speeches comes here. Then both of you will enter.'

"Now, my friends," the Maggid said, "you are probably anxious to know what happened to that man. I can tell you that he is still waiting near the entrance of paradise for a follower whom he had turned into a zaddik to arrive. I can say the same in reference to your new Talmud Torah, which boasts that it will produce scholars of great learning and wisdom. My decision is that we should wait until we see one outstanding personality out of this modern school.

Somehow I feel that we have to wait a long time, like that actor still standing near the gates of paradise."

## FINE FEATHERS

The Dubner Maggid, while visiting a small city, entered a synagogue and heard a preacher deliver a sermon which consisted of his own parables and witty remarks. He waited patiently until the other had finished and then asked permission to speak.

"Once upon a time," the Maggid began, "there was a bird who grew up completely bare of feathers. Her sister and brother birds had beautiful plumage, but she was naked and miserable. The birds of the neighborhood were concerned about their friend's misfortune, so they called a meeting and decided that each one give the wretched little bird one feather. As a result of their decision the naked bird received many feathers and before long looked like every other bird. Soon she forgot that her feathers were borrowed and began preening herself and boasting that she was more beautiful than any of her friends. Once again the birds assembled and brought their haughty friend to trial. This time they decided that each bird should reclaim his feathers. The ungrateful bird, stripped of her borrowed feathers, was left as naked as she was at the beginning. . . . Now, my friend," he continued, addressing the preacher, "the same goes for you. The parables you related in your sermon were not your own. Some were mine and a few belonged to other preachers. I have taken back my feather, and when the others hear you, they will reclaim their feathers too."

## BULLSEYE

The Vilner Gaon immensely enjoyed listening to the Dubner Maggid's sermons. Whenever the maggid came to Vilna he had to visit the gaon and entertain him with his parables. Once the gaon asked him, "How do you always manage to choose an appropriate example, one that is so suitable for the occasion?"

"A wealthy farmer had an only son who was very talented," the Dubner Maggid replied: "He sent him to study in foreign countries, and when he returned home, gave a grand party for him and invited all the neighbors. The young fellow told his guests that besides his fine education he was also a good marksman. He could always hit that which he aimed at or come very close. On returning from the party, the men passed by a fence which had circles on it marked in chalk, and in the center of each circle there was a bullet hole. They gaped in surprise. It was unbelievable. To fire so many shots and still not miss the goal by a hairbreadth.

After some searching they discovered that the marksman was none other than the simple peasant Ivan, the watchman of the forest.

" 'Where did you learn the art of shooting with such precision?' he was asked.

" 'Why,' the peasant replied, 'do you people think that I draw a circle first and then aim to hit the center of it? I shoot first and then draw a circle around the bullet hole.'

"The same is true with me," the Dubner Maggid concluded. "I don't try to find an appropriate parable for

every topic. On the contrary. Whenever I have a suitable parable, I start looking for a topic."

## DOGGED PERSISTENCE

A well-known preacher rose to deliver a sermon in a
hassidic synagogue. As soon as he stepped to the platform,
the people began to stamp their feet and shout, "We don't
want any preachers in our synagogue! We don't need any
sermons!"

The preacher asked the sexton to tell them that he did
not intend to preach a sermon. He merely wanted to relate
an incident that had happened to a Jewish merchant, which
would be worth their listening to. The people consented
to remain quiet, and the preacher began.

"One day a Jew was walking sadly along the street,
when a friend of his met him and asked, 'What has happened to you? Why are you so worried?' 'I am in
trouble,' the Jew replied. 'As you know, I am a merchant
and I have an opportunity to make a good deal of money
from a wealthy farmer. I can make enough to marry my
daughter off and still have a tidy sum for myself. Yet I
can't put the deal through. Whenever I come to the
farmer's house, his dogs become wild and bark fiercely, as
if they wanted to tear me apart. I grow frantic with
fear and run for dear life.' 'Do not be so disturbed,' his
friend consoled him. 'Go there again, and when the
monsters jump at you, say this prayer, "But against any
of the children of Israel shall not a dog whet his tongue.'"
The merchant again went to the wealthy farmer's house

124

and before he had a chance to open his mouth to say the prayer, the dogs almost devoured him. On his way home he met his friend. 'Well, did you say the prayer, and did it help?' the friend asked. 'Perhaps it would have helped,' the merchant sighed, 'but the dogs didn't even give me a chance to begin saying it!' "

## INESCAPABLE

The Kelmer Maggid arrived in a German city, and asked the leaders of the community for permission to deliver a sermon. They agreed, providing he would refrain from ridiculing and criticizing the people because of their sins. However, the maggid gave his audience a severe tongue lashing.

After the sermon they complained: "You promised not to reprimand the people in your sermon; why did you?"

"There was a wealthy farmer," the Kelmer Maggid replied, "who was very stout. He would visit a Jewish bartender, become inebriated, and stretch out on the floor. Since he was so fat, he took up almost the entire room, and whenever the bartender had to pass he unwittingly gave him a shove.

"Enemies of the Jewish bartender told the wealthy farmer about this. The farmer asked the Jew why he must thus dishonor him.

" 'What can I do?' the Jew replied. 'You are so broad and big that you take up the entire room, and wherever I turn you are in my way. Involuntarily I must give you a push!'

125

"The same," the maggid continued, "is true with you, my friends. Your sins are so great that whatever I may speak about in my sermon, I must remind you of them."

## NOMINAL PUN

The Dubner Maggid was a strong opponent of the hassidim and at every opportunity spoke against them. One day he stopped at a small hotel and began to prepare a sermon which he was to deliver that Saturday. Suddenly he heard loud music and dancing on the street. When he looked out, he noticed a large crowd of hassidim singing and wildly pirouetting around their rabbi, Reb Ber Mezeritch, who was staying at the same hotel. The Dubner Maggid wanted to avoid them, but they saw him and began to shout frantically. "Here is the Dubner, our enemy! Let us take revenge!"

Before long they surrounded the maggid and attempted to strike him, but Reb Ber Mezeritch demanded that they do him no harm.

"Do you realize what would have happened to you if I had not intervened?" Reb Ber asked. "If you tell me something that is sharp and witty, I will see that you meet with no disaster."

"I have a wise thought to express," the Dubner Maggid replied, "but I feel that when the hassidim hear it, they will hurt me."

"I promise you that no one will harm you," Reb Ber assured him.

"Today I was more firmly convinced of what I have always said about your hassidim," the Dubner remarked.

"The world of the hassidim is strange and distorted. Throughout the entire country it is customary for the gypsies to play, while the bear dances. With you it is just the contrary. The 'Ber' plays, and the gypsies dance."

## MILKING THE GUEST

The Vilner Gaon invited the Dubner Maggid to his home. As soon as the maggid alighted from his wagon, the gaon asked him whether he had brought some witty stories along.

"Yes," said the maggid. "There was once a poor melamed, who after a number of years managed to save up enough money to buy a goat. His wife was overcome with joy. Now she would have her own milk, cream, but-ter, and cheese for her family. As soon as her husband left for the synagogue to say the evening prayers, she seized a pail and began to milk the goat. To her amaze-ment, it yielded not a drop of milk! In great despair she awaited the arrival of her husband, and as soon as he entered she cried out 'Fool, what kind of goat did you buy? She doesn't give any milk!' 'Silly woman,' the melamed replied. 'You should know better than that. Do you expect the goat to give you milk immediately? First let the animal rest up after her long journey, then give her some food, and after she is nourished and rested you will be able to milk her.'

"That is exactly what I want to say to you," the Dub-ner Maggid then said to the Vilner Gaon. "First permit me to relax after my long trip, then give me something to eat, and afterwards I will give you milk."

## A PARABLE ON A PARABLE

The Dubner Maggid was asked why the parable has such a strong effect upon people.

"I will enlighten you with a parable," the maggid replied.

"Truth once walked along the streets unclad, and none would admit him into their homes. They were terrified and fled from him. As Truth walked about in despair, he met Parable, who was adorned in fashionable and attractively colored clothes.

" 'Why are you so depressed, brother?' he said, addressing Truth.

" 'I am very, very old,' replied Truth, 'and no one wants to recognize me.'

" 'It isn't because you are old that people do not like you,' explained Parable. 'Look at me; I too am very old, but the older I grow, the more people love me. I will tell you a secret. People are partial to everything that is decorative, and a little disguised. I will loan you my clothes, and you will see that everyone will love you.'

"Truth followed the advice of Parable, and adorned himself in his garb. Since that day, Parable and Truth go hand in hand, and the people are quite fond of both."

## THE FORSAKEN

The Kelmer Maggid, Rabbi Moishe Isaac, spent a week-end at a summer resort in Dublin near Riga. On Saturday he noticed that there were numerous Jews in the synagogue without prayer-shawls, because they were too lazy to carry them along.

"My friends, I will tell you a story," he spoke from the pulpit. "Recently while I was spending a Sabbath in Riga, I visited a wealthy merchant and was informed that he was not in. 'Where is he?' I asked. 'He left on a pleasure trip to Dublin,' was the reply. Suddenly I heard sobbing from a nearby chamber. When I entered the room no one was in sight, but I spied a tallis bag hanging on the wall. I realized that the tallis was crying. 'Tallis, dear tallis, why do you weep?' I asked. 'Why shouldn't I cry?' the tallis replied. 'My master left for Dublin and took all his gold and silver, but left me behind all alone.' 'Dry your tears, dear tallis,' I spoke consolingly. 'There will come a day when your master will have to make a much longer journey than to Dublin. Then he will leave his entire wealth of gold and silver behind and only you will be taken along.' "

## HAPPY FAMILY

The people of Vilna decided to engage a preacher, but the communal employees objected. They were afraid there would not be sufficient funds for everyone, and their salaries would be decreased. In spite of their protests a preacher did come to Vilna. They immediately showed their keen dislike for him.

"You are our competitor," they argued. "We hardly get enough to make a living for ourselves, and now you come along."

"Be calm," the newcomer reassured them. "Let me give you an appropriate example. A mistress had chickens which she kept in a coop. Very often she was busy and neglected feeding them. The poor chickens starved quietly. One day the mistress bought a rooster and put him into the coop. From that time on no one went hungry. The rooster would crow loudly, and the mistress remembered to feed the chickens. The same is true with us. When you were alone in the city, no one thought of you; but now, when I start to crow my sermons, they will be reminded of both you and me, and we will all live happily together."

## A MEATY RECITAL

A maggid arrived in a small town and, as was the custom, put up a notice on the wall of the synagogue that he would deliver a sermon that Saturday. Saturday morning the maggid saw that the notice had been torn down. He began his discourse with the following story.

"One day my wife went to visit a relative and I was left home alone. In the afternoon I went to the butcher and bought a tongue. He instructed me how to prepare it, but since I was afraid I might forget what he said, I wrote the instructions down on a piece of paper and pasted it onto the tongue. On the way home I was attacked by a dog, who made a dash to grab the tongue. The mongrel only managed to seize the slip of paper. So I said, 'Dog, you can keep the paper, for as long as the tongue remains with me I'll be able to help myself.' "

## BEASTLY TREATMENT

A rich man entertained a preacher at his home one Sabbath. He treated him nicely, but did not permit him to sit at his table, as he considered it beneath his dignity. Saturday evening, when the preacher was ready to leave, the rich man said, "I hear that you are a preacher. Please say something before you go."

"I'll tell you a story," the preacher replied. "A dog once found a bearskin which he put on, and went to visit a wolf. When the wolf saw him, he noticed that there was something strange about the animal. So he went to the lion for advice. 'I have a visitor,' he said, 'who looks like a bear, but I think he is a dog.' 'Make a party for your guest,' the lion advised, 'then you will know. If he sits at the table together with everyone else, you will be certain that he is a bear, but if he sits by himself, you will know definitely that he is a dog.' "

## SOCIAL JUSTICE

Frequently you will hear people say, "I am doing this to pass time," or "I haven't any time." One has too much time and doesn't know what to do with it, whereas the other has no time at all.

The Kelmer Maggid offered a fine illustration on this subject:

"One day," he said, "while walking along the street I met a heavy-set man, with a massive face, puffing away at a big cigar. When I asked the man why he smoked, he explained that he did it in order to digest the large meals he ate.   Later I met a haggard looking man, and he too, was smoking.   'Why do you smoke?' I asked.   'I haven't eaten yet and I am smoking to drive away my hunger,' was the reply.   'God in heaven!' I called out, 'if that big fat fool would give part of his food to the hungry soul, then one wouldn't overeat and the other wouldn't go hungry!' "

## ON THE OTHER FOOT

The Dubner Maggid overheard a group of freethinkers scoffing at the Jewish religion and at the idea of a Messiah. He turned to them and said, "A hungry fox saw a crow standing on a branch of a tall tree and called up, 'Why are you afraid to come down to me?   The Messiah has come; no animal will now devour the other.   All will live at peace with one another.'   While the fox was talking to the crow, he heard the voices of barking dogs.   He be- came frightened and asked the crow to see where the bark- ing came from.   'Hunters and ferocious-looking dogs are coming this way,' the crow informed him.   Instantly the fox began to run.   'Didn't you say that the Messiah had come?' the crow asked.   'Why are you running?'   'What else should I do?' the fox replied.   'Dogs don't believe in a Messiah!' "

## GOD IS NEAR UNTO ALL

Reb Berish Halpern, the Lubliner Maggid, was inno- cently imprisoned.   He pleaded with the warden to permit him to keep his tallis and tefillin, so that he could pray daily. Reb Berish had a habit of praying very loudly, which the warden of the prison would not tolerate.

"Why must you shout while you pray?" he demanded.

"We Jews pray that way," Reb Berish explained.

"Can't you do it softly, the way we do?" the warden asked.

"You have your God nearby, on the wall, therefore you can pray softly. Our God is far above, in the distant heavens, so we must shout."

## BLOW TORCH

The Dubner Maggid delivered a fiery oration before an assembly of people in Berlin and severely reprimanded their mode of living. Realizing that there was no response on their part, he told them the following story:

"A blacksmith, who lived in a small village, bought a mechanical fire blower for his shop. Until then he had had to blow the fire himself, but now the machine would simplify his task. The blacksmith was delighted with the instrument, but strangely enough it produced no flame when he attempted to use it. He blew and blew but to no avail. He had forgot that the blower could only create fire if there was a spark inside ... So, my friends, since you too do not possess the tiniest spark, of what value is my blowing?"

## BI-GAMY

The Reitzer Maggid, while traveling in a coach with two Reform rabbis, doctors of philosophy, observed how immensely they enjoyed the company of a very attractive young woman.

"Now I realize that such rabbis as you are even more religious than Rabbenu Gershon Meor Ha-Golah himself," the maggid said.

"How?" they exclaimed.

"In the olden days every Jew was allowed to have two women or more. When Rabbenu Gershom came along, he prohibited that. He said that every Jew would have to be satisfied with one woman. Here I see that you are even more severe than he. Both of you are content with only one."

## ZOOLOGICAL QUERY

A maggid went to various people to collect funds for a charitable cause. He entered the home of a miser, who refused to listen to him and ordered him out. The maggid started a fierce argument with the miser until the other called out angrily, "Will you leave, or must I drive you out like a dog?"

"I'll go," the maggid consented, "but you must first listen to me. The world cannot understand why a dog grabs a pig by his ear when he chases him, but I know the reason. The Talmud says that there is no man as poor as a dog and there is no one as rich as a pig. Thus the dog secretly whispers into the pig's ear, 'If you are so rich, then why are you such a pig?'"

## SELF-GLORIFICATION

Reb Mendel Vitebsker, when a young lad, was taught by the Mezeritcher Maggid. One Saturday afternoon the maggid noticed his student strutting around with his hat tilted to one side.

"Mendel," he asked, "how many pages of the Gemara have you studied today?"

"Six," the boy replied.

"Very good," the Mezeritcher Maggid grinned. "If your hat is tilted to one side from six pages of the Gemara, how many more pages will you have to study in order to take your hat off completely?"

## POOR GIVERS

The Kelmer Maggid came to a small town to raise money for a charitable cause. Large crowds of people gathered to listen to his sermons, but did not contribute a penny. Before he concluded his sermon, he turned to his audience directly and said, "The people in your town are permitted to use milk from gentile farmers. Jews are prohibited to drink it because they fear it may be mixed with pig's milk. But according to what I see, you can't get one drop of milk from the pigs in your town."

## SATANIC JUDGMENT

The Dubner Maggid, while walking in the street late one night, was encountered by the town comedian.

"Rabbi," he said, "the Talmud says that a great scholar should not walk in the streets alone at night, because of the devils that lurk in the dark."

"I am not afraid," the maggid replied. "The devils of this town don't consider me a great scholar."

## FAIR WARNING

The Kelmer Maggid, while delivering a sermon, called out, "Listen, my rich friends in the audience! You must see to it that you give charity, otherwise the poor will die of starvation. No doubt you will say, 'What concern is that of ours?' My good friends, it is your concern. The Holy Bible says that the world cannot exist without the poor, and in that case you will have to take their place."

## ACCOMODATING

Reb Israel Horodner, the Minsker Maggid, became blind in his old age. He lived in a small synagogue near a cemetery. When Masliansky came to Minsk he visited Reb Israel, and seeing his great poverty expressed his sympathy. Reb Israel smilingly replied: "I am doing what is right by the Hevra Kaddisha. The cemetery is nearby, and so they will not have to carry me very far."

## PUNITIVE

Reb Jacob, the Dubner Maggid, was asked, "Why is it that you chastise the people and then ask to be paid?"

"Our great Lord acts the same way," Reb Jacob replied. "He too does not chastise for nothing."

## FILTHY LUCRE

The Dubner Maggid once came to a wealthy man and asked a donation for a worthy cause. The man, who was known to be a miser, refused to give it.

"You will always remain rich," the preacher said.

"What do you mean by that?" the miser asked.

"I'll give you an example," the preacher replied. "For instance, if you were to lose a ruble in a filthy place, would you bend down to pick it up?"

"No," answered the miser.

"Well, the good Lord (may He forgive me for the comparison) also lost 50,000 rubles in a dirty place. It will always lie there, for He will never soil His hands to take it out. You will always remain a rich man," the preacher explained.

## CONTENTMENT

A Yiddish speaker held such a long discourse that he went off on a tangent, and forgot what he originally started to say. Finally he thought of how to bring the speech to a close.

"My friends," he began, "you've all probably heard of the oriental riddle: Who is happier, one who has a million dollars, or one who has nine daughters? The answer is: The one who has nine daughters, because he certainly doesn't want any more. My people, I feel that you are in the same position as that father. You don't want any more."

## SOPORIFIC

On Saturday afternoon a maggid delivered a sermon in the synagogue of a small town. Among the people who came to listen to him was a well educated young man. The following day the maggid met this person, and, knowing he had been present at his sermon, asked him how he enjoyed it.

"I can only tell you," the young man replied, "that I couldn't sleep all night after your lecture."

"Why, did my sermon make such an impression on you?" asked the maggid.

"No, it isn't that, but I have a habit that when I have a nap in the afternoon I can't sleep all night."

## ACT OF JUSTICE

The Kelmer Maggid once interpreted a quotation from the Psalms for his people:

"Oh, Lord, break the teeth of the evil-doer." Why the teeth?

When a sinner dies and enters into the other world, he arrives clean shaven. Immediately he is asked, "Sinner, where is your beard?" "I was born without a beard," the sinner replies.

"You were also born without teeth, still you come here with them," the angel demands.

So they grab him and knock all his teeth out.

## LIQUID ASSET

A Jew asked a preacher, who specialized in making eulogies, to deliver one at his wife's funeral.

"What kind do you want?" the preacher asked, "a eulogy with tears or without?"

"What is the difference?" the widower asked.
"The difference is five dollars," replied the preacher.

## JUSTICE

During a sermon a loud snore was heard. The preacher was one of the kind that was known to put an audience to sleep.

"Sexton!" he called out, "wake that Jew up and tell him to leave the synagogue!"

"Why do you send me to wake him?" the sexton angrily retorted. "Since you put him to sleep, it is no more than right that you wake him yourself."

## LONG-WINDED

A maggid preached a sermon in a small town synagogue. Little by little the people began to leave. Only the sexton and a few other Jews, who sat in the corners and dozed away, remained. That did not seem to bother the preacher, who continued with his delivery.

The sexton, realizing that this would never end, went over to the preacher, handed him the key of the synagogue, and said:

"Here is the key. When you finish your sermon, please be good enough to lock the door of the synagogue, and bring the key to my house."

## WORLDLY WISDOM

A father had two sons, Meyer and Herschel. Meyer was a clever chap and Herschel was known to be a fool, whom people shunned because of his folly. Herschel, on the other hand, considered himself a genius and the rest of the world insane. The father, very unhappy over the situation, suggested that his wise son Meyer take the other on a trip around the world. He would then have the opportunity to visit various countries, meet different people, and acquaint himself with their customs and modes of living.

Perhaps Herschel would finally realize that he was not a genius and the others not insane. One day, while the brothers were in France, they passed a furniture factory and saw men chopping up expensive logs of mahogany, cedar, and pine.

"Now, my brother, you can see for yourself that I am quite correct when I say that the world is mad," Herschel exclaimed.

The wise brother remained silent. They walked on and stopped at a silk factory, where they observed through an open window men cutting up luxurious quantities of silks and satins.

"Just look at those lunatics," the fool called out, "ruining such beautiful materials."

"Perhaps you are right," Meyer remarked, "but let us enter the factory and actually see what is happening."

When they went in they saw tailors gather up the cut pieces of cloth, fit them together and produce the most beautiful garments. Herschel was quite amazed and watched the procedure with grave curiosity.

"Come, let us return to the other factory," Meyer suggested.

The carpenters were at work, arranging and nailing together the cut wood in a skillful manner and turning out exquisite articles of furniture. Herschel hung his head in shame, for now he realized that furniture could not be made from wood, nor clothing from silk, unless the material was first cut up. From then on he ceased to insist that the world was demented.

Moral: Men are blind and do not understand the ways of Providence. Very often that which they consider harmful, can yield a great deal of good.

## HEAVY DIET

A wealthy man sought a wet nurse for his newborn son. One day a shabbily dressed beggar woman knocked at his door.

"Madam, would you be interested in a job as wet nurse for my son?"" the rich man asked.

"Certainly," the poor woman replied, "if you will pay me well."

"Ungrateful soul!" the man called out in rage. "You demand a salary? Do you earn more than a few measly pennies and a piece of dry bread a day? You won't have to do any work for me, but eat the choicest food, sleep in a luxurious bed, and actually live like a queen. No, I will not hire you as a wet nurse unless you pay me something in return."

"You are right, my good sir," the woman replied, "but I am very poor. What can I possibly give you?"

"Give me a pawn," the rich man suggested.

Opening her sack, she pulled out her Sabbath jacket and gave it to him.

The wet nurse lived in luxury until the baby became ill. A doctor was called, who declared that the milk of the nurse was too rich for the infant to digest. Instead of butter, cream, and puddings she was to eat simple foods and drink plain water. Soon the baby became well again.

"Now give me back my Sabbath jacket," the nurse demanded of the rich man. "Since I have no more luxuries and my meals are meager, I owe you nothing. Return my pawn."

Moral: Mother Earth is the nourishing center of all living creatures. Man who was created from her is Earth's pawn to God. Mother Earth was content as long as she was blessed, but when the Lord cursed her for the sins of mankind, she rebelled, protesting, "Man, return to me, because the piece of earth from which you are made does not belong to you."

## CROWDING ONE'S LUCK

Itzik was a poor storekeeper, whose wife earned a livelihood for the family, while he sat in the synagogue daily and studied. The woman harassed her husband constantly, because she was the breadwinner, and he never lent a help-ing hand. Itzik always remained silent and bowed his head with shame. On the way to the synagogue one morning, he met an old man with a long gray beard.

"Why are you so despondent, my friend?'" the old man asked.

Itzik immediately recognized the other as the prophet Elijah. "Dear Rabbi," he moaned, "I am very unhappy. Woe to the man who has to live on his wife's earnings. Have mercy on me and bless me with good fortune, so that I may be able to support my family."

"As soon as you reach your house," the prophet replied, "you will have luck in the first thing you touch, and that good luck will never forsake you."

The storekeeper ran home as fast as his legs could carry him, and quickly began to count his wife's earnings for the day. He believed that the money would multiply, and he would count on endlessly.

Suddenly his wife entered, and seeing her husband handling the money, angrily thrust him aside, unleashing a torrent of wrathful words. This time Itzik was courageous, and retaliated word for word. The blessing of the prophet was fulfilled in their heated argument. Husband and wife bickered ceaselessly, and in such a fashion lived for the rest of their days, all because the man did not know how to make a good beginning.

Moral: After the flood, Noah had the task of recon-structing the chaotic earth. However, the first thing he did was to plant a vineyard, into which his entire good luck was sunk. The very same day that Noah cultivated the vineyard, it yielded wine. Noah drank heavily, became intoxicated, and so brought shame unto himself.

## HALVING THE DEBT .

Mendel Krassowitz, a wealthy manufacturer, often sent salesmen across the country to sell his merchandise. It happened that they were negligent and a band of thieves stole their truckloads of merchandise. The agents returned home emptyhanded and despairing. The owner then suggested that they pay a percentage of the loss in monthly installments.

When the first payment was due one of the salesmen gave twice the amount of money that he had to, while another poor agent paid only half.

"Please believe me, my good sir," pleaded the latter to the manufacturer, "it was extremely difficult for me to pay even this small sum."

Those who witnessed the scene observed that the owner was very grateful to this man and spoke kindly to him, whereas he completely ignored the other who had made a large return.

"My friends, I realize that you appear baffled at my behavior," the manufacturer remarked. "Permit me to explain. You must understand that the money I asked you to pay is insignificant in comparison to the tremendous loss I've suffered, due to your carelessness. However, the penalty was to serve as a constant reminder that you owe

147

me something, and that each of you should do his utmost in the interest and to the welfare of the business. I had hoped that this would eventually help to compensate me for my loss. Today I observed that the salesman who made a larger payment than required acted very proudly. His manner was bold, as if he no longer owed me anything, and I am certain that he does not intend to exert any further efforts to save the business. The poor agent, however, feels obligated to me and will earnestly strive to do his very best."

Moral: The rich boastfully donate large sums to charity, while the poor give small contributions apologetically, feeling that they haven't done enough. Thus the charity of the poor is more highly evaluated. It is not the amount of money given, but the heart that gives.

## COMPARATIVE INDIGENCE

A wealthy poritz (householder) lived with his family in a luxurious mansion. One day misfortune befell him and he lost all his money. The creditors seized his mansion along with his entire fortune of gold and silver, leaving him with a humble hut and a small garden. He and his family often yearned for the years when they had had servants, silks, and satins.

One night a fire broke out, consuming the hut and all the poritz's remaining possessions and leaving nought but a heap of ashes. Completely poverty-stricken, he was compelled to sell the piece of land, and with the money he bought a horse.

"There is nothing left for me now but to become a coachman," the unhappy man sighed.

A few weeks later the horse died and the poritz got a job as a porter. He had to lug heavy loads on his back, and the money he earned was barely enough to provide for the scanty necessities of his family. Now the poritz did not complain about his previous misfortunes, but over the death of his horse.

"How happy I was when I was a coachman and had my horse," he would murmur in despair.

One day, while struggling along with a heavy burden on his stooped shoulders, he met an old friend.

"What has happened to you?" the friend called out. "Where are your wealth, your mansion, and your carriages?"

"Why must you remind me of something which I have long since given up hope for and forgotten?" the poritz wearily replied. "I am now mourning the death of my poor horse, as a result of which I had to become a porter."

Moral: New misfortunes dim the old ones.

## SHOW OF LOYALTY

When a gaon, rabbi in a large city, became old and feeble, he decided to change his position for one in a small city. There he would be able to live peacefully and free of responsibilities. The gaon assembled the overseers of the community and said, "My dear friends, I am old and weary. I would like to settle in a small city, where I can live quietly, but I want your permission to do so."

The people, realizing that the rabbi had served them wholeheartedly for many years, consented. The sage immediately wrote to a nearby city, which was in need of a rabbi, and told them he would be willing to accept the position at a small salary, if only he were permitted to live peacefully. The people were thrilled beyond words. They selected the most distinguished personalities of their community and sent them to fetch the rabbi. When the men arrived to take him and his family, the inhabitants surrounded the coaches and began to shout, "We will not permit you to take our beloved rabbi!"

"My people, what is the matter with you?" the gaon pleaded. "Have I not discussed this situation with you previously, and you agreed? Why do you object now?"

"Forgive us, rabbi," they replied; "you are right."

But as the coachmen prepared to depart with the sage and his belongings, several men of the mob seized them and gave them a beating.

"Your efforts are in vain," they cried, "for we will not give you our precious rabbi."

Again the gaon appealed to them. "You have already consented that I go. Why do you behave in such an unruly manner?"

"Rabbi, we did not intend to harm the people," they explained. "It was only an act of graciousness to you. We thought the situation over carefully and decided that the people of the small city might think you had left us because we no longer wanted you. Since we felt they would not give you the honor and respect you are worthy of, we wanted to prove to them how much we treasure you."

Moral: When God decided to give the Torah to the Jews, the angels protested. They did not want to part with the Torah so readily, for fear that the Jews would think the Lord was giving them something which the angels in heaven no longer wanted.

## ACHES AND SHAMES

A baker, while in the market place selling his wares, was approached by a scoffer.

"How much do you want for your entire stock of cake?" the latter asked.

"Not less than two rubles," the baker replied.

"All right," the other agreed; "I will pay you that sum if you eat up all the cakes you have."

The baker approved the suggestion and began to consume the cookies and cake, rapidly. After a while it became difficult for him to force another morsel down his throat, but he summoned up courage and went through with the bargain. With great effort he finished everything.

"How about this?" the scoffer said, pointing to some remaining crumbs.

Perforce the baker stuffed these too into his mouth.

"Now you can pay me," he groaned. The scoffer burst into laughter and disappeared.

"What am I to do now?" the poor baker murmured, stupefied. "I should have known better. I guess I'll just have to grin and bear it, for I dare not relate this absurd incident to anyone." During the night he writhed in severe pain. His stomach rebelled at the mass of sweet food it had consumed.  He screamed frantically for help, for he could not conceal his circumstances any longer.  His pain was greater than his shame.

Moral:  Man is foolhardy when he yields to the Evil Spirit, who urges him to sin.  At the beginning he attempts to conceal his errors, but eventually he loudly bemoans his predicament, for his pain is greater than his shame.

## LIGHTS OUT

Zelig Koppel, who lived in a small Russian city, woke very early one wintry Sabbath morning and decided to peer into the Bible.  It was very dark, but since Zelig could not kindle the light because of the Sabbath, he went forth to wake his neighbor, a gentile, to join him in a drink. Surely Stephen would not refuse; and once Zelig had him in the house Stephen could be made to kindle the light without being told.  When the goy entered, Zelig pre- tended he could not find the flask in the dark.  Stephen understood and put on the light.  The Jew, overjoyed, placed the liquor on the table as if to say, "Here my friend, drink to your heart's content."  Stephen began to gulp down one drink after another.  After he had had his fill, he contentedly smacked his lips, wiped his mustache with the back of his palm, tottered over to the lamp, and with groping fingers put it out.  So the Jew again remained in the dark.

Moral:  We Jews are living through a war through which the world has drunk freely of the blood and sweat of our youths.  As long as they drew from the flask on the table, they kept the lamp of democracy alight. We thought that at last there would be permanent light in our little corner. But as soon as Stephen finished the flask, he snapped off the light—and we Jews are back in the dark again.

## FRUITS OF THE EARTH

A king employed two gardners, a horticulturist who produced luscious fruits, and a simple farmer who tended the vegetable patch. At the beginning of the summer season both men brought their products to the king. The horticulturist had a basket filled with newly ripened fruits, which were delightful to look at and delicious to eat. The farmer brought a selection of new potatoes, crisp lettuce, and sweet carrots, vegetables which had not as yet appeared in the market-place. The king rejoiced in their gifts, and remunerated them generously in gold and silver.

"Let us celebrate the honor the king bestowed upon us," the farmer said to the horticulturist.

"How do you dare to compare yourself to me?" the other retorted, gravely insulted. "You are no more than an ignorant farmer, whereas I am a well learned man and an artist in my profession."

"But," the farmer interposed, "you noticed that the king appreciated my gift no less than yours."

"Wait a few weeks longer, my friend," the horticulturist smiled, "and you will see the difference between my work and yours."

Several weeks later the horticulturist approached the farmer and said, "Come, let us go to the king. I am bringing him ripened clusters of my sun-kissed grapes."

"What can I bring now?" the poor farmer moaned. "The market-place is flooded with vegetables which are cheap enough for any man to buy. It would not be fit to bring the king such a gift."

"Now do you grasp the difference between the two of us?" the horticulturist said. "Your work is appreciated only during a specific season, but mine is always highly appraised and esteemed."

Moral: Some pride is only temporarily justified.

## SELF-SACRIFICE

A wealthy merchant had a servant who helped in his business. The servant did not receive a salary, but worked only for his room and board. One Purim, while the merchant, his family, and the servant were seated at a table bedecked with the choicest foods, a customer entered. The owner did not care to leave the feast and disturb his meal. The servant, however, rose and said, "I will go to the shop and bring the merchandise which the customer desires."

As a result of the servant's efforts, the merchant made a large sale and earned a good profit. Afterwards the proprietor asked his servant, "How much do I owe you?"

"I do not work for a salary," the other replied.

"Well," the merchant explained, "at the beginning I assumed that a meal was the most important thing in your life and that you were content to work only for that. However, I have observed now that you are willing to leave your meal for the welfare of my business. Since you have proven to me that my business is more significant to you than your food, I feel that you should be remunerated accordingly."

Moral: We serve the Lord for our means of subsistence and for furnishing us with the necessities of life. The zaddik, however, would sacrifice his life for God and the Torah, thereby proving that the material things in life are insignificant. Therefore he is bound to receive a greater reward.

## ALL THAT GLITTERS

A king employed a diamond appraiser who was a great connoisseur of gems. One day this man died and the king immediately began to search for another appraiser to replace him. He ordered his most faithful servant to go to the city and take along one of his most precious gems.

"Take this diamond," the king said, "and whoever fully understands its value will offer a great sum of money for it. In order to appreciate the worth of this gem, one must truly be a connoisseur, and in that manner you will be able to select the proper individual for me."

As soon as the servant arrived in the city he announced that he had a diamond for sale. All the dealers immediately surrounded him, among them a very wealthy man who bought diamonds for his personal enjoyment. He possessed a great deal of money but little intelligence, and since he

155

did not know the difference between a genuine diamond and an ordinary piece of sparkling glass the merchants readily cheated him. Now, as always, he began to raise his bid for the priceless gem without knowledge of its value. Whatever the dealers offered, his bid was higher. This continued for a while until the wealthy man finally made a bid which was the actual value of the diamond.

"Now I can see that this man is a great connoisseur," the servant murmured. "The king will be delighted to have a man like him."

When he had to pay the servant, the rich man took out a handful of glass stones from his pocket and said, "My good fellow, instead of money I will give you these precious gems in exchange for your diamond. I have paid huge sums of money for these priceless stones." When the servant saw what the man considered "precious," he regretfully realized the other's ignorance.

Moral: A braggart may often impress people and lead them to believe that he is imbued with a high degree of intelligence, but eventually he will shed his disguise and show his true self.

## MONKEY BUSINESS

A king who had several ministers, admired one in particular more than the others. He never ventured anything without this minister's advice. During these consultations he would even ask his one and only son to leave the room. This made the minister proud, and he would boast to his friends, "The king regards me so highly that when we are in conference he sends his son away. This proves that I am of greater importance to him than his child."

When these words reached the lad's ears he was humiliated and pained. As time passed on the boy became melancholy and finally was confined to his bed. The doctor treating the lad advised the king that the only remedy for his son was that he be cheered with entertainment. The king then summoned his ministers and asked their advice. One suggested that each minister disguise himself as a certain animal, such as a lion, bear, or elephant, and amuse the boy for a day. Since the lad would be aware who the disguised minister was, it would appear comical to him and he would burst into laughter.

The king was pleased, and ordered the ministers to disguise themselves accordingly. He asked his favorite minister, however, to appear as a monkey, because a monkey is bound to amuse a boy more than anything else. The minister had to obey the king, and when the lad recognized the monkey he laughed so heartily that he became well again. Afterwards the other ministers teased their friend the braggart, "The king thinks so highly of you that he made a monkey of you to please his son."

Moral: A braggart should be shown his place.

## TRADE SECRET

A wealthy merchant sent his servant to Leipzig twice yearly to purchase merchandise for him on credit. Each time the servant bought new stock, he paid up the old debt.

One day the merchant devised a plan of going into bankruptcy.

"When you go to Leipzig this time," he said to his servant, "you will buy a tremendous amount of merchandise so that you will not have to travel there any more. You will not need any money, because I've paid enough already."

The servant did not relish his master's suggestion, for he did not want to be an accomplice in the swindle.

"I am afraid that the dealers will not want to sell without money," he said.

"Do as I say!" the merchant angrily shouted.

The servant, having no alternative, went to the dealer in Leipzig and said, "My master has instructed me to purchase a large amount of stock on credit. When I told him that I doubted whether you would trust him with so much money, he asked me to hold my tongue."

The dealer immediately grasped the hint of the honest man and did not sell.

Moral: A word to the wise is sufficient.

## CAVEAT EMPTOR

A man who possessed a pair of expensive, antique watches, bequeathed them to his two sons after his death, with the condition that they were never to be sold. After their father died, the brothers were financially distressed, and they resolved to sell the watches. Each one was ashamed of the other for disobeying the father's instructions, so they sold the watches secretly. One day the brothers met.

"What time is it?" the older one asked.

"I forgot to take my watch," replied the younger. "Where is yours?"

"I also forgot mine," was the answer.

They immediately realized what had happened.

"Did you get a good price?" the older brother asked.

"No, I sold it to a man who could not appreciate its value, and received very little for it."

"You're a fool!" the older exclaimed.. "At least, I sold my watch to a connoisseur of antiques who paid me a good sum of money."

"On the contrary, I was wise," the younger brother explained. "You sold your watch to a man who knows it is a valuable article. If you should ever want to buy it back from him, he will demand a great deal more than what he paid. I sold my watch to one who is ignorant of its value, who will be happy to re-sell it to me for the price he paid."

Moral: He is wise who can foresee the future.

## TAXATION IS VEXATION

A young man inherited his father's estate, which consisted of almost an entire town. Since he had studied in foreign countries for a number of years, he was unfamiliar with the laws of his home town when he returned. He was unaware of the fact that the owners of property situated on his land had to pay taxes. A famous judge moved into the town, and when he realized the circum-stances, explained to the landowner that the residents were obliged to pay him taxes. The young man then hired collectors who conducted and managed the tax affairs.

Some years later, a grandchild of the judge was im-prisoned for non-payment of taxes. One of the inhabitants, and old man, who remembered the way the judge had reinstated tax payments, visited the landowner.

"It is true," he said, "the fellow deserves to be pen-alized for not paying his taxes, but permit me to remind you that it was his grandfather who acquainted you with the fact that you should levy assessments. If it were not for the judge, you would never have received this money. Therefore, in gratitude to him you should be merciful to his grandchild, and reduce his punishment."

Moral: Prior to the days of Father Abraham, the Lord had no income from His people. They did not serve Him then. Abraham taught the people to serve God with prayer and good deeds. Therefore the Lord should be merciful to the children of Abraham if ever they do not fulfill their obligations.

## FOOD FOR THOUGHT

Nachman and Kalman met each other on the street one afternoon. Kalman asked, "Why are you so sad, my friend?"

"My son is ill and I am greatly concerned about him," the other replied.

"Why, I just met him and he seems to be a perfect specimen of health."

"Yes, he looks well, but he refuses to eat," Nachman sighed.

"I will prove to you that the lad will eat," Kalman reassured him.

With these words, he set out to find the boy, invited him to his house, and spread a table of food before him.

"I don't want to eat," the young fellow protested.

"If you'll finish this meal I'll give you a dollar," Kalman proposed.

The lad, spurred by the bribe, hastily devoured all that was put before him. Overjoyed, Kalman ran to his friend and related the entire incident.

"Foolish man," the father replied. "Your story in itself is sufficient evidence that the boy has no appetite and is ill. If he were well, he would eat to satisfy his hunger, and not because you offered him a reward."

Moral: Some people give charity and perform good deeds out of kindness, while others do so to obtain honor in this world and recognition in the next world.

## WHOLESALE

Mendel Berger was a dealer in remnant materials. Two weeks prior to the Passover holiday, his poor uncle approached him and said, "Dear nephew, every year at this time you give me material for a garment without charge. This year, however, my conditions are better, and I want to purchase some cloth."

The dealer allowed his relative to select whatever he desired, and charged him a trivial price. The uncle left very pleased and promised to pay within a few days.

"Why do you sigh, Mendel?" his wife asked. "You should be content that he is going to pay this time."

"On the contrary," Mendel replied. "When my uncle was poor, I used to give him material without money, and it was usually something that was difficult for me to sell. Thus I performed a good deed and it cost me little. Now when he came to purchase something for money, I was compelled to allow him to select the finest piece of cloth at less than cost price. I even doubt whether he will remember to pay for it. Therefore, my dear wife, you can realize my sadness. Not only haven't I performed a good deed, but I may have to stand a loss."

Moral: Many people would rather resort to theft and swindle than to charity.

## RETURN

A father who disapproved of his son's behavior demanded that the boy leave the house. The lad traveled about aimlessly without food or clothing. The father was grieved over the boy's hardships and was also very lonely without him, but nevertheless did not call him back. One day a friend of the family arrived in the city where the exiled boy dwelt. When he saw the lad's sickly pallor and emaciated body he said, "My boy, your father is lonely and unhappy. His health is failing and he is depressed through longing for you. If you follow my plan all will turn out well. Buy a mirror and return home with it. When you approach your father, hang the mirror on your chest so that he will see his own reflection there. Then plead with him, 'Dear father, see how ill you look. Your personality has completely lost its spirit and cheer. Beloved father, forgive me and accept me back into your home. If not for my sake, do it for yours!' "

Moral: Ever since we Jews were driven into exile, we have been yearning for our Father in heaven, and the Divine Presence does not shine as gloriously as it did before. Therefore we pray that our Lord forgive us, if not for our sake at least for His.

## TIGHT FIST

A trapper must be tactful in his methods, because many animals can sense the trap at a great distance and avoid it. The instinct of self-protection is often so developed that some animals can never be caught. The monkey happens to be the most foolish creature, and can be caught without difficulty. The African trapper bores a hole in a cocoanut, scoops out the edible matter and fills the contents with rice. He then chains the cocoanut to the ground. When the monkey scents the cereal he digs his paw into the cocoanut, fills it with rice, and then cannot withdraw his forefoot. Here is a predicament, for he cannot carry the cocoanut away since it is fastened to the ground. If he had enough intelligence to open his paw and drop the rice, he could save himself easily. But his entire being is centered on the rice, which he holds tightly until the trapper comes.

Moral: Some men are no more intelligent than the monkey. They keep their fists closed over their money and cannot permit themselves to part with it. They do not realize that their wealth is a trap through which they lose their entire personality, their freedom, and the love of fellowmen. People cannot respect nor tolerate a man who regards his money above everything else in life.

## WRONG DIGGINGS

A Jewish family on the outskirts of a small village in Russia believed that their grandfather had buried a treasure under a tree along the road from Bialystok to Slonim, when he was fleeing from the Cossacks. One member of the family earnestly determined to find the treasure. He dug under every tree along the road, but in vain. Though exhausted, he continued his search.

An old man, passing, noticed the young fellow with spade in hand, the perspiration trickling down his fore-head. "What are you looking for?" he asked.

"I am searching for a treasure my grandfather buried along this road," was the reply.

"You'll never find it, my son," the aged passerby smiled. "In your grandfather's days people went along the old path, and you are looking along new paths of which your grandfather knew nothing."

Moral: Jews seek spiritual riches along new roads, unaware that the most beautiful treasures can be found only along the old ones.

## MAN IN NEED

There was a rich man whose charity consisted in buy-
ing up implements and tools to loan to needy laborers. One
morning a poor carpenter came to borrow an awl.

"Go up to the attic," the wealthy man suggested, "and
you will find it there."

The carpenter did as he was told, but soon was back
emptyhanded. "I've looked all over," he said, "but I
could not find it."

"Perhaps it is in the cellar," was the reply.

The man was back shortly. "I've searched in every
corner, but did not see it."

"Then try the stable," the other said. "It may be
among the wood."

The carpenter ran from place to place, but to no avail.
The tool could not be found. When he was exhausted
with fatigue, the rich man said, "Here, my friend, the awl
is on the table."

The poor man gaped with surprise. "If the awl was
on the table all the time, why did you tire me out need-
lessly?"

"If affords me pleasure to loan my tools to men who
are in need of them," the wealthy man explained. "There
are, however, some who do not need the implement, but
will merely take it for the sake of borrowing something,
without a definite motive. I tested you to see whether
you really needed the awl, and since that was quite
evident, I gave it to you."

Moral: Sincerity achieves good results.

## TRICKS

A poor neighbor who was in dire need borrowed a silver spoon from his niggardly friend. Several days later he returned the spoon along with another silver spoon of a smaller size.

"What is this?" the miser asked.

"Your spoon gave birth to a smaller one," the man replied, "so I brought you both."

Shortly afterwards the neighbor borrowed a silver cup and a few days later returned two silver cups, with the same story that the small cup was an offspring of the large one. The friend was pleased, and never questioned the veracity of the poor man's explanation.

Some time elapsed and the neighbor ceased coming. "You are free to borrow whatever you may need," the avaricious man suggested. "Just mention it."

"Would you loan me your gold watch?" the pauper asked.

"Gladly," the other assented, and immediately handed over his diamond studded watch.

Several weeks passed by and the poor neighbor did not appear. The indignant niggard went out to search for him.

"What happened to my watch?" he demanded.

"I regret to inform you," the pauper replied, "that your watch has died."

"How can a watch die?" the miser frantically screamed. "Are you insane?"

"If a spoon can give birth to a smaller spoon and a cup can become the mother of another cup," the poor man explained, "then a watch is capable of dying."

Moral: The Lord said to his people, "Thou shalt not add anything to that which is written in the Torah." If one attempts to add a mitzvah that is not specified in the Torah and say that it is the offspring of a mitzvah, then he may also seek an excuse for disobeying an important commandment by saying that it has died.

## THE EYES HAVE IT

Two blind men traveled together begging for alms. One day they arrived in a city where a prominent eye-specialist lived. One of the beggars was an honest man, who grieved over the fact that he had to resort to begging, but the other was a scoundrel, who enjoyed his work. The people of the city advised both men to visit the doctor, who might be able to cure them. The honest beggar, who detested his means of livelihood, joyfully hurried to the physician and was thrilled to learn that his vision could be restored. The other beggar refused to see the doctor.

"If I regain my sight, how will I earn my living?" he argued. "I'd rather remain blind."

Several weeks later both men were preparing to leave the town, one having recovered his sight and the other being still sightless. The inhabitants blessed the sincere, good man and wished him luck in securing agreeable work. The other they frowned upon, muttering, "May he always remain a beggar."

Moral: The wicked are blind, and refuse to open their eyes.

## ADDED BLESSING

A traveler wandering in the desert became faint with heat, hunger and thirst. Suddenly he spied a large, shady tree laden with luscious fruit. Nearby flowed a clear, sparkling stream. The weary man hungrily devoured the fruit, quenched his thirst with the fresh flowing water, and reclined under the shade of the tree. When he prepared to set out again, he turned to the tree and said, "Benevolent tree, how can I thank you? Shall I bless you that your fruit be sweet? Your fruit is sweet. Shall I bless you that your shade be soothing? It is soothing. Shall I wish for water to flow through and nourish your roots? You already have a stream at your feet. There is just one blessing that I can give you. May the twigs which are cut from you and planted in other soil, flourish and blossom like you."

Moral: Thus God spoke to Abraham, "How shall I bless you? Shall I bless you with gold and silver? You already have that. Shall I bestow other blessings upon you? You have everything. However, there is just one blessing which I will give you. May your children be like you and follow in your footsteps."

## CHANGE THE SINNER

A father, enraged at his son's conduct, compelled him to leave the house. The boy wandered about half-starved and dressed in tatters. Finally he approached a neighbor and asked him to plead with his parent for mercy. The neighbor appealed to the boy's father: "Your son hasn't anything to wear and winter is approaching. At least give him a warm coat."

"I'll ask you to give him a coat," the father replied coldly.

The neighbor was baffled and regarded the man with surprise.

"What I mean," the father explained, "is that instead of begging me to have pity on my son, you should have spoken to him to discard his bad habits. Only then will I have mercy on him, for that was my purpose in chastising him."

Moral: When pious men pray to God that He be merciful to the children of Israel, the Lord advises them instead to urge the Jews to become more religious. Only then will He show them mercy.

## POOR JEWS

Zelig Wasserman left his small town for a larger city to seek his fortune. Luck was with him and he accumulated great wealth. Soon all his poor relatives showered him with letters, pleading for financial aid.

Zelig grew weary of constantly giving them contributions, and decided to visit his home town, to see for himself his relatives' condition. He stopped at a hotel, and informed his people that each one was entitled to come to him with one request. There was one cousin who was in dire need, and also very ill. The poor man lacked so much, that he did not know what to ask for. When he saw his rich relative, he burst into tears.

"Why do you cry?" Zelig asked. "Tell me your one desire and it will be fulfilled."

"Dear cousin," the miserable man sobbed, "how can I mention one particular thing, when I am in need of so very much? I don't know what to ask for first, and that is why I cry."

Moral: All races, when they pray, can voice their wishes specifically, but the Jews, who lack so much, must cry out to their Relative in the distant heavens.

## SAFE CONDUCT

A rich manufacturer, who conducted a tremendous business with foreign countries, was traveling across the ocean on a boat heavily laden with his merchandise. He had remembered to take along his tallis bag, with his te-fillin and Bible. During the trip a severe storm arose, and the ship with all her passengers was in danger of sinking.

"You will be compelled to relieve the ship of some of its load,'" the captain suggested to the merchant. "Dump as much as you can into the ocean, otherwise we will all go down to the bottom."

The merchant, paralyzed with fear, seized his tallis bag and was about to hurl it into the water, when his servant grabbed his hand.

"What are you doing, master?" he cried out. "That which you want to cast into the ocean is the very essence of what keeps us alive. It would be more practical to dump some of your heavy cartons of merchandise, for then the ship would become lighter."

Moral: When man meets with difficult economic conditions, he immediately begins to economize on the charity he has been accustomed to give. But charity maintains our very existence. It would be far wiser that he economize on luxuries to ease his plight.

## "ALAS FOR THOSE THAT ARE GONE"

A baroness, a great lover of nature, had a beautiful garden filled with the loveliest and costliest flowers of the world. She was a kind soul, and always gave freely of her flowers to children, for parties and all sorts of occasions. One summer her doctor ordered her to spend her vacation in the country, because her health was declining.

When she returned she found her garden in a neglected condition. The flowers had withered everywhere, but in some forlorn corners a few white roses were still blooming. She gazed at them thoughtfully.

One morning she noticed that a flower was missing and she began to cry bitterly.

"Tell me, grandmother," her grandchild asked, "why do you behave so differently now? I remember when every spring you'd pluck the flowers with your own hands, and give them to everyone. Now you make such a fuss over one flower."

"Yes, my little one," the old lady replied, "there is a great difference between then and now. The warm sun above and the fruitful earth below would yield masses of flowers then. One flower would wither and ten others would sprout up in its place. Today the cruel winds, the bitter cold, have laid my beautiful garden waste until very little remains. When a flower disappears now, there is no other to replace it, and the loss is very great. It grips my heart."

It is the same with us Jews. Once the Torah ruled supremely. With it went happiness, and prosperity. Then many devoted their time and energy to charity and the building of institutions. Such people were plentiful. To-day everything is ruined, and only a chosen few are left. Thus, when one passes away, it is indeed a great loss.

## TREE OF KNOWLEDGE

Two neighbors had trees in their gardens laden with fruit. One of them, a lazy fellow, chopped down his tree when the fruit had ripened so that it would be easier for him to pluck. The other, more cautious and intelligent, shook his tree until the fruit fell down. The task of the first man was easier, but he never paused to think that his tree would never yield fruit again. The other would be compensated for his labor, for his tree would continue to bear delicious fruit every year.

There are two types of parents in America. One, who considers only his personal comfort, chops down the "tree of knowledge" after his son's bar mitzvah, when he sends the boy out to work. The lad's earnings ease the father's financial burden, but the young tree will never yield fruit,

172

for it was cut down at an early stage. Such children will drift away from the Jewish religion and traditions. The other parent, however, decorates his young tree with Torah and learning. He toils on endlessly until it begins to bear fruit, for then he feels certain that in his later years his children and grandchildren will be respectable, learned Jews.

## ETERNAL PEOPLE

Every fruit has its season and climate in which it can bloom and grow. There are some fruits which can flourish only in the golden sunshine and cannot tolerate the cold, bleak wind. There are others which wither and shrivel in the hot weather. However, the esrog is the only fruit which grows both in winter and summer. It is able to survive heat, cold, snow, and rain without injury. As the fruits so are the nations. Each nation has its place and environment in which it can continue to live and multiply. The Jews, however, are less fortunate. They are strewn throughout the world and live under unfavorable conditions and circumstances. Like the esrog, which is the symbol of the Jew, they have overcome all difficulties and managed to survive. The Jew will never become extinct.

## REMEMBRANCES

One Tishah B'ab, Napoleon rode by a synagogue in a small town and noticed the Jews sitting on the ground, wailing bitterly.

"Why are the Jews crying?" he asked a bystander.

173

"They are mourning their land which was destroyed about two thousand years ago," he was informed.

These words deeply impressed Napoleon. "A nation that can mourn over the destruction and loss of their land which occurred two thousand years ago," he exclaimed—"such a people will never perish. They may be certain they will survive and that their land will eventually be restored to them."

## PARTNERS IN CRIME

A deaf beggar and his lame friend became partners. The lame fellow seated himself on his friend's shoulders and they went begging together. People sympathized and contributed. One day the partners passed a house where a wedding was being held. The lame man, hearing strains of music, was seized with an urge to dance.

"Dance for me!" he shouted to his deaf friend. "I feel gay."

But the other heard neither his partner nor the music. The cripple then bought a flask of liquor, which he gave his friend to drink. As soon as the deaf beggar had swallowed a few drinks he became jolly and began to jig. With each he danced the more vigorously. Before long the cripple seated on his shoulders began to shake up and down. So both partners danced—the lame because of the music and the deaf because of the liquor.

Moral: The body and the soul cannot sin individually. Therefore the soul is chastised for the sins of the body, for both are equal partners.

174

## FIRST CONFESSION

A father arrived home from a long trip abroad, and brought an expensive wardrobe for his son. The little boy dressed up, and proudly strutted about in his new out-fit. He tripped and fell into a puddle, soiling his new garments. His friend, an envious little fellow who had witnessed the scene, called out, "I'm going to tell your father and you'll get a good beating," and he made a dash for the house to tell the tale.

The son immediately started to race after the other lad, and rushed into the house before the other, sobbing. "See what happened to me, father! I ruined the beautiful suit you gave me!"

When the father observed his son's tears, and the pitiful expression on his face, he compassionately said, "Do not weep, my child. An accident is bound to happen some-times. You are not at fault. I will cleanse your clothing."

Moral: Instead of giving Satan the opportunity to denounce us before the Lord, that we have blemished our soul, we should hasten to confess, pray, and beg forgive-ness for our sins.

## LIVE AND LEARN

A father chastised his son for his unseemly behavior by compelling him to leave the house. The boy spent his days at the synagogue and ate meals at various homes. The father daily questioned the sexton of the synagogue, "How has my son fared today? Did he study the Talmud? Did he pray?"

When the son learned of the father's inquiries, he ran home in tears. "Dear father," he pleaded, "every day you asked whether I've prayed or studied the Torah. Not once have you inquired whether I ate or had a bed in which to sleep. If you wish to be a parent to me, take me into your house again. You will then see with your own eyes how I pray and study."

Moral: The Jewish people complain to the Lord, "You are concerned as to whether we adhere to your Torah and obey your commandments. If you want to be a good Father to us, see that we are provided with a livelihood, and are reinstated in Your holy land. You will observe then how pious we will be."

## JEWISH ANTIQUITIES

Mordecai Kalish was proprietor of an antique shop. People of the entire neighborhood congregated to admire his exquisite merchandise. One of his friends carelessly broke a costly ornament, and Mordecai vowed that he would never permit him to cross his threshold. Several weeks later the friend, learning that Mordecai had imported some precious antiques, pleaded to be admitted into the store.

"No, my friend," the proprietor replied. "A vow must never be broken."

After a great deal of cajoling, however, Mordecai decided to yield and yet not break his vow. He displayed his new antiques in the show window of his store. The friend was satisfied and the vow was kept.

Moral: The Lord vowed that Moses would not be permitted to enter into the Holy Land. Moses pleaded that he be allowed at least to see it. God told Moses to ascend the mountain peak and from there to gaze down on the land.

## HOME OF GOSSIP

A prominent merchant, whenever he visited Warsaw, always stopped at one hotel, the most elegant in the city. On one occasion, however, he stayed at a very shabby place, much to the dismay of the other hotelkeeper.

The following day the merchant visited the proprietor of the grand hotel and said, "I understand that you are amazed at my stopping at such a filthy and common place. I assure you that you may consider my not staying at your hotel this time as an honor. The Midrash relates that when one comes to a city regarding a shidduch, he should be attentive to barking dogs. I have now come to the city to check up on the reputation of a family, whose daughter was suggested as a bride for my son. Since I know that both your guests and your staff of employees are highly reputed, decent people, who would speak evil of no one, I decided to go to a place where I could obtain such information. I knew that if the bride or her family had any blemish, the dogs there would bark it out."

Moral: Evil talk can be heard only from evil people.

## THE BITER BIT

Reb Nachman, wealthiest manufacturer in his small town, declared himself bankrupt. Widows, orphans, and small business men, who had deposited their monies with him, were frantic with fear, for they now were penniless. They furiously stormed against the bankrupt. A bystander, a visitor in the town, observed one man in the mob who was very calm and nonchalant about the entire affair.

"Did that man also lose money?" the visitor inquired.

"He did," was the reply.

"Then why isn't he infuriated and shouting like the others?"

"He isn't shouting because a few years ago he played the same trick as Reb Nachman and also declared himself bankrupt," was the explanation.

Moral: An honest man refuses to tolerate a wrong deed, but a dishonest man will often remain silent when wronged.

## SOBER RESPONSE

A wealthy landowner and his son were strolling along the street dressed in their Sunday finery. Suddenly a drunkard approached them, seized the landowner by his arm and shouted, "That is my coat you are wearing! You stole it from me!"

"My good friend," the rich man nonchalantly replied, "I didn't steal it. I merely borrowed it from your wife for a day. I will return it to you tomorrow, with sincere gratitude."

When the drunkard heard these words he grew calm and stalked away.

"Father," the son asked, "why did you agree that it was his coat?"

"My boy," the father replied, "it would be useless to argue with a drunkard. If I had denied the fact, it would only have infuriated him the more, and he might have gone so far as to strike me. That is why I put it off for tomorrow. I know that his mind will be less befuddled then and he will forget about the entire incident."

Moral: A soft answer turneth away wrath.

## EVEN RETURN

A king made a feast for his faithful servants, and presented each with a silver urn. One of the servants observed that his gift was not genuine silver, as were all the others. He felt humiliated. Suddenly he had a bright idea. "Your Majesty," he said, "I do not wish to accept a gift for my loyalty to you. It is my greatest joy to serve you. Therefore I will deem it an honor if you accept a silver dollar in return for your gift."

The king was gratified with his servant's offer, but after examining the coin, he exclaimed in surprise, "It is not genuine."

"Your Excellency," the servant replied, "it is like your gift."

Moral: One must be tactful even when exposing the truth.

## DEBTORS

A group of dealers arrived in Warsaw to buy merchandise. They all purchased their stock on credit. Some bought more, others less, but they were very amiable. On the way home, the men observed that one of their friends, who had purchased more than the rest of the group, acted very haughtily.

"Why are you so proud?" one asked. "Do you think that because you have bought more merchandise on credit than we did that you are important? On the contrary, you are only a greater debtor than we are and certainly have nothing to be conceited about. But since you walk about with your nose in the air, it is a sign that you do not intend to pay for what you bought."

Moral: The rich and the poor are alike. God gave them what they possess on credit, so that they might give charity. If the rich are proud, it is a sign they intend to disregard their debt.

## FEED YOUR FOE

When Jacob Karp celebrated his twenty-fifth wedding anniversary, he gave an elaborate feast to which he invited his relatives and closest friends. The host also extended an invitation to his most wicked enemy and ordered his servants to serve this man the very best and choicest food. The other, who had a fierce appetite, consumed all that he was offered. The guests curiously observed their host's attitude towards his enemy, but the following day all was clarified for them. The man, due to his excessive eating, suffered a severe case of indigestion. The people then understood King Solomon's words, "When your enemy is hungry, give him food."

Moral: The Lord permits the evil to fulfill their earthly cravings and desires, for in the end they will suffer and repent.

## LUCKY FIND

Mendel, an indigent farm hand, decided to migrate to another country for better luck. He worked and slaved several years, but was poorly compensated for his efforts and finally determined to return home. A few days prior to his leaving, he found a wallet stuffed with gold coins. Mendel, overjoyed with his good fortune, bought himself an expensive wardrobe, and arrived in his town dressed like an aristocrat, with a tidy sum of money. His friends, marveling at his wealth, were all anxious to go to the same country to acquire riches.

"Be calm, my good people," Mendel smiled. "Miracles do not happen every day, and not every day does one find a wallet filled with gold coins. The hardships I endured there you most certainly would have, but my stroke of good fortune can occur only once in a lifetime!"

Moral: Do not depend on miracles.

## GENIUS

A king possessed a precious diamond. Accidentally it was scratched and a flaw appeared. The king referred to numerous expert diamond cutters, who suggested that the gem be filed down, but that it would never have the same value, as the flaw would still be noticeable. But one

181

diamond cutter, who was considered an artist, undertook to make the defective gem appear even more beautiful than before. After devoting a great deal of effort and time, he polished the diamond to exquisite beauty. When the others observed the man's work, they marveled at his ingenuity.

Moral: Effort can turn a handicap into an asset.

## HUMILITY AND GREATNESS

A wealthy householder gave a feast in honor of his son's bar-mitzvah, and invited many prominent people. Among his guests was a venerable rabbi, a humble man who disliked any token of recognition for his distinguished services. Refusing to occupy the seat of honor, the rabbi placed himself in an inconspicuous spot, at the farthest end of the room near the door. Upon which the host led all his other distinguished guests to where the sage sat and proudly proclaimed, "My friends, this is the seat of honor!"

Moral: Surroundings do not elevate man; man lends merit to his surroundings.

## GEM CARRIERS

A diamond dealer sent his messenger to fetch a suit-case filled with precious gems that he had left at a shop on the road. The dealer stood at the window, impatiently awaiting the return of the messenger with the diamonds. Suddenly he spied the man in the distance, wearily trudg-ing along and carrying a heavy load on his stooped shoulders.

"Woe is me," the merchant cried out. "A great misfortune has befallen me. That fool probably paused to rest on the road, where thieves switched the suitcase of diamonds for one of stones. Man does not moan or suffer when he carries precious gems."

Moral: When modern Jews groan under the strain of Judaism, it is because they have substituted the Lord's precious gems with stones.

## HAPPY EVENT

Two merchants lived in a small town. One had a studious son, of fine bearing and good breeding, who became a rabbi; the other's son was a swindler, sentenced to prison. One day both merchants gave parties for their sons, and invited their friends. One was in honor of the son who became a rabbi, and the other for the son who had been miraculously released from prison. A guest, with a keen sense of honor, attended both events and extended the same wish to the two fathers. "May God help you," he said, "to make the same celebrations for the rest of your children."

Moral: Good fortune varies. There are happy occurrences, however, which one would not want repeated.

## PASSING THE GOAL

A wealthy man hired a private tutor for his son. One day the two went hunting in the forest. The lad spied a fox in the distance and began to chase after him. While running the boy passed the fox, and continued to race on.

"Where are you running?" the tutor called out. "I am going after the fox!" the lad flung back. "Silly fellow," the teacher shouted, "you are not running after the fox, but you are running away from him. The faster you run, the farther away you get."

Moral: People go out of their way to attain honor and prestige, but instead of reaching it, they usually pass it up.

## HEADS AND TAILS

The tail of the snake complained to the head, "Why should you always go first and I have to lag behind? I want to be the leader." "All right," the head agreed, "you may."

Thus the tail went first. Soon the snake fell into a ditch. He wriggled his way out and went a little further, only to become entangled in barbed wire, thorns, and weeds. So, the entire journey consisted of discomfiting events from which the snake emerged bruised and with a broken spirit.

Moral: Great people with great minds should lead the ordinary man.

## WINDFALL

A beggar arrived in a small town, but was ignored by the inhabitants. Occasionally he would receive a penny, or a piece of dry bread. One day the unfortunate man fell and broke his leg, and had to be taken to the hospital. As

soon as the people of the town became aware of the beggar's condition, they were concerned about him. He received the best food and the finest medical attention. When
he was well enough to leave the hospital, they provided
him with clothing and money. In a letter to his wife the
beggar wrote: "A miracle happened to me. I broke a leg."

Moral: People will rather help one who has fallen,
than keep him from falling.

## PUBLIC SPIRIT

A lunatic set a house afire one night while the people
were asleep. The fire spread rapidly to other houses. Each
family ran frantically about, attempting to save its individual possessions. A wise bystander remarked: "You are
silly people. Instead of each one trying to save his own
possessions, why don't you all get together and put out
the fire, so that it will not spread any further?"

Moral: If each man were interested only in his personal welfare, the world could not exist.

## THE PARTING GUEST

An itinerant preacher stopped at a small town and
spent several weeks with a wealthy landlord. The host
was a hospitable person who did everything within his
means to make his guest comfortable. One morning the
preacher packed his suitcase and prepared to leave. Somehow the landlord was suspicious that his guest had taken
along one of his priceless books. The host found himself
in a peculiar predicament and did not know how to ap-

proach the preacher. To search the other's suitcase would be tactless, for if the preacher had not taken the book it would indeed be embarrassing. "My friend," the landlord finally suggested, "you should check the contents of your suitcase before you leave and make certain that you have all your possessions. There is a possibility that you may have forgotten something."

Moral: When one suspects an individual but is not certain of his suspicions, he must use discretion so that he will not offend the other.

## THE POOR MAN'S PURSE

A rich man's son and a poor man's son studied at one school. One day the wealthy lad bought a genuine leather wallet, which was the envy of his classmates. Soon the other pupils managed to save up their pennies, and within a short while they too bought wallets like that of their colleague. All but the very poor youngster who could barely pay for his tuition. He felt like an outcast and was miserable. Finally he decided to go to the storekeeper with the paltry few pennies he had scraped together.

"Good sir," he pleaded, "this is all the money that I possess. I give you my word of honor that I haven't another penny. Please give me a wallet for the little that I have."

"Foolish child," the proprietor replied, "you yourself say that you haven't an extra penny. Of what purpose then is the wallet?"

Moral: Modern Jews donate large sums of money to build beautiful synagogues, but allow these synagogues to remain empty most of the time.

186

## DUNNING THE POOR

A rich merchant arrived in a city to collect the debts his customers owed him. He was severe in his demands for payment with those who owed him large sums, but he did not press his smaller debtors too strenuously. A very poor man he did not bother at all.

One wretched individual brazenly boasted to the others, "See, I am let alone because my credit is better than yours."

"Oh no—that isn't the reason," the other debtors explained. "The merchant does not bother you because you are so poor and insignificant. You have nothing to give."

Moral: Since Moses was so harshly chastised for a minor sin, how much more are we, insignificant individuals, to be punished for sins we constantly commit? But we are only inconspicuous beings, like the poor merchants, who have nothing.

## TOOL OF DESTRUCTION

The Midrash relates that when the trees in the forest heard the clanging of various iron implements, they began to tremble with fear. "Woe is us," they moaned in distress.

"They are preparing to cut off our young lives," one tree called out.

"If it is only the iron that we hear, without wooden handles," another tree said, "we have nothing to fear. They can't chop down a tree with a naked piece of iron. The situation becomes tragic only when the piece of iron is

attached to something which comes from our own kind—
a wooden handle."

Moral: If we Jews were only concerned with the
prayer, "Deliver me from the hands of Esau," our tragedy
would not be so great. The misfortune lies in a handle of
our own kind held in the hand of Esau. Very often we
find a Jew behind the enemy's machinations.


## DE GUSTIBUS

A guest at a hotel ordered that his food should not be
seasoned with pepper. As he passed by the kitchen he
noticed the chef grinding pepper. "What is this?" he
shouted. "I thought I told you that I do not want any
pepper in my food. Why are you preparing it? Is this
the way your hotel caters to its guests?"

"Be calm, my friend," the chef replied. "There are
others who like pepper and I am preparing it for them.
The next time you should not be so hasty in causing unnecessary commotion."

Moral: There are many things on this earth which
we do not relish and we are curious why God created
them. But that which may appear useless to us may be
very important for other purposes.


188

## PARABLE FOR JEWS

A king greatly admired a wealthy man of his city and always cherished his advice regarding various problems. The king's advisers were envious of this man and joined in a conspiracy against him. One day they circulated a rumor that he was plotting to murder the king. When this news reached the king he immediately sent his guards to seize the innocent man and threw him into a dungeon. The unfortunate individual entreated the guards to inform him of what he was guilty. But all his pleadings were in vain and he remained locked behind a heavy iron door. The heartbroken wretch collapsed into a state of inertia which lasted for several days. He would regain consciousness for a short while, during which he was under the impression that it was midnight and he was at home. He seemed to have completely forgotten that he was a prisoner in an underground cell.

Some time later the king remembered his friend and all the evil tales related about him. He resolved to speak to the prisoner and discover the truth for himself. When the king entered the dungeon the prisoner awoke from his stupor and cried out, "How dreadfully long the night is!"

"Fool!" the king shouted. "You imagine that you are asleep in your home, whereas you actually are a prisoner in a dungeon. You have been here several days and several dawns have risen since then. You will never see the daylight here in this gloomy darkness. If you want to see the dawn then put your claims before me and I will set you free."

189

Moral: The Jews sit in the dark and wait for the daybreak. They do not realize that the dawn has appeared numerous times and that they have had countless opportunities to free themselves from their slavery, but have neglected to do so. They could have aided a few million European Jews to emigrate to America years ago, but failed to seize the occasion.

## PICTURE OF LIFE

One bright summer afternoon an artist was standing atop a rocky mountain cliff, painting the beautiful panorama. He was deeply absorbed in his work. With every stroke of the brush, he paused to regard his painting from various angles and smile to himself. When he placed the last stroke upon his masterpiece, the artist began stepping backwards in order to obtain a better view of the completed painting. Little did he realize that each step was bringing him nearer to the edge of the cliff. One more move would prove fatal and the artist would crash into the yawning abyss below. His friend, standing nearby, noticed the artist's danger. Knowing that a warning would be too late, he dashed over to the easel, seized a brush, and smeared the face of the painting. The artist, furious at his friend's behavior, rushed forward to his work and so was saved from destruction.

When the friend explained the precarious position from which he had saved him, the artist was overwhelmed with gratitude and appreciation.

Moral: We find similar instances in life. An individual who has been living in luxury and comfort forgets the rest of the world and his fellowmen. He is completely immersed in his happiness. Gradually he tears himself asunder from his people and his religion. He does not notice that he is stepping further and further into oblivion. Suddenly an invisible hand reaches out and splashes across his canvas of joy, leaving him destitute and forlorn. He is then compelled to return to that which he had previously forsaken—his people and his religion.

## NIGHT THOUGHTS

"I am the finest thing that God created," Night said to man. "Mankind should be very grateful to me, for I bring peace and replenish him with vigor. I soothe the brow of the feverish and ease the pain of the sick. The most unfortunate creature is happy while he sleeps."

"Woe to him who must seek happiness in sleep," Morning replied. "It is true that sleep obliterates man's grief, but it is not fortunate to be unconscious. Night liberates one of sorrow and distress only temporarily. Happy is he who enjoys and utilizes the day advantageously and profitably. Only such a person can obtain complete joy."

Moral: He who must seek happiness in sleep is unfortunate.

## PACK UP YOUR TROUBLES

The inhabitants of Bagdad visited the calif to bemoan their sad plight. Each man groaned that he was more unfortunate than his neighbor, and burdened with the heaviest pack of troubles.

"What would you suggest that I do?" the calif asked.

"There are many wealthy people in your land, who are content and carefree. We too would appreciate a little taste of happiness. Would you grant us the privilege of interchanging our packs with theirs, since their bundles are much lighter than ours?"

The wise calif then summoned all the people to bring forth their bundles of sorrow and pile them in one heap. Before long a huge mass accumulated. The packages were then mixed and tossed around so that one could not distinguish his from his neighbors'. A line was formed to the right and each man eagerly awaited his turn to choose his good fortune. Suddenly they paused, and regarded the peculiar assortment of bundles. They had realized that troubles are plentiful everywhere, since each individual had brought a bundle and each one had come with the intention of selecting a smaller and less cumbersome one. As a result every man took his own pack back, for in comparison to the others his was the lightest. The other bundles were filled with sorrow and anxiety.

Moral: The grass always appears greener elsewhere.

## MEDICAL FALLACY

A famous doctor visited a sick patient, and after examining the invalid, wrote a prescription. He advised the patient to boil it well and then drink the contents thrice daily. The sick man had great confidence in the physician and followed his instructions carefully. But the medicine brought him no relief. His strength gradually ebbed; his heart beat slowly, and his limbs were beginning to lose their powers of sensation and of movement. The family, anxiously gathered around the bedside of the sick man, severely criticized the doctor's diagnosis.

"He is an ignorant fool!" they shouted.

Among those present was a grandson of the invalid, an intelligent young man. "Grandfather," he said to the dying man, "did you take the medicine according to the way the doctor prescribed it?"

"Most certainly, my child," the man moaned. "I took the prescription, placed it in a pan of water, boiled it well, and then drank the water three times a day. The following day I dried the prescription, cooked it again, and again drank the water. And as you see the medicine did absolutely nothing for me."

"But, Grandpa," the young fellow called out in amazement, "you didn't fulfill the physician's instructions. You boiled a piece of paper in the pan and not the medicine. The prescription should have been taken to a pharmacist, who would have given you the appropriate medicine. It was the medicine and not the paper which you should have boiled and taken thrice daily. In that event you would have recovered a long time ago."

Moral: Our great scholars of the past left a prescription which cautioned us not to forget our Holy Land, but our rabbis and leaders did not follow their instructions properly. It is true that the particular phrase was printed in all prayerbooks and we mention it three times a day in our prayers, but that is not the proper medicine for the ailment. To remember Palestine is to think of her constantly and to strive unfalteringly to regain her.

## MAD HATTERS

The elegant stovepipe mocked the little skullcap. "Poor, little, insignificant skullcap," he spoke. "You are only worn by pious Jews and rabbis. You are always an object of ridicule and it is hardly appropriate to wear you in the street. Look at me! I am proudly worn by aristocrats, and the wealthy exhibit me at their most elaborate affairs. See how inconspicuous you are alongside me!"

"Yes, that is quite true," the skullcap agreed. "I cannot deny the fact that you receive great honor and adorn luxurious banquets and parties. But remember, dear stovepipe, that you are empty from top to bottom, whereas I am filled throughout with head."

Moral: Elegance is not always a sign of intelligence.

## SUCCOTH TALE

The lulav reprimanded the esrog for its haughty behavior. "Why do you hide yourself in a box and wrap yourself in cotton? Are you afraid that you may catch a cold or that someone will steal you? You need not fear, for you are not so precious."

"Hold your tongue, long, thin reed," the esrog re-

194

torted. "You can expose yourself to the wind and sleet, because you are dry, odorless, and tasteless. What have you to lose? I am filled with juice and have a delightful aroma, which would quickly disappear if I did not protect it. Therefore I must be very careful and safeguard my valuable qualities."

Moral: The Jew, like the esrog, should not allow himself too many liberties, for fear that he may harm his inherent characteristics.

## QUIET MAJESTY

It was announced one day that the king was to ride through the city where Rav Sheshet lived. Rav Sheshet, who was blind, went along with the other inhabitants to greet the king. A fool who stood near him tauntingly called out, "We are all gathered here because we have eyes with which to see the king, but what is your purpose in being here?"

Suddenly a loud blare of trumpets was heard and a magnificent chariot rolled by. "That is the king!" the fool shouted.

"No, it is not," the blind man calmly replied.

Several other chariots passed, accompanied by bands of music, but Rav Sheshet paid little attention to them. Soon one passed by quietly, without the beating of drums or the blasting of trumpets. Now the blind sage murmured a prayer and said, "Here rides the king."

"How do you know?" the fool asked, in surprise. "You are blind."

195

"Our Almighty God acts in the same manner," Rav Sheshet explained. "There are storms, typhoons, earth-quakes, but Godhood sails in peacefully and majestically, without a sound. Godhood is expressed in peace, for peace denotes all that is great."

Moral: Much tumult about an object rarely signifies value or importance.

## WISE AS AN OWL

A wealthy man strolled through his garden and spied a little bird entangled in a mesh of wire. He freed the frightened creature and held her in his hand. Suddenly the bird began to plead, "Kind sir, please let me go. I will be of no value to you, for I am not beatutiful; I can't sing and I am not edible. If you will set me free I will offer you three valuable pieces of advice."

The amazed man agreed. The bird then spoke, "Do not worry over that which is gone. Desire not that which you cannot obtain. Believe not that which is incredible."

The rich man appreciated the bird's advice and set her free. The wise little bird quickly flew to the highest branch of a nearby tree and laughed heartily.

"Why are you laughing?" the man asked. "I am laughing at you," the bird chirped, "for if you were not such a fool you could have been the wealthiest man in the world."

"How?" the man asked, bewildered.

"Very simply," the little bird replied, "for I carry a diamond the size of a hen's egg within my stomach."

The man was stupified. When he gathered his senses he tried to induce the bird to return.

"Dear little birdie," he called, "your good fortune lies not in your freedom. Soon the cold weather will approach and you will not find a crumb anywhere. Come with me and you will spend your days in warmth and comfort."

The little bird laughed again. "You freed me for the advice I gave you and you immediately forgot it. Remind yourself of what I told you—'First, do not regret that which is gone'—and you already are sorry for setting me free. Secondly, desire not that which you cannot reach, and you want me to return to you, which would mean my instant death. Lastly, believe not that which is incredible, and you are foolish enough to believe that I carry a diamond within my tiny body the size of a hen's egg, when I alone am half the size of such an egg."

With these words the bird spread her wings and sailed off into the distant sky.

Moral: That which is gone never returns.

## ENTOMOLOGICAL NOTE

When God created the world he also created the insects. The Lord then suggested that they find their own means of sustenance. Each species immediately obtained a suitable job, from which to derive individual benefits and self-satisfaction. The bees were the only ones who expressed a desire to serve mankind. They were not concerned merely with their personal interests. Soon a thundering voice pierced through the heavens, "Those insects who seek only to satisfy their own interests and are unconcerned about the welfare of others shall live in the dust and eat of the rubbish. The unselfish bees, however, shall nourish themselves on the nectar of the flowers and thus fulfill their duty towards man, in providing the world with sweetness and honey."

Moral: One also finds among men, cursed insects and blessed bees.

## HORSE AND DONKEY

A wealthy horse trader who was a member of a synagogue, donated large sums of money to the institution. He frequently attempted to take part in various religious controversies, though having no knowledge about the subject. One day, during such an incident, he was asked to be quiet. This audacity infuriated the ignorant trader, and he began to shout, "I have given hundreds of dollars for this synagogue, and what have I? You do not even permit me to voice my opinion. What does the knowledge of your great scholars mean in comparison to me? He is only important who gives money."

The maggid, who was present at the scene, smiled and said, "My dear friend, have you ever heard of the donkey who complained to God, 'Dear Lord, why are we more unfortunate than all the other animals you have created? The beasts in the forest have no master over them. They eat, drink, and live as they wish. Even the cows who have a master laze around in the meadows all day long and have a comfortable stall in the evening. Only we donkeys are denied all agreeable sensations. If we are beasts of burden and must slave all day long, grant us at least the gift of speech so that we may be able to tell our master how cruelly he treats us.' 'Very well,' the Lord agreed. 'Your wish shall be fulfilled. I will give one of you the power of speech and we shall see how well he will exercise it.' This test," the maggid continued, "was made with Balaam's donkey. When Balaam struck the animal three times because he refused to move, God endowed the donkey with speech. But instead of speaking to the point and explaining to Balaam that an angel had blocked his path, the ass began to boast about his heritage. 'I am sorry, donkey,' the Lord called out, 'you will have to remain as you were. An ignorant ass who continues to boast about his material accomplishments must remain a mute animal.' "


## SIAMESE

It is related in the Midrash that Ashmodai brought be-fore King Solomon a man with two heads, whose father had died and left a large inheritance. King Solomon was to decide whether this man should be considered as two people and therefore receive a larger share of the inherit-ance. He suggested that boiling water be poured on the head. If the other head would not object, that would be a sign that they were two different people. However, if the second head reacted to the pain then this meant one individual. The same is true of the Jewish organism, which possesses many heads. They are scattered throughout the world and speak in various tongues. We often doubt whether all these heads belong to one body, and have anything in common. But these doubts disappear when pain is inflicted upon one head. Then all the others immediately feel the agony and rebel against it. Thus we are shown that all are strongly united among themselves and are part of one body and one nation.

## AN APPETIZER

Noah was a wealthy merchant famous for his hospitality. One day he invited a traveler to dine at his home, together with other guests. The others readily partook of the delicious food set before them, but the traveler tasted nothing.

"What is the matter?" his host inquired. "Why don't you eat?" "I am not hungry now," the newcomer explained, "but if you give me a drink of liquor, I'm sure that I will acquire an appetite."

"My custom is to feed the hungry," Noah replied, "not to make hungry those that have been fed."

Moral: God delights in supplying man with his necessities. However, there are some who desire ever more and, when they acquire this they desire still more, like the man who seeks to become hungry so that he may eat.

## DOUBLE TROUBLE

A rich farmer who possessed large tracts of land, vineyards, and orchards, employed many men. These farm hands cultivated the soil, planted the crops, and when the grain or fruit was ripe brought it in bushels to their employer's storehouse. Each one was trusted and their products were never counted. The work was distributed according to the laborer's physical strength. A husky young man was given two or more fields to take care of. An older man was assigned one pasture or orchard to tend. One day an elderly worker complained to his employer.

"Kind sir," he said, "you have given me only one pasture to take care of, and I feel capable of caring for two. Please tell your overseer to give me another field."

The farmer listened and replied, "From the way you entreat me for more work, I understand that you are a thief, and I will deprive you of the one field too. Which man pleads for more work than that which is placed upon him? Therefore your purpose is obvious. If you have another pasture you'll be able to steal more."

Moral: Too much ambition leads to suspicion.

## A LUMBERING MIND

A man worked for his employer for many years. When he grew older, the employer hired a younger person and paid him a higher salary. This hurt the older man's pride, but he said nothing. Finally he could not restrain himself.

"Pray tell me, sir," he said, "in what way does that young chap excel me? I have worked for you over twenty years; he is here only three months and already earns three times as much as I."

"I will show you the reason he deserves so much more," he was told, "but in the meantime go down into the street and find out what all those trucks are doing there."

Soon the old man came back. "The trucks are carrying lumber," he explained.

"What kind of lumber?" his employer questioned.

Again he went down and returned with the reply, "Part of the lumber will be used for furniture and part to build houses."

"To whom does the lumber belong?" was the next query. The man had to go down for the third time to get the name of the owner of the wood.

"Now be seated, my friend, for you must be exhausted," his employer said. "I am going to prove something to you."

He then called in his new employee and sent him to find out what kind of trucks were in the street. The young fellow was gone for a while and finally returned with a complete report. "The trucks are carrying lumber," he explained, "part of which will be used for furniture and part to build houses. Here is the name of the owner and this is what he paid for the lumber. These are his expenses and this is how much profit he intends to make."

"Now, my good friend," the employer addressed the older man, "you have had ample opportunity to note the difference between yourself and this chap. He found out more in one errand than you did in all three. Is he then not worth three times as much as you?"

Moral: It is more profitable to deal with a capable individual.

## DEATH SHOW

There is a legend of Socrates that when on his death-bed he called in his students and said, "I am about to die and I want to depart from this world with a clear conscience. Please be good enough and pay my cobbler the few pennies that I owe him."

His students were impressed with the philosopher's last words and his fine soul. When this reached the ears of Socrates' wife she laughed heartily and said, "I am not amazed at his magnanimity. He may have had an extra-ordinary mind but he was no better than the average individual. He too enjoyed telling little falsehoods and making fine gestures which would help put him in a class above the ordinary man. If he had told me to pay the cobbler, I would have said, 'My darling husband, why have you remembered the cobbler when you owe so much more to the proprietors of the barrooms you used to frequent?' "

Moral: Famous individuals and prominent personalities are like the stars in heaven. We see them from afar and admire their celestial beauty. However, if we would investigate them a little closer our admiration would greatly diminish.

## RAINY DAY

A woodcutter and a thief were neighbors. Both men had daughters. When the woodcutter's daughters grew older they found young men and were married, but the daughters of the thief were unfortunate in this respect.

203

"You are as poor as I," the thief said to the wood-cutter, "yet you are able to give your children a fine dowry and beautiful weddings. I can't understand where you get the money."

"It is all very simple," the woodcutter explained. "As soon as a child was born, I built a small money box and made a lock for it. Every day I would slip a coin through the slit at the top of the box. In that fashion I accumu-lated a tidy sum of money when the proper time arrived. That is what you too should have done, my friend."

When the thief heard his neighbor's story he burst into laughter. "How would I have been able to refrain from breaking open such a small lock, when strong iron locks have no significance for me?"

Moral: When a pious Jew takes an oath he will adhere to it, but a wicked man will not adhere even to the most important laws of the Torah.

## WORKING IT OUT

A *poritz* had rented his land to two farmers. It was a rainy season and the farmers suffered great losses. They owed the poritz money which they could not repay. When the creditor brought suit against them, one farmer sug-gested that he extend the time to keep the land for another year whereas the other offered to work to pay off the debt. Some time later the farmer who had asked for the exten-sion met the other who was working. "I envy you, my friend," the first one said. "With you each passing day makes your debt grow smaller, but with me each passing day makes my debt grow larger."

Moral: The longer we Jews are in bondage, the smaller grows our debt to the Lord.

## HEWERS OF WOOD

A wealthy Pole possessed a beautiful garden to which he devoted his entire energy and time. He imported tropical trees and transplanted them. People traveled from various parts of the country to admire his rare species. During the revolt against Russia, this man's name was found among those of the leaders of the rebellion, and he was compelled to flee from the country.

He called for his tailor and said, "Zelig, you have worked for me for many years and I have found you to be a trustworthy individual. I am forced to leave for an indefinite period and have chosen you to take care of all my possessions. I shall expect you to keep everything in perfect condition, especially my garden."

After the fugitive departed Zelig and his family occupied the estate. Zelig soon made changes in the household to suit his taste. He rearranged the furniture, stuffed the priceless antiques into closets, and chopped down the magnificent tropical trees, which he regarded as useless, and used the wood for fuel. He left only the apple, pear, and cherry trees, which served a purpose for him since they yielded fruit.

Several years later the government exonerated the owner and permitted him to return to Poland. When he entered his house and saw what his ignorant tailor had done he was heartbroken. He sobbed when he found his exquisite garden depleted and shorn of all its beauty.

Moral: We too are heartbroken when we notice how the most beautiful trees of our religious garden are hewn down by the simple people, leaving only the cheap and inexpensive ones. Such individuals do not realize that the laws which are foreign to their sense of understanding are the most magnificent trees in our religious garden.

## STRATAGEM OF CHARITY

There were two neighboring hotelkeepers in a small city. One was a kind and charitable individual, whereas the other was cruel and miserly. A poor traveler arrived in the city and unfortunately entered the hotel of the niggardly proprietor. When he asked for a meal and a night's lodging the other replied, "I will give this to you if you work for me."

The poor man was overjoyed and performed whatever difficult task he was given. At the end of the day, when he was exhausted with fatigue, the hotelkeeper approached him and said, "Now you may go into the next hotel, for I've already informed them to take care of you." The weary man, who was under the impression that the other hotel also belonged to the same proprietor, did as he was told. He was not questioned at this hotel and was given a delicious meal and a comfortable bed to sleep in.

The following day the man thanked the avaricious hotelkeeper for his kindness. The hotelkeeper then suggested that he work for him and in return receive room and board. This appealed to the needy man, and so he continued to work for the miser and be fed by the charit-able proprietor. Several days later he had a conversation with an inhabitant of the city who enlightened him about the situation.

"Do you know that you are working for a devil and receiving hospitality from an angel?" the other asked. "If you had originally gone to the benevolent hotelkeeper you wouldn't have had to toil in vain."

Moral: Man strives and slaves to accumulate money for his family, only to discover later how little it was appreciated and how he has wasted his life away.

## SAINT AND SINNER

When Moses freed the Israelites from bondage in Egypt, he became known throughout the world as a saintly figure. An Arabian king, who had heard of the miracles of Moses, asked one of his famous artists to go to the desert and depict Moses' face on canvas. The artist's mission was to be withheld from the knowledge of others. Several weeks later the artist brought back the painting. The king then invited all the wise men of his kingdom and said, "My friends, observe this painting, study the facial lines of this man, and tell me the type of person he is. Has he any virtues or is he filled with vices?"

The elder of the sages wrinkled his brow and said, "He has an ugly character."

Another said, "He is very proud."

A third one muttered, "He is ill-tempered."

The last of the group confidently replied, "He is the type of man who seeks honor."

207

Finally they exclaimed together, "Such an individual has no love for God or mankind!"

"Hold your vile tongues!" the king called out. "Do you know that this is a painting of the divine Moses?"

"Our decision is as clear as the day," the sages replied, "but there is a possibility that the artist did not paint the portrait correctly."

"That is not true," the artist retorted. "My painting is correct to the minutest detail, but you are not wise men."

The king was baffled, for he knew not whom to believe. He therefore decided to go to the desert himself. When he saw Moses he discovered that the portrait was an identic image, but that his scholars were not skillful enough to detect the fine characteristics. When the king related the incident to Moses the latter wisely smiled and said, "Noble king, your scholars are indeed talented. All the faults that they discovered in me are correct. However, I have overcome the evil characteristics that nature bestowed upon me. As a mighty oak tree grows from a tiny acorn, so have I grown and nourished my soul. I acquired and instilled good habits in myself until the urge to perform noble deeds became second nature with me. That is why I am accepted in heaven as well as on earth."

Moral: Man may overcome and discard his inherent evil characteristics by acquiring good habits.

## USE AND MISUSE

A skillful carpenter made an extraordinary box which was both fire and theft proof. No one but the owner could open it. He made three such boxes and gave them to three different individuals. One was a banker who used the box to keep his money and valuable documents in. The second individual was a poor laborer, and he stored his vegetables and potatoes in the box. The third was a simpleton who did not know what to do with his. He put it somewhere in the basement, where it accumulated dust and became rusty in the dampness. The carpenter was pleased when he learned how the banker had utilized the box he gave him, but sympathized with the laborer who knew no better than to keep vegetables in his. Regarding the simpleton, he was perturbed when he discovered that the man had derived no benefit at all from the box.

Moral: God gave man wisdom and understanding, which the zaddik uses in studying and learning the ways whereby man should live. The Lord rejoices when he observes how the zaddik utilizes his asset. Another, however, uses his gift of God to accumulate vast fortunes. Still the Lord sympathizes with this person, who wastes such an asset for material purposes. But to the evil man who lives like a fool, starving both his body and soul, God angrily calls out, "I have blessed you with the gift of wisdom, and you trample upon it."

## ALL IN THE FAMILY

A father who had a foolish son and a clever one died, leaving his fortune to both with the understanding that they divide it evenly. The shrewd son gradually cheated his brother out of his entire portion of the inheritance. Whenever the poor son, who was in dire need, approached his brother for money, the other never refused, for he knew that it rightfully belonged to him and was not charity. Before long the simple son realized that he had been swindled and he brought his brother to trial before a rabbi. The rabbi decided that he be reimbursed with his part of the inheritance.

"But, rabbi," protested the swindler, "I have given him all sorts of money all along. He will either have to return it or deduct it from his portion."

"It is for these favors that you deserve a harsher penalty," the rabbi replied. "First you did him an injustice when you cheated him out of his money. Then you committed a greater crime when you belittled him by making him believe that he was living on your charity."

Moral: There are those who exploit their fellowmen and then throw them something as charity.

## THE USES OF ADVERSITY

A father who dined with his son's future in-laws noticed that the table was set with costly silverware. He immediately became suspicious that his host had borrowed the utensils in order to impress him. About a year later, when the father again visited the same people, he found them sad and depressed. This time there were no choice meats, sparkling wine, or fancy silverware on the table. Everything was very simple. When the guest questioned his host as to what had happened the other flushed with embarrassment.

"My dear friend," he sighed, "times have changed for me. I've lost all my money in real estate and even had to pawn my silverware to buy food. It is painful to speak about, but since you asked me, I had to tell you the truth."

"You need not feel ashamed of your present condition," the guest replied. "On the contrary, you appear far worthier in my eyes because you were truthful with me. The first time when I visited you and saw the expensive china and silverware I was under the impression that you had borrowed it for the occasion. Now I see it was your own, and it is gratifying for me to know that my son will have in-laws who at least were once wealthy. It is far more respectable to be poor and honest than to be poor and act the part of a rich man."

Moral: Honesty is the best policy.

## TO FIT THE CRIME

Two thieves were caught stealing. When they were brought to trial the judge cross-examined each individually.

"My name is Motke," the first one said, 'and I come from Warsaw."

Upon hearing this several bystanders in the courtroom called out, "We know him very well. He has served many prison sentences. His father and his entire family are thieves."

"My father was a prominent rabbi and my grandfather

was a great scholar," the other culprit declared. "As a matter of fact my whole family is made up of rabbis and sages."

After the judge had listened to both men he passed a verdict whereby the one whose family consisted of thieves was to receive a small penalty, but the other was to be severely penalized.

"Where is justice?" the rabbi's son cried out. "I, who have such a fine heritage, receive a harsher punishment than my partner in crime who is known to come from a family of rascals."

"My decision should not amaze you," the judge replied. "He who was born and raised among thieves should not be blamed so much for his wrongdoing, since he had no one to teach him honesty. But you are a thief in spite of the fact that you were reared in an intelligent environment, and therefore you deserve a greater punishment."

Moral: The Lord chastises the Jewish race more severely than the others for their sins, because of their fine ancestral heritage.

## POOR COUNSEL

A poor man in dire need decided to go seek his fortune. Since he had never set foot outside his small town he asked a wealthy merchant, who always traveled for business purposes, how he should go about it.

"I intend to seek my livelihood in other cities," the poor man explained, "and am certain that you can offer me some profitable suggestions."

The merchant looked at the shabby individual and replied, "Your livelihood will consist of begging for alms. Now what do I know about such things? You should refer to such paupers as yourself. They know where to get a night's lodging and a free meal on the road. That is part of their job, but what advice can I offer you along those lines?"

Moral: Only a saddened heart can understand another.

## INEVITABLE CHANGE

The black hair spied a grey hair in their midst. "You are a traitor," they cried angrily. "We were all born black and intend to keep our hereditary character. It is obvious that something very unpleasant has occurred in your life, that has made you change so suddenly. You put our whole head of hair to shame."

"How ignorant you are, my friends," the grey hair smiled. "That which has happened to me now will eventually befall all of you. It occurred a little earlier with me, but you need not fret, for, good or bad, you will all turn grey."

Moral: The world often condemns individuals who preach premature ideals.

## THREE GIFTS TO HEAVEN

Once upon a time there died a small town Jew. His soul flew to heaven and appeared before Supreme Justice to receive its verdict. There hung a heavy pair of scales upon which good and evil deeds were weighed. The dead

213

man's good spirit appeared with a snow white sack and emptied the virtuous deeds on the right hand side of the scale. Then the evil spirit entered with a grimy bag, placing the wicked deeds on the other side. Nearby the angels stood, breathlessly awaiting the decision. Slowly the scales oscillated and suddenly halted. The good deeds exactly balanced the evil, so that there was not a hair-breadth of difference between the two. Supreme Justice passed the verdict. Since one did not outweigh the other, the soul was neither wicked enough to go to Gehenna nor virtuous enough to be admitted into Paradise. Therefore it was doomed to exile without a place of refuge, until the Lord have mercy upon it and bring it to a haven.

The soul began to sob. "It is far better to endure agonizing torture than nothing at all," it moaned. The sexton of the Beth Din intervened and said, "Go down upon the earth and dwell with the humble people. From there you will bring three precious gifts of unsurpassable value and present them to the zaddikim of Paradise. As a result they will admit you into their domain."

Many years passed and the soul flew, winter and summer, through storms and winds seeking a prize of unusual value, but to no avail. "I am lost forever," the poor soul murmured, "for the world is so poor and the people are so ordinary."

But suddenly it was attracted by a light flickering in a window. There a masked thief was pointing a gleaming blade near the heart of a wealthy man, crying, "One move means instant death."

The Jew stood motionless and silently watched the bandit empty drawer after drawer of sacks of gold, silver, and precious gems. But when the thief seized a little bag, the last item in the commode, the Jew forgot his unfortunate situation, stretched out his hands, and cried out, "Do not touch!"

A stream of blood gushed forth, splashing the knife and the bag. The bandit pounced upon the sack for which the Jew had sacrificed his life, expecting to find something very precious. But there were no gold or gems, nothing of material significance, only a handful of Eretz Yisrael earth, which the Jew had intended to take with him after death and which he wanted to save from foreign hands and eyes. The soul caught a particle of the bloody dust and brought it up to heaven.

The first gift was accepted. "Two more," the angel called out. "The good Lord will help me," the soul responded cheerfully.

Many years passed and the soul still wandered aimlessly, realizing that the fountain of good deeds on earth was running dry. The people became smaller, their sins uglier and larger and their virtues microscopic. All at once the soul heard a blaring of trumpets and shouting of voices. It found itself in a German city before a courthouse. Wild throngs of people surrounded the square, in the midst of which sat the magistrate and his jury, clad in elaborate clothing with shining brass buttons. Nearby stood a pale Jewess, bound hand and foot with iron chains. Several slaves were holding back a wild young stallion ready to break loose. The magistrate, facing the mob, read the decree.

"This Jewess," he roared, "has committed a grave sin, which even our merciful Lord could not forgive. She stole out of the ghetto and walked around on our pure streets during our last celebration. She soiled our holy procession with her shameless eyes, and her cursed ears absorbed the jubilations and songs. Who knows if this beautiful rabbi's daughter is not the devil himself? For she is beautiful, as only a devil can be. Look at her beaming, dark eyes, shaded with fringes of silken lashes. See her alabaster face, which has become paler and thinner with her imprison' ment. Tie the devilish braids of this Jewess to the tail of this wild horse and let him drag her over the streets whereon her sinful feet have trod. Let her blood spurt forth and cleanse the cobblestones which she soiled."

A wild cry pierced the air. When the tumult subsided, the unfortunate girl was asked her last request.

"I want a few pins," she softly murmured.

"She has gone completely mad," the magistrate mut' tered, fulfilling her wish.

In the wild hubbub of the disorganized mob, no one noticed the girl bend down quietly and pin the hem of her dress to her naked legs, plunging the pins into her flesh, so that her body would not be bared to the eyes of the spectators. The wandering soul noticed this, and as the horse dashed wildly through the streets, dragging the limp, lifeless body, it snatched up a bloody pin and delivered it to the zaddikim of Paradise.

216

"Just one more gift," the angel said.

The soul continued to travel round the earth. It was startled by a loud beating of drums. In a prison yard stood two rows of vicious looking soldiers with whips in their hands. A wan, shriveled little Jew in a tattered shirt with a skull cap on his shaven head was being led down the aisle. What crime could this emaciated being have committed?

"Why did they need so many of us?" the soldiers whispered among themselves. "He'll collapse after the first couple of lashings."

The little Jew was pushed ahead and walked unfalteringly amidst the torrent of floggings. The soldiers lashed his emaciated body more and more furiously, until the blood spurt forth from his wounds. One soldier waved his whip high above the Jew's head and tauntingly knocked off his skull cap. After a few steps the miserable, victim realized what had happened. Since he would not walk with a bare head, the blood-stained Jew quietly picked up his skull cap, placed it on his head, and staggered on until he collapsed into unconsciousness.

The soul immediately seized the holy skull cap and flew with it to heaven. The third gift was accepted. The angels then bowed down before the soul, and flung open the doors of Paradise to admit the newcomer.

"These are indeed extraordinary precious gifts," they murmured. "They have no material value, but they are magnificent and beautiful."

217

## THE RING OF FORTUNE

A pious Jew who lived in Warsaw had a large family to support and his earnings were very meagre. One week his income was less than ever before, and he had no money with which to celebrate the Sabbath. The poor Jew was heartbroken.

"Be not sad, my husband," his wife consoled him. "Here, take my coat and pawn it. We will then have sufficient money for food."

The man followed his wife's suggestion, and soon was happily returning home with the money in his outstretched palm. In the meantime a band of Cossacks passed by. Seeing the Jew running, they lashed their whips over his hand, spilling the money into a pool of filthy water.

The Jew cursed the Cossacks under his breath. Bending down on his knees, he began to search desperately for his money. After an hour he managed to find several coins. Perspiring and overheated, he continued to grope in the muddy water until his fingers touched something that resembled a ring. Quickly he pulled it out and a sparkling object dazzled his eyes. It was a ring studded with four large diamonds.

One of the Cossacks had stolen it in Moscow. He had lashed the Jew with such force that the ring, which was too large for him, had slipped from his finger. The Jew, realizing this was a valuable article, brought it to a jeweler, who gave him $5000 for it. He now understood that man should not question why certain things occur, and never again did he curse the Cossacks.

Moral: Misfortune sometimes is good fortune.

## CAST ON THE WATERS

King Louis XII learned that one of his generals was coarsely mistreating the peasants. This grieved the king deeply, and he ordered the servants of the general to exclude bread from all his meals. The general was to have all sorts of delicacies, but no bread.

A year passed, and the general's health began to fail. He became weak and feeble and had no strength to carry himself. He then asked the king to explain why he was denied bread with his meals. His system was accustomed to that staple food, and the lack of it was making him ill.

King Louis XII replied, "Now the general will realize the value of bread and the importance of those who supply us with it by the sweat of their brows."

The general grasped the king's point, and from then on treated the peasants with compassion and consideration.

Moral: Very frequently a scholar will boastfully demonstrate his intelligence before the ordinary man and thus belittle the other. Our heavenly King cannot exist merely among scholars, for they in turn depend upon the layman for their bread.


## ROSEBUDS

Youth danced and frolicked gleefully. "The world belongs to me," she exclaimed. "My future is beautiful and my path is strewn with roses. I am strong and powerful and my energy is inexhaustible. Why should I think or worry my pretty head, when I have today and will surely have tomorrow?"

"My child, be thrifty," Age wisely warned her. "Spend not all your energy at once. Divide your strength equally over the span of seventy years, and you will never feel feeble or unfortunate. However, if you do not preserve your vigor and expend it unnecessarily, your little good fortune will melt away and while still young you will be aged."

Moral: Age is practical and preaches wisely; except that she comes after youth.

## WATERY GLORY

The teakettle puffed its chest and boasted, "All pots have such pungent odors. They reek of that which they cook. Only we teakettles have the good fortune to be odorless."

An old pot standing nearby spurt a sizzling drop on the kettle's head and scornfully retorted, "See how he tilts his crooked nose. What else can you do, my great hero, but spout with steam? That is indeed funny! What do you amount to? Yes, you have no odor because your contents are tasteless and odorless; you boil nothing but plain water."

Moral: To be faultless signifies nothing. It is how important you are and what you accomplish.

## REFLECTION

The book asked the mirror, "Pray, tell me of what your ability consists, that you have acquired so many ardent admirers. There isn't an individual who does not look into you at least two or three times a day. If I had as many devotees as you, I would have freed the world of its ignorance a long time ago."

"What need has man for your literature?" the mirror sneered. "It is my lining that has made me popular with the people. They've discovered that there is silver behind my glass, whereas only plain paper lies underneath your words."

Moral: It is not wisdom but silver that makes friends.

## TENSES

"O King, to what degree are you more fortunate than I," a beggar brazenly asked, as he entered a palace to beg for alms. "Yesterday is lost for both of us. The morrow is concealed in a dark cloak and only God knows on whose head your crown will gleam then. Therefore only today remains. Today the masses bow down before you, but you are only king for a day."

"Tomorrow does not distress me," the king rejoined. "Let it be known to you, my friend, that yesterday helped me to be king today. Today will make me king for tomorrow. You must understand that the past and the future are securely bound together with the present."

Moral: When you can expound the present clearly, it is then obvious what you were and what you will be.

## LOOKING ON

A mirror hanging on a wall in the corner of the room plaintively cried, "I have the power of revealing man's

221

countenance, whether he be ugly or handsome, old or young. But, why cannot I disclose his degree of intelligence? Why does not every mirror also possess the faculty to portray the difference between the sage and the fool?"

Wisdom, hearing the complaint, replied, "You merely see things superficially, and for that reason you can only show the external part of everything. You cannot understand anything profound, because you have no depth yourself. Man's intelligence is too deeply concealed, my friend, to be revealed by you, who are so very flat."

Moral: Many desire to be connoisseurs of things for which they possess no talent.

## FRUIT OF THE VINE

The various fruits had gathered to hold a discussion among themselves. They wanted to discover the reason why no other fruit but the grape contains the juice from which the finest wines are made.

"Her drink is famous throughout the world and exquisitely pleasing to man's taste," they declared. "Why is she more worthy than we to be blessed with this gift of God?"

A cluster of grapes hanging nearby heard the complaint, and replied, "All of you grow individually and produce your fruits independently, but we grapes grow together in bunches and are faithful to each other. For that reason our substance is rich and capable of imparting such distinctive taste and fragrance to our wines."

Moral: In union there is strength.

222

## COMBINED OPERATIONS

Justice said to Power, "It is a well known fact that as partners we go well together. Individually you are of low rank. Quite frequently you commit heinous crimes. Justice without power is still divine and impartial in dealing with man, but power without justice is brutal."

"It does not interest me whether or not you laud me," Power retorted. "Your condemnation does not wound my vanity, for I know that whatever you possess you gain through me. It is rarely that you make a step without me, for justice without power is always humiliated and treated with insolence. If you want to accomplish things you must have me for protection."

Moral: Justice would have to endure torture and bloodshed if Power were not her partner.


## NO CHANGE

Hunger complained to Wisdom that people had no faith in him. When a starved man comes to one who is fed, the latter disregards him and does not want to believe that the other is suffering. "Those who have endured hunger forget that it exists as soon as they have partaken of food."

"Still, you are more lucky than I," Wisdom replied. "You have the occasion to take revenge of your enemies. It frequently happens that those who have been well fed before have to endure hunger, and then you can torture them. As you are aware, I too am not believed, but I can never dream of chastising my enemies. I certainly can never hope to pain the fool."

Moral: The well-fed may become kind and considerate after suffering hunger, but the fool will never grow wise.

## LOVE OF LUCRE

· A bug found itself upon a coin and crawled round and round, murmuring, "This seems to be a tremendous fortune; indeed a huge capital." It was ready to believe the small coin fifty miles long, for there was money wherever she turned. Greedily she hugged the coin, building fantastic ideas to sate her avarice.

Moral: Some individuals, like the bug, feel that a coin is a fortune and refuse to part with it.

GOLDEN CALF

MISERS

# INTERCHANGE

A preacher came for a donation to a wealthy learned man, known to be a miser. During the course of conversation the preacher quoted passages from the Torah and also interpreted them for the rich man. The other listened carefully and then demonstrated his knowledge of the Torah by giving his own interpretations. This kept up for a long time. One attempted to outwit the other. The preacher, realizing that the skinflint was trying to escape giving, told him the following story:

"In a small town there lived a poor man whose family was in dire need. One day his wife said to him, 'My husband, how much longer must we suffer such hunger and poverty? Go forth into the world, as all the others are doing, and try your hand at selling. Maybe the good Lord will help us.' The husband listened to his wife and did as she suggested. He gathered up a few articles of the household, sold them, and with the money bought a sack of onions. Thus he set out on a boat and sailed away.

"During the trip a terrific storm arose, and the boat with all its passengers was marooned on a small island. When the natives of this island beheld the dealer and his sack of onions, they were dumbfounded. Never before had they seen such a vegetable. The man was brought before the king himself to exhibit his merchandise. The king ordered that the dealer be reimbursed in a grand manner. His sack

227

was to be filled with gold coins in place of the onions. Thus the fortunate individual started back home to his wife and family.

"He was now a very rich man. One day he related the story of how he had acquired his wealth to one of his most intimate friends, and advised him to go to the same island. Instead of onions he suggested that he take along a sack of garlic. Since there was no such vegetable there, he would be repaid a thousandfold for his merchandise. The other followed the instructions of his friend. When he arrived at the island he was immediately brought before the king. The king on seeing the rare vegetable the man brought was overwhelmed, and ordered that his servants reward him accordingly. So, for the garlic the man was paid with something that was even more valuable than gold coins, namely onions.

"The same is true with me," the preacher concluded. "When I quote a passage of the Torah, you quote another one. I haven't come to you to be taught the Torah; I possess enough of that without you. I came for money."

## JOINT DISTRIBUTION

A young man, who had come to this country twenty years before, became very wealthy, and decided to take a pleasure trip abroad, to see his home town. When he arrived there, he observed the great poverty of his friends and relatives, and gave them as much money as he could. The people, noticing the large sums this man was distributing, began to gather from everywhere for aid. Not knowing which cause was more worthy than another, he decided to entrust $2000 with the rabbi, to distribute as he saw fit. When the people discovered that the rabbi had all this money, they began to go to him.

One day two well-known misers of the town, who never gave anything towards charity, also came to the rabbi.

"What good news do you bring, my friends?" the rabbi asked in surprise. "You must have something of great importance to tell me, for you've never come to my house before."

"Rabbi, we've come to you, because we have heard that the wealthy American left you money to be used in behalf of the needs of the town. Since the fence of the cemetery is broken, and pigs have begun to crawl on the holy spot, and destroy the tombstones, we would suggest that you give a few hundred dollars for that purpose."

"Yes," agreed the rabbi, with a twinkle in his eye. "That is very important, but I wonder how the pigs learned that I have money, and began to crawl to the 'holy spot.'"

## PENURIOUS LOGIC

A week before Passover a group of men came to a wealthy landlord and asked him to contribute some money, to help the poor buy food for the holiday. The landlord politely refused, saying that he could not give, because he had a poor brother. The men realized that he was right, because a brother is entitled to preference. Passover eve, when the poor came to receive the money collected for them, the landlord's brother also appeared among them.

"We have nothing for you," the committee in charge said; "your brother takes care of you."

"My brother didn't give me a penny," the poor man sobbed.

The committee went to investigate the case. They told the rich man of his brother's complaint.

"He is right," the man agreed. "I didn't give him anything."

"Then why did you say that you had a poor brother?" they demanded.

"What I meant," the rich man explained, "was that if I have a poor brother and give him nothing, I certainly won't give anything to strangers."

## SPONGER

A visitor had dinner at a miser's house. The host served liquor, and advised his guest not to drink it, but to "dunk" his bread into it. The visitor understood his host's purpose, took a large slice of bread and dipped it into the liquor. The bread sopped up all the liquor, so that not one drop remained.

When the miser saw this he said, "My dear guest, if all the Jews had been like you, they would not have needed to have the Red Sea divide for them. They would have dried it up just by dunking."

"Yes," the visitor replied, "but it was Passover, and they didn't have soft bread, only hard matzoth!"

## HIS OWN LAST

A wealthy, miserly Brisk Jew, who never gave charity, remained at the synagogue Yom Kippur eve and prayed all through the night. Reb Yoshe Ber, the Brisk Rabbi, approached him and said, "In the army there are various kinds of soldiers. Some are in the infantry, others in the cavalry. Each one does his duty under supervision of his commanding officer. If an infantryman should attempt the work of the man in the cavalry, he would be penalized. The analogy I give you," Reb Yoshe Ber continued, "is identical in the case of the Jew. We Jews are God's soldiers. A scholar must study, in order to spread his knowledge and wisdom. The rich man must give charity, and help others. If he who belongs to the division of charity givers takes to study and prayer, and does not fufill the duties of his own position, then he too will be punished."

## SWEATING IT OUT

A wealthy miser became very ill. The doctor who diagnosed the case said that the man's life could be saved only if he were to perspire. All methods were tried, but to no avail. The sick man could not perspire. Meanwhile some friends came and suggested that the man write a will and leave a certain amount for charity.

"With the help of God you will get well and live to a ripe old age," they consoled him. "One should give charity while he is alive. Give and you will get well."

The miser finally consented to donate an old dilapidated house, situated in a forlorn section of the city. The men breathlessly wrote down every word, when suddenly the invalid cried out, "Stop where you are! Write no further! I am perspiring!"

## NO CHANGE OF SPOTS

Several men paid an unexpected visit to a penurious rich friend, who had no alternative but to receive them. The rich man told his wife, who was not as miserly as he, to prepare some food. She set a beautiful table, with a delicious meal, which the guests enjoyed immensely. They began to think that a great change had come over their friend. Ordinarily he would allow no one to approach his threshold.

"We arrived unexpectedly," one of the guests remarked, "and still you were able to entertain us in such a grand fashion. Imagine what you would have done if you had expected us."

"If I had expected you," the wealthy man coldly replied, "I certainly would have bolted my door."

## ULTIMATE PROOF

A wealthy miser died. While the corpse lay at home the son did not shed a tear. As soon as the men began to flourish their charity boxes the son began to cry bitterly. The bystanders asked him why he was so heartbroken now and not before. He replied, "When the men call for charity, and my father does not run away, then I know for sure that he is dead."

## ETIQUETTE

A shadchan visited a wealthy miser to speak of a match. When tea was served, the shadchan used several teaspoonfuls of sugar, which greatly annoyed the miser.

"Do you drink tea at your house in the same manner?"

"Well, you know how it is," the shadchan replied. "At home one can conduct himself in any manner he desires, but among strangers one can't be a pig."

## THE RIGHT MEN

The child of a wealthy miser became ill, and the doctors gave up all hope for her. Since nothing else could be done, the father remembered that there is an old Jewish custom to pray in such an event. It was midnight and very cold when he woke the sexton of the synagogue and asked him to secure a minyan to pray. The sexton was very angry for being disturbed at such a time of the night, but had to do as he was told. So the two set out to look for a minyan. In the distance they noticed some people and started to walk toward them. As the sexton was about to speak to them, the rich man pulled his sleeve and whispered:

"They are the thieves who robbed me several weeks ago."

"Really?" the sexton replied. "Then they are excellent for the purpose of our minyan. They can accomplish things even when all doors are closed."

233

## IT ORPHAN HAPPENS

Two Jews came to a wealthy miser and asked him to give some money for the poor. After much pleading and coaxing he gave, but very little.

"Don't be angry with us," one Jew remarked, "but your son donated very liberally, and you gave so very little, toward such a worthy cause. We cannot understand."

"You say that my son gave more than I did?" the wealthy miser cried out. "How can you compare me with him? He has a wealthy father, but I am an orphan."

## GREAT GIVER

A beggar came to a wealthy miserly Jew for some money. The wealthy Jew, on seeing the beggar, clasped his hand warmly and welcomed him to the city.

"How did you recognize the fact that I am a stranger here?" the beggar asked in surprise.

"Oh, I am very sure of that," the miser replied, "because all local people know that as for coming to me for charity, there is nothing in it for them."

## EQUINE BRAINS

A wealthy land owner had an ignorant son. One day he came to town to get a teacher for him.

"How much do you want for teaching my son?" the father asked one instructor.

"400 zlotys," was the reply.

"So much!" shrieked the man. "For such a sum I can buy the best horse."

"Well, do that," replied the teacher calmly. "You will then have two."

## FOOD FOR THOUGHT

Among the hassidim of the Kozshnizer Maggid there was a very wealthy Jew, a known miser. One day when he visited the preacher, the other asked him:

"What do you eat every day?"

"My meals are frugal and meager. I eat nothing but bread and salt."

The preacher became enraged, and ordered him to eat meat every day, with a glass of wine after every meal. When the rich man left, the hassidim eagerly inquired:

"Rabbi, please explain what your purpose was in instructing that man to eat such good food?"

"What is there to understand?" the rabbi replied with a shrug. "If that rich miser will eat meat and drink wine every day, he will realize that the poor are at least entitled to bread and salt. But, when he eats bread and salt, then he thinks that the poor should eat stones."

## GIVING TILL IT HURTS

A wealthy miser became ill. He was burning up under a high temperature, and the doctors said there was no hope for him. His wife and children gave fifty dollars for charity in his behalf, and asked that prayers be said for him. When the miser became well and found out that fifty dollars had been distributed in charity he became wild with rage and screamed:

235

"How did you dare do such a thing without my knowledge?"

"What do you mean?" his wife asked.

"You yourself told us to give that amount for charity."

"I was delirious when I spoke," he angrily snapped, "and you believed me."

## GOLD IN THEM HILLS

Reb Joseph Saul, a well known comedian, once said to an old miser, who had just become rich:

"It is said that in America gold lies in the streets. In our town I see greater miracles! Here we find gold lying in the worst filth and mud."

## HIDDEN SAINT

When the gaon Rabbi Yom Tov Lippman was rabbi of Krakow there lived a very wealthy man in that city, known as "Stingy Simon." He was despised by all the inhabitants because he never donated any money for charitable purposes. However, his servant Shloime was well liked, since he gave large sums for the poor. No one ever questioned how he obtained his money, nor what business he conducted. He had been a servant at the home of "Stingy Simon" for a number of years, and when he retired took greater interest in the poor than ever before. Every day he invited groups of men to his home, where they received a wholesome meal and some pocket money. People admired Shloime's devotion and loyalty to the poor. One

236

day it became known that "Stingy Simon" had died. No one attended his funeral and very few people of the city mourned him.

In punishment for his niggardly behavior he was buried in a section of the cemetery reserved for the wicked. But soon after his death Shloime ceased to give charity. The poor moaned that they would starve now because Shloime had been their sole support.

They appealed to Rabbi Yom Tov Lippman for help. He immediately summoned Shloime the servant.

"Why have you stopped giving charity?" the gaon asked.

"Rabbi, I want you to know that the money which I gave was not my own," Shloime explained. "It was 'Stingy Simon' who gave me the money under oath that I would not reveal his name. I was to distribute the charity, inasmuch as he did not seek honor. He dealt out his entire fortune through me, and now he is dead I have nothing to give."

The sage was astonished and impressed with the secret Shloime had divulged. "Now I understand what the Talmud meant when it said, 'And a servant to run before him.' Here is the shining example of Reb Simon who sent his servant to aid and guide the poor."

The distinguished rabbi then requested that he too be buried near "Stingy Simon."

# ATHEISTS

## CYCLORAMA

Non-believers say that the earth revolves around the sun, and the hassidim maintain that the sun revolves around the earth. When Reb Shmuel, the hassid, spent a few hours with the rabbi, and gulped down several glassfuls of liquor, he grunted, "Rabbi, I am prone to believe that the atheists are right. I can actually feel and see the earth turning round and round."

## REFLECTION

An atheist came to a rabbi and ironically asked him to interpret a dream.

"What did you dream?" the rabbi asked.

"I saw an angry dog gnashing his teeth at me and straining to free himself from his leash. It was horrible!"

"Don't be frightened, my child," the rabbi replied, "you have nothing to fear. You only saw your own shadow."

## NO JEST

An atheist came to spend Passover eve with a rabbi, so that he might have the opportunity to scoff at him.

"Rabbi, what part of the Haggadah are you up to?" he jokingly asked as he entered.

"I am up to," the rabbi retorted, " 'The dog came' " (in the song Had Gadya—An Only Kid).

## THE ATHEIST

"Young man, you say that you are an atheist, and you don't believe in anything?"

"I believe only in that which I can understand," the young fellow proudly replied.

"Now I see," the other smiled, "why you believe in nothing."

## HORRIBLE THOUGHT

An atheist was asked why he feared thunder and lightning.

"I am afraid," he said, "that God may give us another Torah."

## FEARFUL SIN

A hassid met Adam HaKohen Levinson walking with a cane on Saturday.

"Aren't you afraid of God? Why do you carry a stick on the Sabbath?" asked the hassid.

"I carry a stick because I *am* afraid of God," replied the freethinker.

## FINE DISTINCTION

A father, who was a freethinker, found his daughter lighting the stove one Saturday morning, and became very angry with her.

"Why do you smoke a cigar?" she asked.

"Listen to the comparison!" the father replied. "That I can't do through someone else, but lighting the stove—could surely have been done through a goy!"

ANECDOTES

# A CONTRACT FOR A CANTOR

The city Slonim was famous for her fine cantors, but they never stayed long. As soon as a cantor became prominent, representatives of a larger city would offer him a larger salary, and he would leave. When Yoshe Slonimer came the people wanted to make certain that he would not be taken away. They called a meeting, and decided that the cantor sign a contract that would bind him to Slonim for a number of years. The chairman went to Reb Eisel Charif for advice on how the contract should be worded, in order to assure themselves of the services of the cantor.

"I'll tell you a story," Reb Eisel said:

"A new cemetery was established in a city. As is the custom no one wanted to be the first to buy a plot there. The Chevra Kaddisha informed the people that the first corpse would be buried without charge, and his family would receive 100 gulden. Some time passed and the cemetery still remained vacant. Everyone who died had willed that he be buried in the old cemetery and not in the new one.

"In that city there lived a poor Jew, a happy-go-lucky fellow. When Passover approached and he had not a penny for the holidays, his wife began to nag him. 'What

245

are we going to do? Passover is almost here, and there isn't a sign of the holiday in our house.'

" 'I have an idea!' the husband exclaimed. 'I will pretend that I am dead, and you go to the Chevra Kaddisha and say that before I died I agreed to lie in the new cemetery. You will then get 100 gulden, and we will have a happy Passover.'

"His wife did as she was told. The husband dressed in shrouds and the wife ran moaning to the sexton of the Chevra Kaddisha and told him what had happened. The woman's story made the sexton very happy, and he immediately gave her 100 gulden, and sent his men to take care of the corpse.

"The funeral was small, with only a few inhabitants of the city present, who dropped out gradually, one by one, until only the sexton and the coachman remained. When they passed a bar on the road they left the hearse outside, and went in to have a drink. As soon as they were gone, the 'corpse' jumped out of the coffin and ran home.

"After a while the men returned, a little drunk. Unaware of what had happened, they continued to the cemetery. When they began to lower the coffin they almost fainted, for the box was empty, and the corpse was gone. That same day the presumed corpse bought matzoth, fish, and wine for the holiday. The whole city was aflutter with the trick the Jew had played on the Chevra Kaddisha.

"Some time later a poor man died. Again the funeral was small, and again the sexton and the coachman were

the only ones left with the hearse. On the way they passed
the same bar, and this time too were tempted to go in for
a drink. 'Now we will make certain that the corpse does
not escape,' they said. They took a heavy rope, and began to tie up the coffin. Nearby stood a wise man who
laughed at the peculiar sight. 'You men are such fools,'
he chuckled. 'You should have tied up the other one, who
was alive, so that he would not be able to run away. This
one is a genuine corpse. You don't have to tie him up;
he will never run away from you!'

"Now do you understand?" Reb Eisel continued, wink-
ing slyly. "The other cantors you should have tied up
with a contract, which would have prevented their running away from Slonim. This cantor you don't have to
tie up. He will never run away. No one will snatch
him."

## THE IDOL-BREAKER

During the years when idolatry was practiced, two
Jewish children studied in a religious school in the City of
Eshad, under a very pious teacher. One of the children
always argued with his friend that Jewish learning held
no future, therefore he was going to enter a hellenic
school, and become a follower of the Greeks.

After a few years he became a priest, and rose higher
and higher until finally he was made a hierarch over an
entire section, in which the city of Eshad was also included.

Once, while on an inspection tour, he rode into Eshad.
There recollections of his youth and of his school days

came back to him. He thought of his friend Pinchas, and was most anxious to learn what had happened to him.

Finally, he was brought to Pinchas's home, where he found him poverty-stricken, earning his livelihood by teaching.

The hierarch asked permission to spend the night with his friend, so that they might discuss the memories of their childhood together, and other incidents of their past lives. The following morning the hierarch left very early. On making his bed, Pinchas's wife found a small image made of pure gold lying among the sheets. Both she and her husband immediately assumed that this was an idol which their friend worshiped, and had probably forgot. On looking further, however, they found a note which said they should consider the little god as a gift from him.

Pinchas broke off one arm, brought it to a jeweler, and received a large sum of money. With this he purchased clothes, and food for the entire family. Then he chopped off another hand, and sold that. With the money he received he was able to start living in a wealthy fashion. For the diamonds that made up the eyes of the image, he bought property, gave charity, and became very well known. Little by little he broke, and sold the entire idol.

A few years later, he was again visited by his friend, who this time found him quite prosperous.

"Now, Pinchas, you must confess that I am right," the hierarch said. "You say you have a God that is great for the entire world. What has He ever given you? Poverty, hunger, and a miserable existence. Then I gave you my god, in a very small form, and see what he has done for you. Now, I ask you, whom would you rather serve and pray to?"

"You are not right, my friend," replied Pinchas. "You call that a god! The only way he can benefit you is when you break his hands and feet, pierce out his eyes, and pull out his teeth, until he is completely destroyed, and you no longer have what to worship. But our almighty God, when he gives, gives bountifully, and of his own good will. He gives both life and sustenance. He is eternal, and will live forever. No, my friend, I will never change my God for anything else in this whole wide world. Neither I, nor any of my people."

## EXPERT PURLOINMENT

One day a judge in Mexico City arrived late at court and found a crowd of people already waiting. Nonchalantly he reached for his watch to see the correct time, but to his dismay discovered that he had forgotten it at home.

"In my great hurry I left my watch under my pillow," he said.

Among the audience there was a well-known thief who had come to court to ply his profession. As soon as he heard the judge's words he ran out, bought a large turkey, and with it went to the judge's home.

"I met your husband on the way to the courthouse," the thief explained to the judge's wife. "He told me to bring the turkey to you and ask you to give me the watch that he left under his pillow."

The woman did not doubt the varacity of the story and gave him the watch. When the judge came home for dinner, his wife thanked him for the turkey.

"What turkey?" the judge asked in surprise.

His wife then related the entire incident.

"A watch that I have treasured for so many years has fallen into the hands of a scoundrel," the judge sighed.

"Do not reproach yourself," his wife consoled him. "You will buy a much better one. Meanwhile I will prepare the turkey and you will invite the attendants of your courthouse for dinner tomorrow evening."

The thief, who was in the courthouse at the time, heard the judge extend the dinner invitation to his friends and immediately ran to the judge's house. He rang the doorbell and in a disguised voice told the wife that her husband had sent him to get the roast turkey with all the plates and silverware, because the judge had decided to serve the meal in the courtroom. The woman believed the thief and gave him what he asked for. When the judge and his company of friends arrived at the house for supper they were astonished to learn of the new trick the villain had again played.

"My dear wife, it is your naiveté that is the cause of all this trouble," the judge scolded.

Several days later the judge received a letter of consolation from the thief with the following notation:

"An exchange is not a theft, and the turkey is mine because I bought it. Instead of using it for the enjoyment of you and your friends, it is better that I eat it to still my hunger."

## PROUD MORTAL

A poor farmer suddenly acquired great wealth. He built a beautiful house, bought luxurious furniture, and gave a large party. All his friends ate, drank, and were merry, but the teacher, who had taught the farmer's children, was the merriest of all. The farmer could not understand what made him so joyful.

"Why do you dance so much and why are you so thrilled with the house and furnishings?" he asked. "Soon your time will be up and you will have to leave."

"What of it?" the teacher replied. "Does it make you any less happier now because your time, too, will eventually be up?"

## NO BELIEF IN SIGNS

A fish dealer hung out a sign, "We Sell Fresh Fish Here." A customer came in. "Why do you need the word Fresh? Who says that you don't sell fresh fish?"

"You are right," the dealer agreed. "I'll cross it out."

Another woman asked, "Why do you write the word Here? You certainly don't sell fish anywhere else."

"Yes, I'll erase it," the dealer said.

A Jew came in. "Of what importance is the word Sell?" he demanded. "Everyone knows that you don't hand it out for nothing."

"All right, I'll rub that off immediately," the owner replied. And only one word remained—Fish.

Finally another customer walked in, and asked, "Mister, why do you need a sign which reads Fish, when your fish smells a mile away?"

## BREAD AND PHILOSOPHY

Two yeshivah boys set out to hike from one town to another, and on the way became very hungry. They spied a loaf of bread on the road. The poor boys were over-joyed at the seeming miracle.

One of them was ready to tear the bread in half, and begin eating, but the other stopped him and spoke very seriously.

"How can a person be so anxious for food? Before we fill our stomachs, let us fill our eyes with the beauty of the loaf of bread. It is good to look at. Do you realize that everything on this earth should be counted as two, instead of one, because there is the object itself, and the thought that it exists? In that respect we now are in the possession of two breads. We have the bread, and the thought of it, in our minds."

"Well, now that you've given me such a grand philos-ophical explanation, I think we can start eating," the first boy replied.

"You may eat," the other suggested; "as for me, I am going to meander around a bit before I start."

As he walked away, his friend devoured the bread, leaving not a crumb.

"Where is my portion?" he demanded on his return.

"Why, didn't you say that we had two breads?" the other replied. "I just ate up one, and left the second bread for you."

## COMEDY OF DUPES

Two wealthy men stood near the entrance of the market place of a small town, where a sale of horses was going on. They noticed the way two gypsies were putting over a deal between themselves. One was tall and massive looking, while the other was short and puny. The short fellow sold the other one a horse for twenty zlotys. The men looked on and decided to discover who was the greater swindler of the two. They called the gypsies over and offered them food and drink.

"We know that you are both swindlers," one said, "but we want to find out which one of you is the greater cheat. The one who will prove himself such will receive a prize of fifty zlotys."

"Good," both gypsies agreed. "Try us out."

So the two wealthy men approached the short fellow. "We saw you sell the horse to your friend and receive a banknote of twenty zlotys for it. That is a very small sum. Didn't he fool you?"

"No, my good man," the short fellow replied. "That was not little money; on the contrary, it was a very high price. I fooled him because the horse limps."

"Then how did you permit yourself to be cheated like that?" they asked the taller one. "For a crippled horse, that will not be able to perform any work, you paid so much money?"

"It is true, the horse does limp," was the answer, "but the little fool didn't notice that there was a nail stuck in

253

the heel of the horse's foot, which caused him to limp. I just have to remove it and the horse will be in perfect condition."

The wealthy men then turned to the other, saying, "Didn't you notice the nail in the heel? Your certainly were taken in, little man."

"It is true that he is much taller than I," the short gypsy remarked, "but his stupidity is there to mislead him, because the horse is really crippled."

"Well, what have you to say now? Your friend certainly did fool you," the two men laughed.

"It is useless for the pigmy to attempt to outdo me in lying," the tall gypsy replied. "I foresaw the lameness of the horse, because the banknote that I gave him is counterfeit."

## GLUTTON FOR PUNISHMENT

A Jewish dealer visited the home of a wealthy poritz with whom he had a business transaction, and found him eating his dinner. The table was spread with delicious roast meats and sparkling wines. The poritz bade the Jew be seated and placed before him a plate of the choicest meats. The Jew politely thanked his host, but refused to eat.

"Why? Doesn't it smell good?" the poritz asked.

"Indeed it does," the Jew replied, "but we Jews are forbidden to eat it."

"Oh, I see," the other said, laughing heartily, "it isn't kosher."

Later the poritz poured a glass of wine for himself and his guest. The Jew again refused with the words, "It is not allowed."

Finally the poritz could not tolerate the situation any longer.

"Listen here, Jew," he exclaimed, "your God is entirely too cruel. He hangs heavy stones upon your necks which are absolutely beyond all human endurance. What would you do if you were lost in the woods, on the verge of collapse for lack of food, and someone approached you with a dish that was not kosher?"

"Well, if it is a matter of life or death," the Jew replied, "one is permitted to eat according to our religion."

Suddenly the poritz, his face distorted and his eyes lit with a fiendish gleam, jumped up and pointed a gun at the Jew, shouting, "Drink the wine instantly, or else I'll shoot you!"

The Jew seized the glass and gulped down the wine. Another glass was poured for him and he also drank that. When he was finished the gentile put down the gun and amiably said, "I merely acted that way in jest. Are you angry with me?"

"Angry? Of course, I'm angry with you," the Jew retorted. "Why didn't you play the same joke on me when you served the delicious roast meats?"

## SIMPLE ACCOUNTING

A poverty stricken Jew was unusually distressed. Passover was almost here and he had no money with which to buy anything.

"Why are you so worried and downhearted?" a friend asked.

"Alas," the poor man sighed, "it is very bad for me. I have a thousand worries on my mind and they are driving me mad. There is no matzoh, meat, or wine in the house. The children have no clothes, and my wife hasn't even a dress for the holidays. My head is just splitting with all my worries."

"But, my good friend, you don't have to have so many worries," the other replied. "Here, take a pencil and paper, and figure up just how much you will need for Passover. Matzoh, five rubles, meat and wine, six rubles, shoes and clothing for the children, four rubles, a dress for your wife, three rubles. Now how much does that amount to all together? Eighteen rubles. See, here you have it. The entire thing adds up to just one worry. Where will you get the eighteen rubles? One worry, and that is the end of your entire problem. Now you don't have to rack your brain with all the other nine hundred and ninety-nine worries!"

## KISMET

The two pious brothers, Reb Elimelech and Reb Zusha, while in exile, traveled over the whole world as two simple paupers. One day they stopped at an inn, where a wedding was being held. The brothers entered and sat down in a corner of the room, in such a position that Reb Elimelech faced the wall and his brother Reb Zusha the guests. When the farmers became merry, they decided to make sport of the two beggars. They seized Reb Zusha, who was facing them, placed him on the floor, and after every dance, each one gave him a slap on the back.

This continued until finally Reb Elimelech said to Reb Zusha, "Why should you take all the punishment? Let us change places so that they will take me instead." Reb Zusha agreed. While the inebriated guests were dancing, Reb Zusha took his brother's place facing the wall, and Reb Elimelech sat facing the guests. When the dance was finished, they again approached the beggars.

Suddenly one of the guests called out, "Brothers, it isn't fair to take the same one all the time! Let us take the other one now, the one facing the wall. Let him also get a beating, and remember that he too was at a wedding!"

Again Reb Zusha was the victim. When they were through with him, and Reb Zusha sat down again near his brother, he said, "Now, my dear brother, you can see very clearly, that he who is destined to get a beating, cannot buy his way out of it."

## VERBAL LEGACY

A wealthy dealer became ill in a small town, far from his home. He had $10,000 with him, and was in fear that the hotelkeeper might take it from him if he should die. At last he devised a clever scheme to protect his money. He called over the owner of the house and told him that he was going to will him the entire $10,000 because of the good care he was giving him. He asked him to bring in a notary and a witness to prepare the will.

The will was made, with only one condition that the hotelkeeper had to carry out. On the death of the dealer he was to go himself to Bialystok, Poland, and bring the sad news to the widow. He should also give her as much money as he himself would want.

The man died, and the owner of the hotel went to find the bereaved wife. He arrived at the city and immediately went to the rabbi, with the money and the will. The rabbi read the will and sent for the widow. When she arrived, he asked the hotelkeeper how much money he was willing to give her. The mercenary man replied that he intended to give her $100. Then the rabbi gave his decision—that according to the will he would have to give the woman $9900, and keep $100 for his expenses.

"What do you mean?" shouted the hotelkeeper. "How do you gather that from the will?"

"It was cleverly worded," the rabbi replied. "It is distinctly written that you are to give this woman such a sum as you would want yourself. It is very obvious that you want $9900 for yourself, which remains when one deducts the $100 you so good-naturedly offered the widow. So, my good man, pay up."

## SEE YOURSELF

In a forlorn section of Asia, far from civilization, lived a young married couple. The woman never went beyond the boundary line of her city, and was completely ignorant of any kind of progress. One day her husband had to go to the big city with a petition to the governor. When he was ready to leave, he bade his wife farewell and asked, "What kind of gift would you want me to bring you back from the big city?"

She remained silent and did not know what to ask for. Suddenly she spied the crescent moon, and very happily called, "Oh, bring me a comb shaped just like the moon above."

"Very well, my dear, I will bring you such a comb, and you will wear it in your beautiful hair."

Some time passed, and the husband, having accomplished his mission, was ready to start his journey back home. He remembered that he had promised his wife a gift, but he did not recall just what she wanted. He went to a nearby store and looked around.

"What do you want, sir?" the proprietor asked.

The poor man only looked puzzled and could not answer. Then looking up at the beautiful full moon, he remembered that she had asked for something that would be similar to the moon. Filled with joy he exclaimed, "I want something for my wife that resembles the moon!"

"Good," the storekeeper replied. "Here you have a mirror that is as round as the moon. I feel certain that your wife will like it."

The man bought the mirror. On his arrival he gave his wife her present. Very carefully she took the mirror in her hand, and began to look at it with curiosity. Suddenly, she spied the image of a very pretty young woman there. She became frantic with fear, and ran to her mother, weeping bitterly.

"Mother, mother, my husband has brought a beautiful woman home with him. He does not love me any more. Look and see for yourself!" And she handed the mirror to her mother.

The mother looked into it, and seeing the reflection there, very confidently said, "My daughter, you have nothing to fear. She is an ugly ancient creature."

## CLOTHES AND THE MAN

A father had several sons who were quite wealthy and lived in different cities. One day he invited them to the wedding of their youngest brother. All responded immediately that they would come, but the poorest of the lot wrote asking what kind of clothing he and his wife should take with them. The father, under the impression that he was the wealthiest of all, made up a list of the most expensive wardrobe. On the day of the wedding the rich sons arrived, dressed very fashionably, but the poor son and his wife were garbed in silks and satins. The family accepted him as a man of high rank and showed him great respect. Toward the end of the evening they discovered that he was as poor as a churchmouse.

"I can't understand your motive in asking me the kind of clothes to bring. You could have come in whatever you had," the father said.

"My dear father," the son replied, "I haven't even a pair of shoes to wear and my clothes are covered with holes and patches. I would have had to borrow clothing regardless, so it might just as well be the best."

## THE BOGEYMAN

A traveler spent a fortnight at a hotel, and when he was about to leave the proprietor presented him with an exceedingly high bill. Since there was nothing he could do about it, he grudgingly paid. The hotelkeeper suggested, if he visited the city again, that he make it a point to stop at his hotel.

"I'll be frank with you," the traveler replied; "it would be pleasant to stay at your place if you didn't have such a large number of mice."

"What can I do about it?" the proprietor asked.

"I can give you a very good remedy," the guest suggested. "Just show them your rates and they will run away, never to return again."

## NO CHANGE

A Jew dined at a small hotel. For the entree he was served a portion of fish. He tasted it, grunted, and pushed it aside with disgust.

"What is the matter?" the hostess asked. "Why don't you eat the fish?"

"It has a foul odor," the Jew replied.

"You ate here a week ago, and you praised the fish very highly," the woman remarked.

"Yes, then it was very good."

"I give you my word of honor," the lady solemnly extended her hand, "that it is the very same fish."

261

## INESCAPABLE

A newlywed young woman, who did not know how to cook anything but bean soup, fed her husband with it day after day. The husband was a patient fellow, who loved his wife dearly, and he did not complain.

One day he went to a restaurant to eat something different. The waiter handed him a menu. Not knowing how to read or speak English, he pointed to something. It was bean soup! When the waiter arrived with his portion, the poor fellow sickened at the sight of it; but since he had no alternative he forced it down his throat.

At a nearby table sat another customer, who when the waiter asked what else he desired cried, "The same!" He was served a portion of noodles.

When the waiter approached the young fellow, who was struggling with his bean soup, the latter also said, "The same," thinking that it meant noodles. When he saw that he was being served bean soup for the second time, he excitedly jumped up, paid for the two portions, and started back home, muttering, "Misfortune seems to follow me all over. If I am doomed to eat bean soup, I prefer eating my wife's!"

## A MYSTERY

A Jew had to go to a city on an urgent matter. It was autumn and the weather was miserable, for it rained continuously. The roads were slippery, and to travel by horse and wagon was dangerous. Since the Jew had no alternative, he offered a coachman ten dollars to take him there.

262

They started on the journey. When they reached a hill, the coachman asked his passenger to get out and help him push the wagon up, because the old mare wasn't very strong. In spite of the heavy downpour they pushed the wagon to the top. After that, the Jew started to get back into the coach.

"What? You are going to sit down?" the coachman called in surprise. "Can't you see that we have to go downhill now? You must help me hold the wagon back."

After a few hours of such torture, they reached their destination, drenched and very tired. The entire trip had consisted of pushing and pulling the wagon.

"There is something that I can't understand," the Jew said to the coachman. "I rode in this weather because I had to attend to an important business deal. You went because you earned ten dollars. But pray tell me, why did that old horse go?"

## THREE POOR MEMORIES

When R. A. Broides was a young man, he and two of his friends, atheists like himself, would shut themselves in a small house on Saturdays, and smoke to their hearts' content. One Saturday afternoon a Jew passed by and noticed what the boys were doing. He began to shout, and a large crowd gathered, broke open the door and dragged the fellows out. One of the boys, realizing that he was in for a beating, pleaded, "Please let me go. I am innocent. I forgot."

"What have you forgotten?" the Jews asked.

"I forgot that today is Saturday," he said.

"Perhaps that is so," one Jew agreed, and they decided to let him go.

The next fellow gave the same excuse. He too had forgot.

"Now what did you forget?" the crowd asked.

"I forgot that one is not allowed to smoke on Saturday."

The people felt sorry for this boy too and forgave him.

Finally they came to Broides, the leader of the group. "And you, my fine lad," they sarcastically called out, "you probably also forgot!"

"O course I forgot," Broides retorted.

"What?" they cried.

"I," replied Broides calmly, "I forgot to pull down the shades."

## COMPARATIVE VALUES

Two immigrants, simple Jews, came to America and built a synagogue. One was the rabbi and the other the cantor. One Saturday a young man entered the synagogue and observed the positions the two men held. At a meeting the following day he discussed the impression they had made upon him.

"Torah, Prayer, and Charity," he began, "the foundations of the world, complained that their end was near. People did not pray, they had ceased learning, and did not give charity. Torah spoke up, 'What will happen to the world?' 'Don't worry,' a voice from above called back; 'as long as there is a rabbi the Torah will exist!' Then Prayer

264

complained that people had stopped praying. 'You have nothing to fear,' the voice replied. 'While there is a cantor they will pray.' Charity added plaintively, 'People don't trust one another and do not give charity. What will happen to everyone?' 'Do not be so concerned,' the voice consoled him. 'As long as a pinch of snuff exists, charity will remain.' 'Great God in heaven,' Charity moaned, 'my friends you give two important men, the rabbi and the cantor, and with me you settle for a pinch of snuff!' 'Be calm, my friend,' the voice called back. 'The cantor and the rabbi aren't worth even a pinch of snuff!' "

## MONEY BACK

Chaim noticed a coat in a shop window, which he admired, but could not afford. The temptation was great and he decided to buy the garment. When he showed it to his wife she became enraged at his extravagance.

"Return the coat immediately," she demanded, "and get a refund!"

"What if the merchant refuses to accept it?" Chaim mumbled.

"Find some fault with the coat," the woman suggested, "and he will be compelled to return your money."

The poor man went to the store and found the owner busy with several customers.

"Give me back my money, for I've discovered a damage in the garment!" Chaim bellowed.

The proprietor did not utter a word and immediately refunded the cost of the coat.

The customers present were baffled. "Why didn't you give him another garment in exchange if his was damaged?" they asked.

"If the man had come and told me there was a flaw in the coat and then asked for his money, I would have persuaded him to take another one. When this individual immediately demanded his money, I knew his claim was a pretense, and that he probably regretted the deal. I did not care to waste any time with him, so I returned his few dollars and got rid of him."

## COMPENDIOUS INSULT

Hershel Astropoler stood on a street corner, trembling with hunger and cold, staring into space. A heavy-set, miserly landowner of the city passed by, noticed Hershel, and gave him a hearty slap on his back, saying, "Hershel, what are you thinking about?"

"I was just thinking about you," Hershel replied.

"About me?" the other asked in surprise. "May I know what?"

"I presume you know," Hershel began, "that a duck is fat on his stomach and lean on his back. An eagle, on the contrary, is fat on his back, and lean on his stomach. Do you know why that is so? A duck swims on the water, and is afraid of no one underneath her, so her stomach grows fat. From above she is afraid that she may be shot, and that is why her back is lean. The eagle is not afraid that he may be shot from above, because no one can fly higher than he, therefore his back is fat, and his stomach lean. When I look at you, I see that you fear neither the One above, nor anyone beneath, and that is why you are fat, greasy, and rounded out on all sides like a pig."

## HYPERBOLE

An elderly *shadchan* was instructing a younger man in the business. He took him along to all his deals and taught him the rules and regulations of the profession.

"The most important thing to know in making a shid-duch is not to lie," he explained. "Remember, you have to assent to everything I say."

"All right," the younger agreed.

The following day they went to a wealthy man's home, to speak of a *shidduch* for the son.

"The girl I have in mind for you," the older shadchan said to the son, "comes from a very fine family."

"A fine family indeed!" the young shadchan called out. "The finest in the world."

"And they are wealthy!"

"Wealthy? They are millionaires!" the young one agreed.

"And the girl is pretty!"

"What do you mean pretty? She is an outstanding beauty!"

"The only fault is that she has a little hunch on her back," the older shadchan continued.

"A little hunch?" the young shadchan became enthusi-astic. "Why, it is a hunch the size of a monument!"

## THE ROYAL POWER

Years ago, when Jews were not allowed to practice pharmacy in Austria, Joseph Perel sent his son to study that profession. When his studies were completed, the king granted him the privilege to practice. As soon as it became known that a Jew was to be a pharmacist, there were protests. The noblemen asked the king to withdraw the right he had extended to Joseph Perel's son. The king sent for Perel and said, "There is much excitement in my kingdom. All the noblemen are frantic. I wouldn't like to withdraw the privilege that I gave you. Please be good enough and give it up yourself. If you oblige me, I will grant you any other thing that your heart may desire."

"Then," Perel replied, "I want the king to give my son back the years that he spent studying."

"That no man can return," said the king.

"Since a king himself cannot grant a person all that he desires," Perel returned, "he should not take away that which he once gave."

Thus did Joseph Perel win the right for his son to practice pharmacy.

## THE ULTIMATE

A well-known contractor once confided to a friend of his.

"Everybody thinks that because a contractor runs around and is always flustered, he is doing a wonderful business. They are under the impression that he is making buckets full of gold on every enterprise he undertakes.

I tell you it isn't true. There is not one job that one does not lose money on. Earning a living is out of the question completely."

"Tell me then," his friend asked, "where do you get so much money if you lose all the time?"

"I'll let you in on a little secret," the contractor whispered. "Each time I take on a larger enterprise, so that I will have enough money to cover the previous ones."

"But it must come to an end sometimes," the friend replied.

"Sure," replied the contractor, "with the help of God one can suddenly drop dead right in the middle of everything!"

## THE ROAD BACK

Count Patotsky, the proselyte of Vilna, had a friend Zaremba who followed Patotsky's idea—his wife and he converted themselves to the Jewish faith.

After they became Jews Zaremba said to his wife, "Let us get a divorce now. You marry a real Jew and I'll marry a Jewess, and in that manner we will be rooted into the Jewish race."

Zaremba's wife smiled wisely.

"Two people were once stranded in a desert," she said, "and lost their path. They wandered aimlessly together, suffered hunger and thirst and were tortured by the burning sand and blistering sun. Finally a miracle happened and they found the road back to civilization. When they reached their destination, they clasped each other's hands and said, 'When we lost our way we suffered great pain and agony together. Now that we have found a place of refuge, is it wise that we should part? Is it fair?'"

## REQUIESCANT

Yossel the philosopher suffered a great deal and was very unhappy, because his parents were constantly quarreling. His environment was miserable, and when he grew older he left home. He felt sorry for his father and mother, who lived so unhappily. When his mother died, Yossel said Kaddish religiously. But when his father died, he refused to say Kaddish at all.

His neighbors reprimanded him. "What is the matter, Yossel? Why don't you want to commemorate your dead father?"

"I have been told," Yossel said, "that when one says Kaddish, it brings the dead into Paradise. I've said Kaddish for my mother for a whole year, and I know that she is there already. I wouldn't want to bring my father there too. They quarreled enough while they were alive; let them at least be at peace in death."

## RATIONING

A merchant entered a hotel in a small town and asked for something to eat.

"What would you like?" the hostess asked.

"Meat or fish," the guest replied.

"We haven't any fish," the woman explained, "because there is no river in our town. Meat we can only obtain on Saturdays."

"In that case bring me some butter, cheese, and cream."

"We haven't that either, my friend. Our cows have stopped giving milk."

"Then give me a herring."

"I'm sorry, but my husband hasn't come back from the market place yet."

"Have you any bread?"

"My heavens!" the mistress incredulously murmured, scratching her head. "I've never seen such an appetite in all my life!"

## CORRECT

A modern teacher, who taught his pupils other subjects besides Jewish studies, was discussing nature with them.

He called on Yankele: "Tell me, my boy, what is the purpose of sheep?"

The youngster remained silent.

"What do we get from sheep?" the teacher persisted. "Wool."

"What else?"

The boy was quiet.

"You are a fool," the teacher cried impatiently. "What is made from wool?"

The lad bowed his head in embarrassment. He didn't know.

"Stupid child!" the teacher shouted, "From what is your jacket made?"

"From my father's old pants," Yankele mumbled.

## HOW TO CHOOSE A BRIDE

Young man: You, as an experienced man—tell me how should I choose a bride.

Old man: Have you ever seen a flock of geese?

Young man: Yes.

Old man: Well, when you see a flock of girls, dash in as you would among a flock of geese, and grab the first one you can reach for.

Young man: But which one?

Old man: Which one? I would advise you to close your eyes.

Young man: Then I may catch a snake.

Old man: And if you look with open eyes, do you think that you'll find something better? They are all the same, like geese. Therefore, it is best not to pick.

## SAUCE FOR THE GOOSE

A debtor asked his friend to advise how to escape the fury of his creditors. His friend suggested that he put on an act of insanity when his creditors came, and begin dancing, whistling, and laughing before them. They would then become frightened and cease annoying him. Much to the debtor's delight, the plan worked out beautifully. When the men saw his actions, they fled as fast as their legs could carry them.

This debtor also owed his friend some money, and when he came to claim it, the debtor began to dance, laugh, and sing as to the others. His friend was flabbergasted.

"Ungrateful wretch," he furiously called out, "I advised you to act this way to save you from your other creditors, and now you dare to use it as a weapon against me?"

## THE MATERIALISTS

Motel Kamenetz was a wealthy contractor in Kiev. Many people derived benefits and favors from him. One day he lost a fortune in real estate, and his friends began to avoid him. But luck was with him and his business again began to flourish. Soon he became rich and his friends again recognized him. One holiday they all decided to visit him. When Motel saw them coming, he ordered his gentile servant to place his money box on the table. The crowd entered the house and cheerfully wished him a happy holiday, but on seeing the box of money they asked, "What does this mean?"

"My friends," Motel replied, "I am well aware that you have not come to greet me. The fact is that you have come to greet my money. Pray sit down, my good people! Here is my money and rejoice with it."

## A BINOMINAL THEOREM

A Jew came to a judge and asked for permission to change his name. The judge wanted to know the reason for his request.

"I live in an Irish neighborhood and deal with Irish people," the Jew explained. "It seems that my name is harming my business."

"What is your name?" the judge inquired.

"Izzie Rabinovitch."

"What do you want to call yourself now?"

"Patrick Gilligan."

The judge granted the request. Several months later the Jew was back in court. This time he wanted to change his name from Patrick Gilligan to Donald O'Brien.

"What is the matter now?" the judge asked. "Why isn't the name Patrick Gilligan suitable?"

"Yes, but the trouble is," the Jew complained, "that my Irish customers keep asking me constantly, 'What was your name before?'"

## COMBINED OPERATIONS

Two policemen came to the home of a poor melamed and took away his pillow and his candlesticks in payment for taxes he owed. The following morning, when the melamed went to the synagogue, he related the incident to the sexton.

"I can't understand which opinion the two policemen adhere to," the melamed said. "There was one rabbi who said that the night was created for sleep. If they are his disciples then they had no right to take my pillow. Another rabbi said that the night was made only for study. If they believe in his teachings, they should not have taken my candlesticks."

The sexton, a clever old man, quickly found an excuse for the behavior of the policemen.

"The wisdom of their actions lies in the fact that they came together," the sexton replied. "The one who holds the opinion that the night was made for sleep, took the candlesticks, and the other, who believes the night was made for study, took the pillow."

## COOL AND COLLECTED

A beggar stopped at an inn and asked to be served a good dinner. In the evening he ordered the best food and drinks in the house. The next morning he ate a hearty breakfast. As he was about to go, the owner of the inn stopped him and asked:

"How about paying for your room and meals?"

"Don't worry about that," the beggar replied; "the money is as safe as if it were in your own pocket. I am not running away. I have come to this city to collect donations. That is my business. Yesterday I was very tired from my journey, but today I am going to start working. You can be sure that I will repay every penny that I owe you."

"What do you mean, I can be sure?" the innkeeper shrieked. "I certainly can't be sure!"

"Well, if you are skeptical and don't believe me, come and we will go begging together."

"What! Are you insane? I will go begging with you?"

"Oh, you are ashamed to go with me? I'll tell you what, then. Here is my sack, and go yourself."

## PERPETUAL MOTION

Two poor Jews were lying on the hard benches of the synagogue, discussing how well and contentedly the rich man lives.

"Do you know Chaim, the rich man of our city?" one of them remarked. "He puts on a white shirt every Saturday."

"And Brodsky, from Kiev?" the other asked.

"What a question! He can afford to put on a white shirt twice a week."

"And the minister?"

"Oh, he? Every day."

"What about the king himself?"

"Twice a day."

"Now let us take Rothschild for example. What about him?"

"Rothschild? Who can compare to Rothschild? He puts on shirts and takes them off; puts them on and takes them off all day long!"

## THE RITUALIST

A religious Jew arrived in Vienna and asked where he could find a kosher hotel. A place was pointed out to him. He observed that the mistress was koshering meat according to the dietary laws. The Jew decided to remain. The next day he again saw the woman bring meat into the house, but this time she merely washed it and immediately put it up to cook. The Jew was confounded.

"I should like to ask you something," he spoke up.

"Why did you kosher the meat yesterday, and today you did nothing of the kind?"

"For the simple reason," the woman replied, "that yesterday I bought *trefah* meat, and I had to kosher it. Today I bought kosher meat, so why should I bother koshering it again?"

## FOR THE BLIND

A beggar put on a pair of dark glasses and disguised himself as a blind man. With his dog alongside, he parked himself on a street corner. On his chest he hung a sign with the following inscription:

"Please have mercy on an unfortunate blind creature."

Before long he had collected a tidy sum of money, but the police were soon on his trail. They were informed that the man was not blind, because people had seen him counting his money. The beggar was arrested and brought before the judge.

"Why did you fool the people and swindle money from them when you are not blind?" the judge asked.

"I didn't fool anyone," the beggar deftly replied. "The blind creature is my dog. I was begging for him and not for myself."

The judge laughed heartily and dismissed the case.

## A NEW COMMENTARY

Two yeshivah boys, who constantly sat in the synagogue studying were arguing with each other over a certain commentary in Rashi. In the midst of their argumentation a fine looking Jew entered who seemed to be a learned man. The boys immediately approached him and asked that he give his opinion as to which was right. The Jew, who was only a small-town storekeeper, and hardly a learned person, looked at the Rashi and finally said:

"Do you know, it seems to me that there is still another question to be answered."

"Another one?" the boys asked in surprise. "Do you mean that there is a third question?"

"Yes," the intelligent looking Jew replied. "Since the words are so small, I can't understand—how do you read them?"

## SPEECH UNSPOKEN

Two small Jewish merchants were walking together when one pointed out:

"Do you see that long-legged man there? He comes from England, and under no circumstances will he speak anything but English. Looking at him, one would think that he is a respectable man, but he once insulted me when I was in his place of business."

"What do you mean?" the other asked. "Did you understand his English?"

"Of course, I understood. When he seized me by the collar with one hand, and showed me the door with the other, I immediately understood what he meant."

## NOT SO DUMB

A shadchan, after listening to a young man describing the kind of fiancee he would like, finally became angry, and impatiently called out:

"Young man, forgive me, but you want a girl who has everything. She must be beautiful, of a fine family, and must also have money. I'll tell you, my good fellow, she would have to be insane to want to marry one like you."

"Oh, that wouldn't bother me. If she has all the qualities I mentioned, she may be insane. I wouldn't mind," the young man replied calmly.

## ETERNITY

A speaker addressed a large audience, where the chairman was a young, clean-shaven man. Several prominent people were seated on the platform, and when the chairman was called to the telephone, he asked one of them, an old man with a long gray beard, to take his place. The speaker, being absorbed in his speech, did not notice what had happened. Suddenly, he turned around, stared, and rubbed his eyes in amazement, saying:

"My friends, I know that I have a habit of making long speeches, but have I really spoken so long that the chairman has grown a beard?"

## DIVINE JEST

A fire broke out in the middle of the night in Chaim Yankel's store. It happened a few days after his insurance had lapsed. When Chaim Yankel saw the flames consume his entire business, leaving only ashes, he called out frantically:

"God, I wish you would strike me dead, so that there would be an end to all my troubles!"

He had hardly spoken these words when a brick, which broke loose from the wall, struck him on the head. For a moment he was dazed, and when he regained his senses he cried out:

"Dear Lord, can't you take a joke?"

## ASSURANCE

A young woman insisted that her husband take out a life insurance policy. She always argued with him, and called him an egotist, saying that he didn't care about her. What if something should happen to him?

She then pointed out her friends as examples, because their husbands were insured.

"But," said her husband, trying to squirm his way out, "what are they getting out of it? They pay and pay, and have nothing."

"Who knows?" replied the wife. "Perhaps I may be more fortunate than they."

## INTENT

Yossel related this incident to a friend of his:

"Last evening I was at the home of a wealthy farmer with whom I was to transact a business deal. We argued for a long time, when finally the farmer became angry and wanted to slap me."

"How do you know that he wanted to slap you?" his friend asked.

"How do I know? That is a funny question. Take a look at my cheek, and you will see the mark even now."

280

"Then he really did strike you! Why do you say he wanted to?"

"Well, if he didn't want to, he certainly wouldn't have done it."

## KOSHER

Several Jews and gentiles were traveling in a train. One of the gentiles, who sat directly opposite a Jew, started to insult him and call him names. Suddenly the Jew opened his mouth wide and yawned.

"Shut your mouth!" shouted the other. "What do you want to do, swallow me?"

"God forbid," replied the Jew. "You know that we Jews are forbidden to eat swine."

## RARE BIT

A mistress once gave a yeshivah student a plate of noodle soup. The young man put his ear to the plate and listened closely.

"What are you listening to?" the woman asked.

"I hear the noodles talking," the boy replied.

"Really, what are they saying?" the woman picked up her ears.

"One noodle is calling to the other, 'Where are you?' " was the reply.

## BUDDING BAHAIST

A policeman stopped a beggar who was standing near a synagogue, and shouted:

"What are you doing near a synagogue now? Only yesterday I saw you begging near the entrance of a church. Are you a gentile or a Jew?"

"I am a Jew," the beggar replied, "but it is very difficult to earn a livelihood from one religion nowadays."

## LAST RESORT

A teacher who had taught a whole winter in a small town was going home for Passover. While traveling he noticed that his wallet, which contained the few rubles he had saved up, was missing. He searched every corner of the wagon, but to no avail. The poor man began to sob loudly and throw his arms about in desperation.

"I won't live through such a misfortune," he cried.

One of the passengers who saw his despair tried to calm him:

"My dear fellow, maybe your wallet is in one of your pockets. Take a good look."

"What are you talking about?" the teacher wailed. "That is the only bit of hope I have. Do you want me to lose that too? Then I am a ruined man."

## HIS ROUNDS

Two beggars met one day.

"Congratulate me, brother," one of them said, "I have just married off my older daughter. Do you know who my son-in-law is? He is Fishke, the hunchback, and is in the same business as we."

"Oh, of course I know him," the other replied. "A very

fine son-in-law, indeed. What sort of a dowry did you give?"

"Don't ask. He is a very shrewd fellow. I had to give him all of Lita, and Zamut, with all the houses in that territory. Now I dare not even come near there."

"I only wish that when I marry off my younger daughter, I should be able to give her a dowry as fine as that."

## A CARD

Mr. Rosen, a good friend of Dr. Berg, came to Canada to sell the doctor's books. He went into the home of a wealthy Jew, and began to discuss Dr. Berg's brilliant writings and his accomplishments in cultural Judaism.

· "Who the devil is that guy, anyhow?" the Jew cried out. "I never heard of him!"

"Don't you know?" Mr. Rosen replied. "He is the dis-coverer of pinochle."

"Oh, is that so? He certainly is a great man! I'll buy all his books," said the rich, informed man.

## SAMPLE

Baruch was elected president of a Talmud Torah be-cause he had a great deal of money. At the end of the term, when the children were to be examined, he and other members of the board visited one of the classrooms. One student was asked several questions, and the answers he gave were very satisfactory.

"Come, let us go to the other classes," the president urged his friends.

"What about the other children in the room?" the teacher asked.

"A class can be compared to a barrel of herring," the president replied. "You know that I sell wholesale. When I take out one herring, and see that it is good, I know that the whole barrel is good."

## NOMINAL CHANGE

Two Jews, Goldberg and Steinberg, were partners in business, and when their business went bad, they decided that one of them should change his name. So Goldberg changed his name to O'Reilly. As soon as business improved, the other partner also changed his name from Steinberg to O'Reilly. Now the concern was called O'Reilly and O'Reilly. One day a customer called up, and asked to speak to O'Reilly. One of them, who answered the telephone, asked:

"Which O'Reilly do you want, Steinberg or Goldberg?"

## FAST REPARTEE

During the Fast of Gedaliah a man visited a friend and found him eating.

"Fie, it is a shame," he called out. "You are a Jew. How is it that you eat during the Fast of Gedaliah?"

"I do not fast for three reasons," his friend retorted. "First, Gedaliah will not come back to life through my fasting. Secondly, if I were to die, Gedaliah also would not fast, and thirdly, wherein is the Fast of Gedaliah more important to me than Yom Kippur?"

## SPREADING IT THICK

A poor man began to criticize a loaf of bread:

"I don't understand," he sighed, "why you avoid my house, while you go to the rich every day."

"Why shouldn't I avoid you?" the loaf of bread called back. "When I come to the rich, they spread me thickly with butter, cheese and other delicacies, but when I come to you once in a great while, the entire household grabs hold of me, tears me into pieces, and dunks me into a watery barley soup."

## SINGLE THOUGHT

A woman lying on her death bed called her husband and whispered faintly:

"Moishe, you can see that my days are numbered, and I will soon have to leave you. I want you to marry my sister Deborah, after I die."

"My dear, dear wife," the husband replied, "bless your kind heart. I thought about that a long time ago."

## LET IT RIDE

The son of a wealthy man was about to become bar-mitzvah. The father, not knowing of a suitable gift to buy his son, referred to the Hebrew teacher for a suggestion.

The teacher advised him to buy the boy an encyclopedia. The word "encyclopedia" left the father dumbfounded, as if he had been hit with a hammer over the head.

"No, I won't get him that," he snapped. "God forbid, that rascal might have an accident with it. Let him walk."

## INTOXICANT

Two Jewish youths, just arrived in New York, decided to walk around and look at the big city. They passed by a place and saw a sign, "Beer and Billiards."

"Yankel, let us go in, and drink a glass of billiard. Beer we drank in the old country. I would like to taste something different."

"All right," the other replied. "We'll have a few glasses of billiard, if it isn't too expensive."

So they entered, and ordered two glasses of billiard. The waiter, realizing the type of customers he had, filled their glasses with water.

"Do you know?" said Yankel, smacking his lips, "it is quite a good drink, but if I didn't know that this was billiard, I could have sworn that it was water."

## DUMB ANSWER

"Moishe, tell me why does the whole world speak so highly of the Rambam? What if he did write the Kuzari? Does that make him such an important person?"

"The Kuzari?" Moishe asked in surprise. "The Rambam didn't write that; Yehudah Halevy wrote it."

"What! do you mean to say that he didn't even write

286

the Kuzari? Then I still have a greater reason to ask why the world makes such a fuss over him."

## MULTIPLICATION

A shrewd youngster explained the following to a coach-man near the station:

"If it takes one hour to ride with two horses from the city to the station, then four horses could make the trip in a half hour. So use six horses, and you'll save yourself the trouble of traveling at all."

## PULLING A FAST ONE

A wealthy American Jew hired the sexton of his syna-gogue to fast for him in memory of his dead. During the afternoon he entered a restaurant, and found the sexton eating a very hearty meal.

"What do you call this?" the wealthy Jew shouted. "You are nothing but a common swindler."

"I'll be frank with you," the sexton replied. "The gabbai of the synagogue also hired me to fast for him. Now I ask you, have I strength to fast for two people? Look at me, all skin and bones. So I made a decision. I'll fast for you, but for the gabbai I'll eat."

## SELLOUT

A Shylock, strolling along the street with a friend of his, called out:

"Do you see that man walking over there? I want you to know that it was I who put him on his feet."

"How?" his friend inquired.

"Well," replied the financier, "this man used to ride around in his own beautiful carriage. Since I took it away from him in payment of a debt, he is back on his feet again."

## MATHEMATICS

"Why are we so poor?" a wife once asked her husband who owned a liquor store. "It seems to me that we shouldn't be poor at all. To the liquor we always add half water, and besides, you always write down a larger amount on the bill than the customer actually purchases. How is it then that we are not making any money?"

"Yes, my dear wife, that is all very true," the husband replied. "But we don't add one drop of water to the liquor we add on to the bill."

## EASY MONEY

A famous author met a friend of his, a laborer.

"How are you?" the laborer asked.

"Making a living," the author replied. "And how are you?"

"Oh, I have a great deal of trouble. Tell me, how do you earn your living?"

"From writing," was the reply.

"Is that so!" his friend said, looking at him quizzically. "From writing? That is very funny. Do you know? It never entered my head to take up such a business."

## PANTOMIME

A woman, just arrived in America from a small town in Poland, became mistress of her son's home. It was difficult for her to shop, because she knew no word of English, and had to point to everything she wanted. One Friday morning she set out to buy a chicken, but didn't know how to ask for it. When she came to the butcher she began to wave her hands in the air, as a chicken flaps its wings. To make it clearer for the butcher, she began to crow at the top of her voice. Now she was certain he would understand.

"Madam," the butcher said in Yiddish, after observing her peculiar behavior, "do you want something? Tell me what it is?"

"God bless you, my friend," the woman gleefully exclaimed. "You can speak Yiddish! Then why should I bother to speak to you in English?"

## BUSINESS IS BUSINESS

When a notorious New York gangster died his friends arranged a very respectable and honorable funeral for him. As is the custom at all such funerals, charity collectors came with charity boxes for contributions. The gangster's friends deposited liberal sums of money in every box.

At the cemetery a young woman with a box in her hand collected for some institution. One of the thieves deposited a five dollar gold piece in it, but on his way back, snatched the box from the woman's hand.

The woman ran after him and called:

"I do not understand such actions. You gave me a large donation. Why do you grab the entire box away?"

"Charity is charity, but business is business," the gang- ster replied.

## A CEMETERY FOR GUESTS

A stranger came to a small town which was inhabited by only ten Jews, but had both a synagogue and a ceme- tery. The guest, who was in high spirits, thought he would poke fun at the Jews about the size of their town.

"Tell me, good people," he asked, "why do you need both the synagogue and the cemetery? There should be either one or the other. If you all live, of what use is the cemetery? On the other hand, if one of you should die, you won't have a minyan; then your synagogue is unnecessary."

"You are quite right," answered the snappy overseer. "With God's help, we will all live and be well; so in that case we do need a synagogue. But we also have a ceme- tery because we want to be prepared. What if a guest should come here and die?"

## LET THEM EAT CAKE

A poor man visited his wealthy neighbor and found the family eating pancakes. When he came home he told his wife to prepare the same dish for him. The poor woman explained that she would need flour, eggs, and milk, which they did not have.

"Don't worry about that," the husband reassured her:

"Make it without milk and eggs. You'll be able to scrape up a little flour from the bottom of the trough."

The wife followed her husband's advice and made the pancakes accordingly. Without the eggs and milk the pancakes, of course, tasted quite flat. As the poor man bit into one of them he remarked, "The devil only knows what the rich make a fuss over and what they can enjoy eating!"

## HIS FIRST CASE

A pauper suggested that his wealthy relative, a prominent business man, give him a job.

"What sort of position can you hold?" the relative asked. "Do you know bookkeeping?"

"No," the other replied.

"Can you write letters?"

"No, I can't do that either."

"Well, what can you do?"

"I see that your business needs an expert adviser," the pauper answered, smiling ingratiatingly. "Without overestimating my ability, I can verily say that there is no better man for that position than I."

"Really?" the rich man jumped up gleefully. "Then pray give me a sample piece of advice. How can I get rid of you?"

## NO RECOUNT DEMANDED

A cantor held a position in a synagogue for a number of years. The people became tired of him, but the president didn't dare to tell the cantor openly that he wasn't wanted.

It was decided that this question should be taken to a closed ballot at a meeting. After the vote was cast, it was discovered that there was only one man who had voted for the cantor; all the others were against him. The cantor felt humiliated and turned ghastly pale. The people, seeing the reaction, regretted the entire incident, and each one approached the cantor appologetically, saying:

"I gave you my vote. That individual vote was mine."

Thus every person gave the same excuse. Finally the cantor said:

"Yes, my friends, individually you are good, but all together you are good for nothing."


## CORRECT PROCEDURE

Moishe spent Saturday on a small farm. During the afternoon he had a yearning for a glass of beer and asked the farmer if he had some. The farmer, to oblige his guest, sent his son to buy beer.

When the lad returned Moishe asked, "How old is the boy?"

"Seventeen," the farmer replied.

"You permit a seventeen-year-old fellow, who prays with tefillin every day, to buy on Saturday?" Moishe reprimanded him.

"You city people think that we farmers have no sense at all," the other replied. "I deliberately don't allow him to pray and use his tefillin, so that he may buy on Saturday."

## OLD RELIABLE

A young coachman asked his colleague to loan him his horse. The other, not wanting to, told him the horse was in the pasture. Suddenly a neigh was heard from the stable.

"I can hear that your horse is in the stable," the young fellow said.

"Now I ask you, are you sensible?" the other coachman replied. "Whom would you rather believe, the foolish horse, or me, a good friend?"

## PAYMENT IN KIND

A woman wired her husband, "Can't pay hotelkeeper. Send money immediately."

To which the husband replied, "Haven't any at present. Will send some in a few days. Meanwhile I am sending you one thousand kisses."

Several days later another telegram arrived from his wife, "Don't need money. Gave the hotelkeeper a few of your kisses."

## HE LOST

"I've heard that you played cards on the Sabbath day," a rabbi rebuked a member of his community. "Are you aware of the fact that you have committed an unpardonable sin?"

"Rabbi, please believe me," the other sighed, "I paid heavily for that sin."

293

## MISTAKEN IDENTITY

A new president was elected in a modern congregation. During the prayers, when the cantor began "Barechu," the congregation rose. This irritated the president very much. How did they dare rise without his permission?

"Why did you all get up?" he bellowed.

"Barechu"—they answered him.

"Who the devil is president here?" he roared with rage —"I or Barechu?"

## AND THEN WHAT HAPPENED?

The professor was discussing one of his theories and paused to elucidate the theory of time and eternity.

A Jew in the audience, who was sitting alongside a heavy looking, clumsy woman, called out:

"If the professor had lived thirty years with my wife, he would not have much difficulty in explaining the meaning of eternity."

## TOPSY-TURVY

"You should always remember," a learned man said to his friend while they were studying the Talmud, "that bread and butter will always fall with the buttered side downward."

"Not always," spoke up the other; "I have seen bread fall with the buttered side up."

"It is impossible," the scholastic insisted. "The bread must have been buttered on the wrong side."

## POST HOC

Two travelers, a doctor and a chef, met in a hotel. The doctor was looking for a town where he could practice his profession and the chef was seeking a place where he could open a restaurant.

"Since we have met," the physician suggested, "let us both establish ourselves in one town."

"That is hardly advisable," the chef replied. "You need a town where the inhabitants are weak and ill, but I require a place where the people are robust and strong, with healthy appetites. We could never get together on that."

"That does not matter," the doctor interposed. "If you cook, I will have patients."


## SO HE FOUGHT ON

An Irishman and a Negro had a dispute as to who could take a better beating. They decided to fight, and the one who felt himself growing weak should call out "Sufficient!" They kept pounding away at one another for quite a while until finally the Irishman called out "Sufficient!"

"You devil!" the Negro bellowed, "I wanted to say it an hour ago, but I couldn't think of the word."

## JEAN VALJEAN

A beggar entered a home and asked for something to eat. The woman, a good-natured soul, told him to wash himself, and then served him a hearty meal. When the beggar was through, he wished the woman luck and set off.

As soon as he left the mistress noticed that a silver spoon was missing. She ran after the beggar, shouting, "My friend, I want to tell you something!"

"What is it?" the beggar called, trembling with fear.

"Please don't forget that the spoon you took is a *milchige!*"

## A TRUTHFUL MAN

Lawyer: Gentlemen of the jury, my client is a poor man. Hunger and need compelled him to steal the wallet with thirty dollars from the drawer. You have sufficient proof of his character, in that he didn't take the wallet which contained $200, in spite of the fact that it was lying in the same drawer.

Judge (turning to the defendant): Why didn't you take the wallet with the $200?

Defendant: Your honor, I didn't see it.

## LEGAL REPARTEE

When the witness finished his story, the plaintiff's lawyer assumed cross-examination.

"What is your business?"

"I am an entertainer in a cafe."

296

"Don't you feel that isn't a very respectable job?"

"Possibly," the other remarked, "but in comparison to the position my father held, I can be proud of my work."

"What was your father?"

"My father," the witness calmly replied, "was a lawyer."

## DUSTY ANSWER

An old melamed enjoyed stopping youngsters on the street, plying them with questions. One day he met a little boy playing near the synagogue.

"Come here, my child," he said. "What is your name?"

"The same as my grandfather's," the lad replied.

"And what is your grandfather's name?"

"The same as mine."

"I mean, what are you called at home when you have to eat?"

"I am never called to eat," the little fellow replied, "because I am always the first one at the table."

## TIME WELL PLANNED

An American Jew, president of a synagogue, asked the cantor, whom he disliked intensely, how he spent his time. Since he prayed in the synagogue only on Saturdays, what was he doing the remainder of the days?

"I will show you how I am kept busy every day," the cantor replied. "In the morning, before I can prepare myself, it is eleven o'clock and I have to eat breakfast.

After breakfast I practice singing for two hours. When I am finished, I have my lunch; and from three o'clock till supper my time is taken up with hating my president."

## COACH AND EIGHT

A cantor, who had his own carriage and coachman, traveled with his choir from city to city. Friday evenings the people invited the choir to spend the Sabbath at their homes. The cantor, not wishing the coachman to be deprived of this hospitality, placed him in the choir also. A landlord, thinking the coachman one of the singers, chose him as his guest.

"Why were you quiet while the rest of the choir sang?" the landlord asked. "Why does the cantor need you?"

"I," the coachman exclaimed, "am more important than the cantor! The cantor conducts only the choir, whereas I conduct both cantor and choir."

## THE OPTIMIST

The Jewish philosopher Mendelssohn worked as a bookkeeper for a wealthy merchant in Berlin. The ignorant merchant transacted important business deals and employed many people.

"God is not just," a friend once said to Mendelssohn. "You, who are so educated and intelligent, are employed by such an illiterate person who is so very rich."

"On the contrary," Mendelssohn smiled, "God is just. Since I am educated and can be a bookkeeper, I can always earn my livelihood, but what would my employer do, poor soul, if he were not wealthy?"

## THE PROPOSAL

An elderly widow with a keen sense of humor complained to her doctor that she was very nervous, and did not know what really was the matter with her.

"The best remedy for you would be to get married," her doctor advised.

"Doctor, how about you marrying me?" the widow brazenly asked.

"My dear lady," the doctor smiled, "we doctors only write the prescriptions; we don't take them."

## RITUAL BAN

A beggar was about to enter the home of a wealthy man. As soon as the rich man spied the beggar he left the house. .The beggar could do nothing but himself depart. Later, when the rich man returned, his wife asked, "Why did you leave when you saw the beggar?"

"There is a saying in the Talmud, that a beggar is equivalent to a dead man," the husband explained. "Since I am a priest, I am not permitted to remain in the same house with a corpse."

## AUDACITY

Cantor Zallel Odesser was a very clever man with a keen sense of humor. A young fellow said to him one day, "Tell me, cantor, what is the idea of holding your finger under your chin while you sing?"

"Is that what you want to know?" Zallel replied, feigning surprise. "You certainly are an audacious young man! For fifty years I've been holding my finger under my chin, and I still do not know the reason for it, and here comes a young rascal and wants to know the reason in one moment!"

## DIETARY LAW

A rabbi's wife was concerned that her daughter be religious and adhere to all the Jewish traditions and customs. She taught her all the necessary laws and stressed that she must not mix the *milchige* dishes and silverware with the *fleishige*.

One day the rabbi's wife became ill, and the doctor was called. He wanted to look into the woman's throat, and asked the daughter for a spoon. She hurried into the kitchen, but soon came back.

"Doctor," she asked, "should I bring a fleishige or a milchige spoon?"

## YARD GOODS

A peasant came to the priest of his town for confession.

"What have you done?" the priest asked.

"I've stolen ten yards of linen, holy father," the peasant replied, with downcast eyes.

"You are a sinful soul," the priest rebuked him.

"How can I repent for what I've done?" the peasant pleaded.

The priest was thoughtful for a moment, and then said,

"You must bring thirty yards of linen for the church."

"But, father," the peasant moaned, "I am a poor man; where can I get it?"

"Get it," the priest advised, "where you got the ten yards."

## TOTAL LOSS

A merchant, whose business was on the verge of bankruptcy, awoke one morning with his hair full of feathers. He was so upset that he did not realize it.

One of his friends noticed him and asked in surprise, "What do you call this? How did you ever walk out into the street and forget to comb your hair?"

"I will confide in you," the merchant smiled, "because I know that you can keep a secret. Lately I've accumulated many debts, more than I can bear. It has actually reached a point where even the hair on my head does not belong to me. So why should I bother combing someone else's hair?"

## THE BOASTER

The sexton of the Chasam Sofer had an uncle who was a wealthy banker. He would often boast of his fine heritage and great capabilities. Not only did he work for the Chasam Sofer, but he also had a very rich uncle! Before long these words reached the ears of the sage.

"Why are you so proud, my good fellow?" he asked the sexton. "I could understand the reason if you were as learned as I or as wealthy as your uncle. But since you are as learned as your uncle and have as much money as I, what have you to brag about?"

## DOUBLE DUTY

A merchant riding along the road met a poor man struggling with a heavy load on his back. He invited the man to ride with him to the city. After a while he noticed that the poor man was still holding the load on his back.

"My friend," he said, "why not set it down in the wagon and make yourself comfortable?"

"Good sir," the man replied, "isn't it sufficient that you are kind enough to carry me? Must you also carry my load?"

## SOLUTION

Boss: Do you know bookkeeping?

Bookkeeper: Of course I do.

Boss: Then figure this up for me quickly. How much would a pair of trousers cost me if I used 1¼ yards of material at $3.75 per yard, and paid $5 for workmanship?

Bookkeeper (scratching his head): What good are the figures? A clever person would know just what to do.

Boss: What would he do?

Bookkeeper: He'd buy a ready-made pair of pants.

## ARITHMETIC

Hershel Astropoler came into a hassidic synagogue one day in high spirits.

"Why are you so happy today, Hershel?" he was asked.

"Why shouldn't I be happy? Today I realized that for two kopeks I can get a good drink of liquor!"

"For two kopeks?" the hassidim asked in amazement. "Where do you get such a drink?"

"Well," Hershel drawled, "the day before yesterday, I bought a drink for five kopeks, and it was actually money thrown out. Yesterday I paid seven kopeks for a drink, and that too was no good. Today I paid nine kopeks for a drink, and that I enjoyed immensely. So I realized that it only cost me two kopeks, because the other seven were wasted anyhow."

## VOCATIVE

A cantor visited Professor Friedman, the cantor of Budapest, and asked for a singer for his choir. He was to pray before a new congregation and lacked one man.

"Let me hear your voice," Professor Friedman asked, "then I will know what kind of singer to give you."

The cantor started to sing, and Professor Friedman listened. The man had no voice nor could he carry a tune.

"From what I see," Friedman smiled, "you do not need a singer for your choir, but you do need a cantor, and I haven't one for you."

## THE CONTAINER

Motke Chabad, while visiting a friend, slipped and fell down the entire flight of stairs. There was a terrific

303

noise, and all the tenants ran out. They saw Motke standing at the foot of the steps.

"What happened?" they asked.

"Nothing," Motke assured them. "My coat fell down the stairs."

"Then why was there such a noise?"

"Oh," Motke smiled, "that was because I happened to be in the coat."

## A STRIKING RITUAL

An ignorant farmer who did not know how to conduct the Seder services sent his wife to observe his neighbor. The woman looked through the neighbor's window and saw the man beating his wife. She ran home filled with fright, and dared not tell her husband how a Seder was conducted.

"Well, my wife," the husband asked, "what did you see there?"

The poor woman was still afraid to tell. In exasperation the husband beat her a few times.

"If you already know," the poor wife sobbed, "why do you ask?"

## GOOD OLD AGE

Baron Rothschild's mother lived to a ripe old age. At ninety her health began to fail, and she visited a prominent specialist, who advised a series of treatments. Several months passed and Madame Rothschild still showed no signs of improvement.

"Doctor," she said, "it seems that you are not administering the correct treatment in my case."

"Forgive me, madame," the doctor replied, "but one cannot make an old person young."

"No, dear doctor," Madame Rothschild smiled; "on the contrary, I am not thinking of becoming younger; I want to grow older."

## UNHANDY

The telephone, when first discovered, was an odd piece of mechanism. Reb Velvel the melamed had no idea how it was to be used. A guest who stayed at his house became ill one night, and Reb Velvel had to inform his relatives, but did not know how to go about it. He asked one of the people present to explain the procedure.

"First turn the handle with one hand," he was told; "with the other hand hold the phone near your ear."

"Then," Reb Velvel asked in surprise, "with what will I talk?"

## INTROSPECTION

There is a legend in Prague that has remained with the people through the ages. It is told that the Gaon Maharil created a golem which performed all sorts of tasks as if it were a human being. People say that this figure still lies on the roof of the synagogue.

One day a visitor came to Prague and asked the sexton of the synagogue to show him the golem, promising to reward him liberally. The sexton brought the visitor into one of the rooms on the upper floor. When they entered, the sexton pointed to a large mirror which hung upon the wall and said, "Look into that and you will see the golem."

## CIRCLE OF BRIBERY

During the reign of Nicholas I there was a vacancy for a high official. The minister selected a man who was very intelligent, but very wealthy. When the Czar discovered this, he called in the minister and said, "I give you my word that I will not penalize you, but tell me the truth. Why did you choose that man?"

"I'll be honest with you," the minister replied. "He gave me 25,000 rubles for the position."

"So you sell your country for money?" the Czar furiously assailed him.

"What could I do," the minister pleaded, "if I still owed a debt for what my own position cost me?"

## CAUGHT NAPPING

A famous author and economist lectured on the Marxian theory one Sunday afternoon. The day was warm and a number of people in the audience dozed off. Some even started to snore. The lecturer asked the chairman to tell the audience that it was impossible for him to speak under such conditions.

"Ladies and gentlemen," the chairman began, "those of you who want to sleep will kindly go home, so that our speaker may proceed with his lecture."

Suddenly one of the audience sprang up and shouted excitedly, "Mr. Chairman, where do you get the nerve to drive people out of here? We are all hard working men, who slave all week long. When Sunday comes and we want to have a nap at a lecture, you have the audacity to tell us to leave. Where are we anyhow? in Hitler's enslaved country, or in free America?"

## NOT ENOUGH FOR THREE

A man who had several yards of cloth went to a tailor and asked if that would be enough for a suit.

"No," the tailor replied, examining the material.

But another tailor told the man that this would be sufficient, and that he could call for the suit in a week. When the man came for it, he was surprised to see the tailor's small son wearing a suit of the same cloth as his. He became curious, and asked why the other tailor had told him he would not have enough, while he even had enough material for his son.

"The explanation is simple," the tailor replied. "I have only one son, the other tailor has two."

## SKIN DEEP

A hassid, traveling in a coach, found a beautiful woman sitting directly opposite him. Every time the hassid looked at her he made a grimace and muttered "Pfui!"

A passenger sitting nearby heard the strange utterance. "Why do you act so oddly? If you don't like the woman why don't you change your seat?"

307

"On the contrary, my good man," the hassid replied, "that woman is very attractive. I am not saying 'Pfui' at her, but whenever I catch a glimpse of this beautiful individual I think of my wife."

## PUBLICITY

"Please give me something," a poor man pleaded with a diner in a restaurant. The guest was irritated and, to get rid of the beggar, gave him a slice of bread. The poor man seized the newspaper on the table and quickly wrapped up the piece of bread.

"What do you call this?" the guest cried out. "I give you a slice of bread and you are brazen enough to grab my paper!"

"When a man like you gives something," the beggar replied, "it should immediately be put in a newspaper."

## FAIR ENOUGH

A cantor prayed before a congregation one Saturday. He chanted extremely well and felt that he had made a good impression on the people. He was confident that he would be accepted for the position. When the congregation informed him that he was not suitable he was astonished. The following day he inquired of the people where he could buy a donkey.

"What do you know about donkeys?" he was asked.

"If donkeys are judges of a cantor," he snapped back, "then I am a judge of donkeys."

## GATES OF MERCY

A poor farmer, having committed a felony against his landowner, anticipated a severe penalty. After long brooding he decided to go and plead for mercy. The landowner learned of this and ordered his servants to shut all his doors. Since his estate was very large and consisted of many entrances he had to place a guard near each one.

A friend, who observed the landowner's methods, wisely remarked, "Why must you inconvenience yourself by closing so many doors, and placing guards at each one, when you can merely close the one door of the poor farmer's hut and set one guard there?"

## A JEWISH CUSTOM

Czar Nicholas I was known to be an anti-Semite. His foremost aim was to convert all the Jews into Christians. One day a young Jewish girl, whose father had been innocently imprisoned, came to the Czar and begged that he be released. A gold image of Jesus was standing on the table. The Czar gazed at the Jewish girl for a few seconds.

"First kiss the groom," he said, pointing to the figure.

"There is a custom among the Jews," the girl retorted, "that the groom must kiss the bride first."

## BODY AND MIND

Reb Zalman Poizner, in spite of the fact that he was a very wealthy farmer, dressed in an old fashioned and sim-

309

ple manner, but wore an expensive sable hat. A Polish farmer, a friend of his, asked him one day:

"Why is it that you wear ordinary clothes, but an expensive hat on your head?"

"The reason is simple," Reb Zalman smiled. "To your people the body is the principal thing, so you dress it in the finest and costliest clothes. The head is unimportant, there-fore you leave it uncovered. With us Jews it is the oppo-site. The body is not very important, so we clothe it in any sort of garment, but the head! Ah, that is paramount, and we must dress it most elegantly."

## COMPARATIVE VALUES

During the reign of Alexander III of Russia there was a Minister Ignatoff, who was a cruel enemy of the Jews. It was whispered in Petersburg that the Jews were accu-mulating money to bribe the Minister. One day Ignatoff met Baron Ginsburg on the street.

"I have heard that you are contemplating giving me money," he smilingly remarked. "How much, for instance, would you give me?"

"My dear Minister," the Baron humbly said, "as much as the Jews are worth to me I cannot afford to give you, but as much as the Jews are worth to you, that I will read-ily give."

## UNSOCIAL MEDICINE

Two poor friends who lived in Warsaw for several years met on the street one day.

"How are you, my good fellow?" said one to the other. "I haven't seen you in such a long time. How do you like Warsaw?"

"Oh, I'm just getting along; I suppose it is better than being dead," the other replied. "I wouldn't have been doing so badly, but I was ill for two months, and that cost me two hundred rubles."

"Really! two hundred rubles! That is too bad. I tell you, as sure as I am living, in Lithuania you could have been sick for two whole years for that much money."

## THE ACCUSED

The president of an American Talmud Torah visited the classes of his school. The teacher, on seeing him, became very nervous. Trying to make a good impression, he called on one of the pupils:

"Izzie, who wrote the Psalms?" Due to his nervousness, the teacher's voice was rasping and highly pitched. Izzie became frightened and cried:

"Teacher, I didn't do it."

The president, seeing Izzie's predicament, called out angrily:

"Why do you pick on that poor boy? He wouldn't do such a thing. I know his parents well, and they are very respectable people."

## WRAPSODY

During the Succoth holidays a Jew was walking through the street, carrying an esrog and a lulav. A worldly friend of his saw him and asked:

"Aren't you ashamed to carry the esrog and the lulav through the streets?"

"What then should I do?" the first replied. "I have to bring them to the synagogue."

"Well, the least that you can do is to wrap them up in a paper," the aristocrat advised. "Must you advertise the fact that you are a Jew?"

"Then why don't you wrap your nose up in a paper?" the first one replied.

## PERSPIRATION

Several Jews were traveling together in a train and, as usual, were discussing their business problems.

"Some people say that I don't work," one Jew called out. "They say that I live on air. Don't believe that, my good people. I live by the sweat of my brow, and I suffer plenty until I earn my bread."

"And I," another said, "I also live from sweat, but not my own. Someone's else.

"What do you mean?" he was asked. "Are you a manufacturer and do you exploit your workers so that you live off their sweat?"

"God forbid! How do I come to be a manufacturer?" the Jew answered. "I am simply a bath-keeper."

## BUSINESSMAN TURN OVER

Two friends went to the city on a business trip and, in order to save expenses, rented a small room with a single bed. At night, when they went to sleep on the narrow bed, they realized they had no room to move arm or leg.

They lay in agony for a few hours and could not fall asleep. Suddenly one got up and started to crawl out of bed.

"Where are you going?" the other asked.

"Where do you think I'm going? To turn over on my other side, of course."

## PIE IN THE SKY

The famous Slonimski, who had a great reputation in the field of astronomy, lived in need during his youth. One day, as he sat absorbed in thought, trying to discover a new planet, his wife approached him and asked:

"What are we going to do, my husband; I need a few rubles. We have nothing in the house."

"Be patient, my dear," he replied. "As soon as I discover the planet our condition will improve."

"Yes," his wife wearily sighed, "it is much easier for you to find a star in the sky than a ruble on earth."

## A THOUGHTFUL BROTHER

A poor man visited his wealthy brother and spent a few weeks with him. Before leaving he collected as much as he could of everything, wished his brother good luck, and departed. The next day he was back again. The rich brother stared at him in great surprise, as if to say, "What are you doing here? You just left!"

"My good brother," the other explained, "I thought

things over and came to the conclusion that when I leave, you celebrate. So I said to myself it isn't really right for me not to be present at my brother's home when he has a celebration."

## THE DISGRACE OF IT

During the night thieves broke into the house of Reb Mordecai. They began to search through the closets and along the walls, thinking that they would find clothes, linens, or silverware.

Reb Mordecai's wife heard them groping in the dark and awakened her husband, whispering:

"Mordecai, do you hear? There are thieves in the house!"

"Be still," her husband warned. "My face is burning with shame! They have nothing to take, and you shout yet. It doesn't even bother you!"

## PROPERLY PLACED

A small town coachman became very wealthy and bought a seat for himself in the synagogue, where only the important people sat.

One Saturday a man who had once worked with the coachman entered in the synagogue and, noticing the place the coachman occupied, asked one of the men in amazement:

"How is it that you allow a coachman to have a seat near the Mizrach wall?"

"Don't be surprised," the other replied. "Those who

314

sit there are all horses, and they really are in need of a coachman."

## ALL IN ONE

A shadchan once inquired about a certain young man as a prospective groom.

"I'll tell you," the other said, "this particular fellow is entitled to a large dowry. He is a very rare piece of merchandise nowadays. A horse that would cost twenty-five rubles years ago now costs one hundred. The highest price paid for a pig then was ten rubles; now it is three times as much. A young man who got one hundred rubles dowry money now gets several hundred. Now figure this out for yourself. How much should one pay for something like this: You can't find a horse in the entire world to compare with him. As for a pig, he is the best of its kind, and to top it all off, he is a young man."

## FISHY RETORT

A poor man came to a house and told the owner that he had not eaten for several days. The rich man, on seeing the other's pitiful expression, gave him a ruble. A few hours later, entering an exclusive restaurant, he found the same poor man eating a large portion of fish. The rich man became furious and asked harshly:

"Is that why you beg from door to door, so you should be able to eat such portions of fish?"

"I can't understand what you mean," the beggar angrily replied. "Before I had the ruble I couldn't eat such a portion of fish; now that I have a ruble I am not allowed to eat it. Pray tell me, when will I be able to eat fish?"

## TALMUDIC WISDOM

A teacher sat with his American pupil and studied a part of the Mishnah,

שנים אוחזין בטלית זה אומר אני מצאתיה וזה אומר אני מצאתיה

(Two men in court hold a coat; one says, "I found it," and the other says, "I found it.").

The teacher became incensed at the pupil's indifference. He wanted the young boy to understand and remember. The boy paid very little attention.

"I don't want to learn such Gemara," he complained, "where two argue over one coat. I know that within a short while they'll probably start to fight over it. My mother always told me never to stay near where a fight is going on."

## VISITATIONS

A farmer came running home one day with news.

"Do you hear, my wife? There is a rumor in town that the Messiah is coming this year. Woe is me! What will we do? I invested so much money in the farm, rebuilt the house, and cultivated the fields. Now we will have to leave everything behind and go."

"Don't worry, my husband," his wife consoled him. "We Jews have gone through so much suffering. We had a Pharaoh, and a Haman, and the good Lord helped us get rid of them. I am sure that he will also help us get rid of the Messiah, too."

## SABBATH LAW

A foreign Jew, who had recently come to New York, saw his friend alight from a trolley car one Sabbath afternoon.

"How can you do such a thing?" the foreigner reproached his friend. "Think of the religious father you have."

"Ah, you are still a foreigner," the other replied. "This is a Shabessdige car."

"What! Are you crazy?" the foreigner laughed

"Well, take a look, then. Can't you see the sign in the car which says, 'No Smoking'? That means today is Sabbath, and smoking is not allowed."

## A DOCTOR'S FEE

A wealthy old man of Krakow, who was a great lover of gefillte fish, was eating his favorite dish one Friday night and was almost choked by a bone in his throat. He could neither disgorge nor swallow it. His life was in grave danger. Dr. Kirschenbaum was called to save him. The doctor hurriedly arrived and found the wealthy man half dead.

With the aid of a small plier he quickly removed the bone. The wealthy man was overwhelmed with joy.

"Herr Doktor," he said, "with the help of God you saved my life. How can I ever repay you?"

Upon which the doctor very calmly replied:

"Just give me half of what you would have given when the bone was stuck in your throat."

## BUSINESS TO THE END

A Jewish storekeeper was lying on his deathbed. His entire family gathered near his bedside. His wife, a sorrowful sight, was crying painfully:

"Jacob, Jacob, have mercy upon us, open your eyes. To whom are you going to leave us? Have pity, and look at us. We are all here around you. See—Morris, Harry, Rebecca, and Sarah!"

Jacob rose with a start: "If you are all here," he demanded, "then who is in the store to wait on customers?"

## DISHING IT

A shadchan approached a carelessly dressed and filthy looking yeshiva boy concerning a match with a beautiful girl who had a dowry of one hundred rubles. The fellow became very anxious, and immediately wanted to see the bride.

"How can you go in such clothes?" the shadchan asked. "Wash yourself, comb your hair, and clean your clothing. When you look presentable you will be in a position to see the bride."

"What if she should not like me?" the fellow questioned.

"If she should not like you," the shadchan replied, "you will always be able to dirty yourself up again."

## A HARD LIFE

A Hebrew teacher visited a father to talk over the instruction of his son.

318

"I am not a novice," he introduced himself. "I've been in this profession for twenty-five years."

"You don't look it at all," remarked the father.

"What do you mean?" the teacher asked.

"You look well. You seem to be quite healthy. Among Jews it is a known fact that after teaching a few years, a good teacher must have acquired either a weak heart or tuberculosis!"

## INSECT CORTEGE

A visitor spent the night at an inn in a small town. During the night he was greatly annoyed by the bed-bugs, and did not sleep a wink. The next morning the mistress of the house asked him how he had slept.

"Not so well," was the reply.

"Why not?"

"I don't know. I found a dead bed-bug in my bed."

"You complain about one bed-bug, and a dead one at that! What harm could it do?" .

"Yes, it is quite true, but the dead bed-bug had a very large funeral, and what a long procession of living, well-fed friends there was!"

## UNKNOWN QUANTITY

In the days of the Jewish philosopher Mendelssohn there was a law in Berlin that whoever wanted to enter the city had to give his name and state his business. At the entrance to the city the official approached Mendelssohn and curtly asked:

"What do you deal with?"

"I deal with that which you do not," Mendelssohn replied. He continued to give the same answer to every question asked. Finally the official became exasperated and cried out:

"You filthy Jew, what do you deal with?"

"With intelligence," Mendelssohn calmly replied.

## GIVE AND TAKE

A talented actor who earned a good salary was always short of funds, because he spent all his money on women. There was a beautiful actress in the same theatre who did not earn as much as this artist, yet was very wealthy. She had many admirers who showered her with gifts.

"It is very puzzling," she once told the highly paid star, "that I who earn only half your salary should possess so much more money than you."

"Yes, my dear," the actor sighed; "that which makes you rich, makes me poor."

## OFFICIAL MADMAN

The overseer of a small town reproached a tailor who was reputed to be very impudent.

"Your children lack breeding," he said. "All day long they shamelessly chase after the town lunatic."

"That is your own fault," the tailor retorted. "What can you expect when you take a common cobbler and call him the town lunatic? How can my children respect him? If you were to accept that position yourself and become the town lunatic, you would observe how my children would esteem you."

## MAN AND BEAST

A notorious imposter would travel to small towns and present himself as a prominent personality, in order to swindle money. One day he arrived in a village and introduced himself as a venerable rabbi. Soon he had many ardent followers who showed him great respect and honor. A few farmers paid him tribute by unharnessing the horses of his wagon and starting to pull it themselves. A bystander who recognized the imposter approached the gasping farmers and said, "My good men, the rabbi is a counterfeit, but the horses are genuine."

## INSIDE INFORMATION

A guest complained to a hotelkeeper, "Your servant stole several things from me."

"Yes, I believe you. There is no doubt that you are right," the hotelkeeper agreed. "Those hotel servants are wicked people. They are all thieves. I know them very well, for I was a hotel servant once myself."

## THE SALESMEN

Two merchants were boasting about their clever salesmanship.

"I could sell you ten times before you'd sell me once," one bragged.

"You are right," the other replied. "For you, no one would even offer a penny."

## TOPSY-TURVY

A Frenchman, while spending a winter in Russia, was attacked and bitten by a dog. In his fury he reached for a stone to hurl at the animal, but the stone was frozen to the ground.

"What a miserable country this is," the Frenchman exclaimed. "Instead of tying up the dogs they tie down the stones."

## GOOD COMPANY

Isaac Mayer Dick, the famous Hebrew-Yiddish author, much absorbed in a problem, walked along the street talking to himself. A friend met him and said, "Isaac Mayer, do you realize that you are talking to yourself?"

"Listen here," Isaac Mayer retorted, "if I want to speak to an intelligent person must you come along and interrupt me?"

## THE HELPER

A poor man awoke one night and heard footsteps in his room. "Who is there?" he called out.

"A thief," was the reply.

"What are you searching for?"

"Money."

"Just a minute," the poor man replied; "I will light a candle and search with you."

322

## MISFORTUNES

"I am a very unfortunate man," Chaim moaned to his friend Moishe. "My first bride died, the second one left me, and the third — "

"Well, what happened to her?" Moishe eagerly asked.

"The third one became my wife!"

## THE BAREFOOT MAN

A *kohen* was asked what his thoughts were while he stood concealed in his tallis, giving the priestly benediction from the *bimah*.

"I have been doing it for the past fifty years," the *kohen* replied, "and there has always been but one thought in my mind, — that no one should steal my shoes."

## BLACK ART

A fortune teller informed a customer that she was going to inherit a fortune of a million rubles. The customer, quite content with the prediction, prepared to leave.

"Madam, you have not paid me," the fortune teller said.

"Since you can foresee the future," the customer retorted, "you should have known that I wouldn't pay."

## BIBLE PATTER

The German poet Schiller, when a young man, enjoyed playing the harp, much to the annoyance of his neighbor.

"Herr Schiller," the neighbor said, "you play like King David, but not as well."

"And you," Schiller replied, "speak like King Solomon, but not as wisely."

## EYE TROUBLE

"A terrible misfortune has befallen me, Zorach," one friend said to the other. "My wife's eyes became bad, and it cost me over $200 to cure her."

"That's nothing, my dear Baruch," the other spoke. "My wife's eyes cost me a good deal more. She cast her eyes on a pair of diamonds, and it cost me more than ten times as much as it cost you."

## TOO CHEAP

It was harvest time, and a landowner did not have enough help. He noticed a tramp on the road, and asked if he would like to work.

"How much will you pay me for the day?" the tramp inquired.

"As much as you are worth," the landowner replied.

"I'm sorry," the tramp said, scratching his head. "I can't work so cheaply."

## RACIAL SATISFACTION

The famous atheist, Berel Lidner of Vilna, was brought to trial and sentenced to a number of lashes. When he arrived home an acquaintance asked how he had felt during the flagellation.

"The pain was great indeed," the atheist replied.

"Every lash left a burning sting on my back. The only thing that gave me courage to endure it was that I knew they were smiting a Jew."

## CLEVER TURN

A Jew and a German were sitting in a restaurant. The Jew ate a portion of fish, and the German ate a portion of ham. The Jew wanted a drink of liquor, and he called to the waiter, "The fish wants to swim."

The waiter understood, and immediately brought him some liquor. The German admired the Jew's clever remark, and called out, "Waiter, the pig wants to drink."

## BUSINESS MEN

A schnorrer came into a store late one night. When the owner saw him he asked, "So late you go to schnorr?"

"Why do you keep your store open so late?" the schnorrer rejoined.

"This is my business," the owner said.

"Well," the beggar retorted, "schnorring is my business."

## DOUBLE ERROR

Two men were traveling in a coach. One realized that his wallet was missing and immediately suspected his neighbor. Soon he discovered that it was in another pocket of his suit.

"I beg your pardon," he said, addressing the other: "I made an error in suspecting you."

325

"We both made an error," his neighbor replied. "You thought I was a thief and I thought you were a gentleman."

## WINDY

At a special gathering one of the guests was holding a long discourse.

"Take a rest," a listener suggested.

"No," the speaker replied, "I am not tired."

"In that case," the listener remarked, "allow us to take a rest."

## JOKES

A visitor entered a home while the owner was eating dinner.

"If you can take a joke," the owner said, "come and eat with us."

"If you can take a joke," the visitor replied, "hearty appetite!"

## UNSPENT ENERGY

Two Jews spent the night together at a hotel. They turned on the table lamp to see how to undress. For some time afterwards they could not fall asleep because the light was glaring in their eyes. A few hours passed, and finally one whispered to the other, "Do you know, Yankel, we should put out the light, — only I am too lazy to get out of bed."

"I thought of that a long time ago," Zalman replied, "only I was too lazy to speak up."

## DEEP ENOUGH

"Tell me, Kalman, do you know how deep the earth is?" one friend asked the other.

"I don't know," was the reply. "Do you?"

"Of course I do. The earth is so very deep, that my grandfather, who went there twenty years ago, has not returned yet."

## NO HONOR

A thief was brought to court. At the trial, the judge said, "It seems that you committed the theft yourself."

"Of course I did it myself!" the thief exclaimed. "Who can get an honest partner nowadays?"

## EXPENSE

A worldly fellow was once asked why he did not go to tashlich on Rosh Hashanah.

"I have paid very dearly for my sins," he replied, "and it would really be a shame to just take and throw them into the water."

## SUSPICION

A farmer was afraid to say "Had Gadya" at the Seder, on Passover eve. He said that the whole story appeared very strange and suspicious to him:

"In the middle of the night a young goat is sold for only two gulden. Who knows, maybe it was stolen."

## LIFE GOES ON

A judge asked a spinster, who had appeared as a witness, her age. Filled with fear she gazed at the judge but did not reply. "How old are you?" the judge insisted. The spinster flushed with embarrassment and still did not answer. The judge, grasping the reason for her silence, called out, "Miss, your silence is only making the situation worse, for the longer it takes the older you are growing!"

## EFFICIENCY

A mistress entered the kitchen and saw the maid standing, eating her dinner.

"Mollie, why don't you sit down while you eat?" she suggested. "You'll digest your meal more readily."

"I can't, madam," the maid replied; "the chair is dusty."

## NO HEALING

A farmer's wife, visiting the large city for the first time, fell and broke her arm. Frantic with pain she ran in search of medical help, and saw a house with a sign reading "Doctor." "Please help me, doctor!" she pleaded.

"My dear woman," the man replied, "I am not a doctor of medicine. I am a doctor of philosophy."

"What sort of a disease is that?" the woman asked.

## VISIONARY

Mrs. Levine admired a fur coat she had seen in a department store, but did not know how to approach her husband for it. Suddenly a bright idea flashed through her mind.

"Do you know, darling, last night, I dreamt that you bought me a beautiful fur coat."

"That is fine," her husband replied; "in your future dreams you will wear it."

## CONGESTION

A young man entered a coach crowded with passengers and carelessly sat down on someone's foot.

"My friends," he called out, "whose foot am I sitting on?"

"If the foot has a red sock," an elderly Jew replied, "it is mine."

## EXPLANATION REQUIRED

One Jew asked another, "Why are four questions asked on Passover, and no questions on Yom Kippur or Rosh Hashanah?"

"Because," the other replied, "to see a Jew wail and moan is not unusual, and raises no questions, but to see a Jew happy—that demands an explanation."

## WEATHER NOTE

The famous philosopher Socrates had an ill-tempered and shrewish wife, who made his life miserable. He would always listen to her calmly and remain silent. One day she raved on more furiously than ever before, and when finished poured a pailful of water on his head. Even this act did not seem to distress him. When Socrates' pupils asked him how he could tolerate so much, the philosopher laughingly replied, "Why are you so surprised, my friends? Don't you know that rain comes after thunder?"

## COMPLIMENTS

A prominent cantor, who was also a witty fellow, was talking to a few of the trustees of the synagogue when a dog started to bark.

"That dog is practicing to be a cantor," one of the trustees said.

"Yes," the cantor snapped back, "but meanwhile he is barking like a trustee."

## RESURRECTION

"Did you write this poem yourself, or did someone else write it?" a critic asked a young writer.

"I wrote it myself," was the answer.

"Really! Greetings! Let me look at you! That means that you are the poet Yehudah Leib Gordon, and I thought that you died in 1892."

## TIGHT SQUEEZE

A tailor made up a very narrow pair of trousers for a professor, which he refused to take.

"This is the latest fashion," the tailor explained. "One must keep up with the rest of the world."

"Yes, but pray tell me," the professor protested, "how

will I be able to run after the rest of the world in such narrow trousers?"

## FAIR CHOICE

Mr. Levy met a friend in the street one day and immediately asked him for a loan of twenty-five dollars. His friend remained silent and would not utter a word.

"Why are you so quiet?" asked Mr. Levy. "Say either yes or no."

"I'd rather owe you an answer than have you owe me twenty-five dollars," the other returned.

## C R U C I F I X

A fire broke out and burnt down the houses of a Jew and a gentile. The gentile was downhearted and walked about as though the world had come to an end.

The Jew, on the other hand, was happy and carefree.

"I can't understand it," said his neighbor. "I am so unhappy. I feel as if I'd lost everything, and you don't even seem to care!"

"I'll tell you," said the Jew. "In your case, not only was your house burned, but your God, too, was destroyed. My God is still alive, so I still have hope."

## A REASONABLE VIEW

In a small village a hog dealer held the position of chairman of the school board. While he was out walking, a school teacher passed by and did not greet him. The chairman felt slighted and said to the teacher:

"You haven't acted respectfully to me. How is it that you don't greet your breadgiver?"

"If you earn your bread from pigs," the schoolteacher asked, "do you greet them?"

## SEDITIONIST

A Jew, walking along the edge of a river in Russia, accidentally fell in. Frantically he cried for help.

Two policemen standing nearby recognized the Jew by his beard and pretended not to hear.

"Let the Jew drown!" they sneered.

The Jew, on seeing the reaction of the police and realizing his own danger, shouted:

"Down with the Czarist regime!"

He was immediately dragged from the water and brought before the police.

## THE TAKER

A beggar came to a wealthy man for money, and when he was refused, threatened to send his brother-in-law to him.

"Who is your brother-in-law?" the rich man inquired with curiosity.

"The angel of death, who took my sister," was the snappy reply.

## WRONG MAN

In a small town in Lithuania a gentile died in the month of Nissan. A Jewish woman who saw the funeral sorrowfully murmured:

332

"If one had to die in the month of Nissan, why couldn't it have been a Jew?"

Note: There is a belief that one who dies in Nissan goes directly to heaven.

## FORCE OF HABIT

A well-known liar of a small town near Vilna was once asked:

"Why must you travel to Vilna all the time, and then tell such stupendous lies about the city, when you could just as well stay home and tell the same lies?"

"If I were not to go there, I might slip up and tell the truth," the liar explained.

## EROTEMATIC

A Jew was summoned to court as a witness.

"Do you know Baruch Finkelstein?" the judge asked.

"How should I know him?" the witness replied.

"Did he ever attempt to borrow money from you?"

"Why should he borrow money?"

The judge became provoked with the Jew's replies and demanded:

"Why do you answer every question with another question?"

"Why not?" the Jew replied.

## NUMEROLOGY

A wealthy, ignorant manufacturer arrived late at a concert one evening, because his wife had taken a long time

333

to dress. When they entered the concert hall, the husband asked the usher what part of the program was being played.

"They are playing Beethoven's Fifth Symphony," the usher whispered.

"It is your fault," the husband angrily nudged his wife. "Next time see that it doesn't take you so long to dress. Four symphonies we had to miss."

## TIME AND ETERNITY

A Jewish woman became acquainted with a famous professor of astronomy at a banquet.

"Tell me, professor, what is the difference between time and eternity?" she asked.

"Madam," the professor replied, "if I should devote all my time to explain the difference to you, it would take an eternity for you to begin to comprehend."

## CRUELTY TO ANIMALS

The commissar of a small town brought a circus into town to amuse the inhabitants. Selig, the sexton, and his wife were also among the crowds of people. They strolled about and examined the animals and circus people with great curiosity. When they came to the camels Selig tugged at his wife's sleeve:

"Look, Sarah," he whispered, pointing to the camel, "—see what the Cossacks did to a poor horse."

334

## DEAD BEAT

A Hebrew teacher asked his pupil why Adam was driven out of Paradise.

"Because he didn't pay his rent," the pupil replied.

## FROM THE GRAVE

A farm contractor told his wife that while he was negotiating with the landowner he saw Berel coming to rent the farm for a cheaper price, but as the latter approached the place the owner's two dogs made a dash to attack him.

"Do you think that those were ordinary dogs?" his wife wisely asked. "They were the spirits of my mother and father, may they rest in peace, who spoke up for us."

## A SMALL REQUEST

In a small town there lived a poor Jew by the name of Yossel Lattutnick, who had a keen sense of humor. Every day he would pray to God:

"Dear Lord, you just give me a piece of bread to eat, and a suit of clothes to wear. That is all I ask of you. Liquor I will buy myself."

## CANINE WISDOM

A Jew visited the home of a friend. The owner's dogs, seeing the Jew enter the yard, began to bark loudly. The Jew became frightened and cried for help.

"Don't you know that barking dogs never bite?" the master of the house asked.

"Do the dogs also know that?" the Jew replied.

## COSMIC WAIT

The famous English author, Sir Walter Scott, met a beggar. Scott reached into his pocket for a coin, and found nothing smaller than a five dollar gold piece, which he handed to the beggar, saying:

"Here is five dollars, but remember to return it to me some day."

"May the good Lord bless you with long years," the beggar fervently invoked, "because it will take long, long years before I remember to return this money."

## MARK-UP

One of the members of the Rothschild family spent a week-end on a small farm in the country. When the owner gave him his bill, he was startled to see the amount he was charged.

"What!" Rothschild exclaimed in surprise; "four francs for an egg? Have you such a scarcity of eggs?"

"Not of eggs," the owner replied, "but we have a scarcity of Rothschilds."

## CORRECT TIME

Late one Saturday afternoon a young man visited his friend and found the wife furiously cursing and shrieking at her husband. The young man carefully lit his pipe and began to smoke.

"You have no right to smoke," his friend chided him; "the stars haven't appeared yet, therefore the Sabbath is not over."

"When hell opens up," replied the visitor, "the Sabbath rest is over."

## CONJUGAL BLISS

A man had a very ill tempered wife with a sharp tongue,who would curse and call him names all day long. One day, while she was in a fit of rage, she noticed that her husband did not answer her. Whereupon she started to swear at herself. Hearing this, her husband seized a stick and began to beat her, saying:

"When you cursed and insulted me, I kept quiet, but when you call my wife such names, that I cannot tolerate!"

## A BAD EGG

Emperor Francis Joseph of Austria visited a prison, and asked every prisoner why he was there. Each one defended himself, saying that he was innocent, but had been imprisoned on false accusations. One prisoner confessed and said that he was serving a sentence because he had committed a theft.

"Such a scoundrel can contaminate all the good people here," exclaimed the Emperor; "throw him out immediately!"

## LESS LOSS

A father and son came to the city of Lodz to purchase textile materials. The son noticed that his father was bargaining more than ordinarily with the dealer. He kept on haggling with him over a penny.

"Why do you bargain so much?" the son asked. "You are not going to pay him anyhow."

"The dealer seems to be a very honest man," the father quietly replied, "and I don't want to do him much harm."

## PICTURE READER

Two illiterate shoemakers went to the country for a vacation. There they met a group of intelligent people, and, in order to show that they, too, were educated, took an English paper and pretended to read.

"Do you know that you are holding the paper upside down?" one said to the other.

"How do you know? You can't read either!"

"Yes, but I can see that there is a pair of shoes advertised in the paper, and you are holding it so that the heels point upward."

## RESIDUE

A woman with a wicked disposition was operated on for gallstones. One day the doctor met her husband on the street. He seemed to be much worried.

"What troubles you now?" the doctor asked. "The operation was very successful."

"For me hardly so," the man sadly replied. "It is true, you did remove the stones, but the bitter gall was left."

## WHO WOULD?

A shadchan took a young man to meet a young lady. "Well, how do you like her?" the shadchan afterwards asked. "See, I didn't fool you. They are wealthy people. Did you notice the silverware on the table?"

"Isn't it possible that they might have borrowed it from a neighbor?" the young man inquired.

"What are you talking about! Such foolishness! Who would trust so much silverware to such people?"

## POLITIC

Dr. Bull, a famous politician and a well known lawyer, was once visited by a small town wealthy man who was to be tried. During the course of conversation the wealthy man kept on calling the lawyer "Dr. Ox." Finally, Dr. Bull asked:

"Why do you call me 'Ox' when my name is 'Bull'?"

"I knew you had the name of an animal," the other innocently replied, "but I forgot what kind of an animal it was."

## CURSED FATE

One holiday, in the middle of the cantor's prayers, a man noticed his friend fold up his tallis and prepare to leave.

"What is your hurry, Reb Kalman?" he asked. "Don't you want to wait a while?"

"What is there to wait for?"

"What a question, Reb Kalman; the kohanim will bless you."

"That isn't necessary. I have a wife who blesses me more than enough."

## A WAG

A young man was walking along the streets of Warsaw when he met an old lady who was a complete stranger to him.

"Mazel tov, dear lady," he called.

"Young man!" the old woman exclaimed, "why do you say Mazel tov to me? I don't even know you!"

"Because this is the first time that I've seen you since your wedding," the young man quickly replied.

## BESIDE HIMSELF

A hassid who enjoyed drinking liquor was asked how one person could drink as much as he.

"What do you mean, 'one person'?" the hassid exclaimed. "You should know that after every drink I take I become a new man, and I am sure that this other man can also enjoy a good drink of liquor."

## CATECHISM

A Jew came to court to become an American citizen.

"Where is Washington?" the judge asked.

"Washington? He has been dead a long time."

"I mean, where is the capital of the United States?" the judge insisted.

"Every state has a capital," was the reply.

"Do you undertake to support the constitution?"

"Have mercy, judge," the Jew pleaded. "I have a wife and a half dozen children to take care of!"

340

## CONSIDERATE

A young man, seated in the front row of a lecture given by Dr. Nachum Syrkin, fell asleep and started to snore loudly. Interrupting his speech, Syrkin jumped off the platform, ran over to the sleeping man, and started to shake him.

"Young man, young man, wake up! Do you think it is comfortable to sleep with your clothes on?"

## SHARP ANSWER

At a convention a prominent lawyer, holding his hands in his pockets, approached the guest speaker and said:

"I must congratulate you. This is the first time I've heard you make such a fine speech."

The speaker looked at the lawyer very intently and quickly replied:

"Well, I, too, must congratulate you. This is the first time I have seen a lawyer with his hands in his own pockets."

## ORDERS ARE ORDERS

A Russian general inspected a division of his soldiers and found them to be very dirty. He issued a command that every man must change his underwear.

"But we have no other clothes," the colonel replied.

"That is no excuse," the general angrily retorted. "You must do as I say. Let the soldiers change their underwear with one another!"

341

## YEARS OF EARS

"How are you, Mr. Kilker?" a young man greeted an aged friend of his.

"Quite all right," replied the greyhead, "only that I am a little deaf in my left ear."

"That's nothing unusual," the young man said, "for a man of your age!"

"Age, bosh!" the old man angrily replied. "My right ear is as old as my left one, and it is still good."

## MAN OF EXPERIENCE

A schnorrer came to a wealthy man for money and acted very brazenly. The rich man remarked that one should not act in such a manner when coming to ask another for money. The schnorrer became very indignant:

"Well, how do you like that? I didn't learn how to schnorr only yesterday, you know. Thank God, it is twenty-five years that I am in this business, and now in my old age I have come to you to teach me how to schnorr?"

## HEAVENLY RULERS

During the reign of King Ludwig XV, the counselors of the various monarchies gathered at a conference. That evening the moon was shining very brightly. The counselor of Austria, raising his glass of wine, drank a toast and said:

"I drink to the health of her Majesty, Queen Elizabeth Maria Theresa, who shines like the moon."

The Russian counselor said:

"I drink to my Czar, who can compare to the sun."

"And I," the English Counselor said, "drink to my king, who is like Joshua who stopped both the sun and the moon."

## A P O L O G Y

A liberal member of the Russian Duma jumped out of his seat and very excitedly shouted:

"It is outrageous! One half of the Duma are perfect donkeys!"

The members present protested and demanded that he withdraw his words and apologize.

"All right, I take back what I said," the member replied. "One half of the Duma are not donkeys."

## SMALLER LOSS

Said one liquor dealer to the other:

"It is very rarely that I sell liquor on trust. But when I do, I charge any price I see fit."

"And I," the other said, "do just the opposite. I charge less when I trust than when I sell for cash."

"What's the idea?"

"The idea is very simple. Often I am not paid back. In that event I lose less than I would otherwise."

## INHERITANCE

A merchant invited an elderly Jew to spend a Sabbath at his home. Friday evening, when they were coming home from the synagogue, a young man followed them.

When they entered the merchant's home, the young man also went in with them.

"Who is he?" the merchant asked.

"Do not be surprised," answered the elderly Jew, "that "I have come here as two instead of one. This is my son-in-law, and I am still supporting him."

## A GOOD REASON

A poor man who was present at the funeral of the wealthy Brodsky of Kiev kept moaning and sighing in a pitiful manner.

"Why do you sigh so painfully?" one of the bystanders asked. "Was the dead man closely related to you?"

"No," the poor man replied, "the wealthy Brodsky was absolutely no relation of mine. That is why I sigh."

## TRUE PATRIOTISM

During the war a soldier deserted his regiment. When brought before the general he was upbraided and called the vilest names for betraying his Fatherland.

"I did not betray my Fatherland," the soldier pleaded. "I love my country, and would even sacrifice my life for her, but I had to run because I despise the enemy so much that I couldn't stand the sight of his face."

## GREETINGS

Ludwig of France was a fanatic Catholic. One day he asked his house doctor, Reb Tobiah:

"Why have I never seen you greet the holy image that stands near me?"

"I once did greet the holy image," Reb Tobiah replied, "but it did not answer me, so I understood that the image didn't consider it an honor to be greeted by a Jew."

The king remained silent, and smiled.

## BOOZE HOUND

A drunkard placed a bottle of whiskey near his bedside before he went to sleep, and said to his wife:

"I am going to sleep, but wake me up as soon as I want a drink."

"How will I know when you want a drink?" his wife asked.

"You know, my dear wife, that whenever you wake me, I will want to drink," replied the drunkard.

## NATATORIAL

A Jew, who was known to like liquor, explained that he drank only to drown his troubles.

"After you drown them, why do you continue to drink?" he was asked.

"You don't know my troubles," he sighed. "You just leave it to them. They are excellent swimmers. I try to drown them, but they swim right up again."

## GOD IS JUST

At a conference of physicians it was revealed that the largest percentage of diabetics were Jews.

"God is just," one of the doctors remarked. "Since the Jew's life is embittered with hatred, pogroms, and cruelty, He at least sweetens his death."

## PERPETUAL MOTION

A schnorrer entered a place of business late one evening.

"You schnorr so late at night?" the owner asked in surprise.

"Don't worry about that," the schnorrer replied; "I also schnorr during the day."

## THE OBVIOUS

A well-dressed blind beggar walked along Park Avenue, with a sign which read:

"Kind people. You may even give me a penny. You have nothing to be ashamed of. I can't see."

## TOO TRUE

A young doctor noticed a new medical book advertised, entitled, "What To Do Until the Doctor Comes."

"The devil with such books," the doctor called out angrily. "Why doesn't someone write, What to do until the patient comes?"

## BLOOD WILL TELL

While taking his patient's pulse, Dr. Eselkopf said, "Somehow, I feel that you think I am a fool."

"My good doctor," the patient replied, "this is the

first time I have met one who can read another's thoughts through his pulse."

## IT IS TO WEEP

A lady of ugly appearance found a little girl crying on the street. "Hush, child, don't cry," the lady said. "Children who cry become ugly."

"Then," the little girl sobbed, "you must have cried a great deal when you were a child."

## ROYALTY

"May I look around in this palace?" a tourist asked.

"Please do," the owner replied. "I will show you everything of importance."

"That isn't necessary," the tourist said. "I was king here a few years ago."

## MEDICAL FEAT

A poor Jew boasted to a friend that his daughter had married a doctor.

"A doctor!" the other exclaimed in surprise.

"Yes," the Jew replied, "he took a hunch off my back."

## LIFE WORK

Two friends who were attending different colleges, returned home to spend their vacation.

"What is your ambition in life?" one asked.

"To live and let live," was the reply.

"Then why are you studying to become a doctor?"

## BIG BUSINESS

Pincus the Melamed told a friend that he had given up his profession and was now dealing in furniture.

"How much furniture have you sold already?" his friend asked.

"So far," Pincus replied, "only my own."

## GET A LOAN

"You complain," said one Jew to another, "that you have no business. I have a business for you that will last a long time. You just loan me a few hundred dollars, and, with the help of God, I promise you that you will have business with me for many, many years to come."

## SATISFIED CUSTOMERS

A visitor in Sing Sing asked the warden if death by the electric chair was not painful.

"Until now," the warden replied, "no one has complained."

## AN EYE FOR AN EYE

"You stepped on my wife's foot. Can't you see where you are walking? Apologize to her immediately."

"Why should I apologize? There is my wife sitting in the corner. Go over and step on her foot."

## REVENGE

A father became angry at his daughter and slapped her in the face.

"Isn't it enough that my husband strikes me—do you also have to strike me?" the daughter cried.

"Yes," the father replied, "let that fine husband of yours know. He hits my daughter; I will hit his wife."

## DUNCE

"Why did you have to stay in school an hour later than all the other children?" a father asked his son.

"Because I didn't know where the Dardanelles are," was the reply.

"It serves you right," the father warningly shook his finger. "Next time remember where you put things away."

## INSECTIVITY

In the morning the innkeeper approached his guest and asked: "Did you sleep well last night?"

"Yes," replied the guest, "I slept very well, but the poor bed-bugs were up all night."

## ADULT TASK

A mother was sobbing loudly over the death of her young son.

"Yossele, my poor soul, when you go to heaven, pray for all of us here."

"On such an errand you send a child? Why don't you go yourself?" her husband demanded.

## HELPFUL

A man was drowning and began to shout desperately: "Help! I can't swim!"

A Chelemer Jew passed by and heard him.

"Is that why you make so much noise? Why don't you get out and learn how to swim?"

## NOT CLEAR

A guest was given barley soup at an inn.

"Did you strain the water?" he asked the mistress.

"Why do you ask such a question?" the mistress angrily demanded.

"Well, there is a barley swimming around," the guest retorted.

## HOW SAD

Why must a cantor, according to Jewish law, be married?

Because he has to pray before the people with a broken heart and a plaintive voice.

## INSUFFICIENT AUTHORITY

The priests of Yekaterinoslav once sent a protest to Alexander II of Russia asking that he intervene and prevent the Jews from erecting a synagogue that would be taller than their church.

"I rule only over the length and width of the Russian land," replied Alexander. "Above there is another Ruler."

## FOR THE DEAD

The sexton of the synagogue called the congregation to order, saying:

"My good people, the president of the synagogue has to say Kaddish today in commemoration of his dead. Let everyone wait for him. After him everyone may say Kaddish."

## IT ALL DEPENDS

A man, after visiting an elderly woman in the hospital, called the doctor aside and asked, "Doctor, is the case critical or is there still hope?"

"That depends," the doctor casually replied, "on whether she is your mother, or your mother-in-law."

## DUST TO DUST

"The rain is worth a fortune," said one friend to another, while standing on the doorstep. "Now the earth will yield all that she possesses."

"May God have mercy on me!" the other exclaimed. "I have three wives there."

## PROMPT REMITTANCE

A Jew was called up to the Torah, and before he began to say the prayer, pulled a roll of bills from his pocket.

"How much is it?" he asked.

"Today is Saturday," the sexton answered; "you can pay the next day."

"I don't know of such business," the Jew hastily replied. "When I buy junk I pay cash."

**351**

## SELF-POSSESSION

A lunatic once caught hold of his neighbor who lived on the second floor, and said:

"Come, let us jump out of the window."

"Why should we jump down?" his neighbor asked. "We can go down, and try to jump up."

"A brilliant idea!" the lunatic enthusiastically agreed.

## ON THE ALERT

A citizen of Chelem came to Warsaw, and wherever he walked he carried a pencil and notebook in his hand. A friend met him and asked what his reason was.

"Well, when I cross the street, and an automobile runs me over, I will immediately be able to mark down the license number!"

## PEDIGREE

A student told his father that he was studying Darwin's theory, according to which, his teacher said, man originally came from a monkey.

The father didn't approve of such teaching and scornfully said:

"Don't believe such idiotic talk. I certainly do not come from monkeys. Maybe you do."

## THE MOST DIFFICULT AND THE SIMPLEST

A wise man once asked:

"What is the most difficult thing in the world, and what is the simplest?"

The most difficult thing is to find one's own faults; the simplest thing, to find others' faults.

## PICKING ON FEIVEL

When Feivel Phist boasted in the synagogue that he had been chosen as chairman of his organization, one wise man remarked:

"It is a well known fact that in selecting peas the wormiest are picked out."

## AND HE BURNED

"Do you think that I have put enough fire into my lecture?" a speaker asked one of his listeners.

"My suggestion is," the other replied, "that it would be much better if you put your lecture into the fire."

## GREAT DIVIDE

A pauper prayed in a plaintive voice:

"O God, give me $200,000. I assure you that I will give one half to charity. If you don't believe me, then divide it yourself, and give me only $100,000."

## COMPARE

The medical doctor heals the sick body, the preacher—the sick soul. The difference between the two is that when the doctor says he is through, there is grave sorrow. When the preacher says he is through, there is great rejoicing.

## SAGE REPLY

Father: "Why do you complain to me about your wife? Why didn't you ask me for my opinion before you married her?"

Son: "Did you consult me before you got married?"

Father: "Did I have to ask you? I married your mother, but you went ahead and married a total stranger!"

## DECADENT

Mistress: "One can hardly depend upon you, Reb Getzel. The apples you sent me are all rotten, and I have brought them back to you."

Reb Getzel: "Why did you have to bother bringing them back? I would have believed you. To me your word is as good as the apples."

## CRITICISM

A young poet came to a well-known critic with a book of poetry. While listening to the poorly written verses the critic dozed off. The poet noticed this and asked:

"How can you pass an opinion on my writings when you are sleeping?"

"To sleep is also an opinion," the critic replied.

## STRANGER

A pious Jew wanted to say the benediction for the new moon. He was standing on the street looking up at the sky, but the moon was nowhere to be found.

"What has happened that the moon has not appeared yet?" he asked a bystander.

"I don't know," the other replied. "I don't live here."

## MATERIALIST

A woman put ten cents into a charity box and whispered:

"Dear Lord, I am giving this ten cent piece as charity in the name of my daughter who is ill. Just as this money is going to Jerusalem, so on the same trip, send her sickness also there."

## PANIC

A man complained to a good friend of his that everything was going against him. He wanted to know where he could go to find a good business, something really worthwhile.

"I'll tell you," the friend replied, "go to the devil. The best business is going there nowadays."

## IRREPLACEABLE

A teacher asked his pupil why he had arrived at school so late that day.

"I was busy at home," the boy replied; "my father needed me."

"Couldn't your father have used someone else instead of you?" the teacher inquired.

"No," answered the honest pupil, "I had to get a spanking."

## SQUEEZE PLAY

Stingy people are like sponges. They sop up a great deal, and, unless one presses hard, yield nothing.

## SLUMBER ON

In the middle of his speech the lecturer began to feel cold. Turning to one in the audience, he said:

"Please be good enough to close the window."

"Let it stay open," one of his listeners called out; "I am accustomed to sleep with open windows."

## MENDELSSOHN'S ANSWER

"Will the time ever come when we will be able to eat together?" a Catholic priest once asked Mendelssohn.

"Yes, at your wedding," Mendelssohn quickly replied.

## WHEN TO EAT

The Greek philosopher Aristotle was asked what he considered the correct time for one to eat dinner.

"The rich man should eat when he has an appetite, and the poor man when he has food."

## SLAPHAPPY

A Jew, walking along the street, saw a man who appeared familiar. He ran over and slapped him across the face. Then to his utter amazement he realized that the other was a total stranger.

"Pardon me, sir," the Jew spoke in embarrassment. "I thought you were my neighbor Chaim."

"And if I were he, would that warrant your slapping him?" the stranger angrily retorted.

"Why should it concern you," the Jew rejoined, "if I want to slap Chaim?"

## BRONCHIAL DUTIES

A father and son stopped overnight at a hotel in War-saw. The father had caught a bad cold, and during the night was seized with a terrific fit of coughing The land-lord, in an adjoining room, was annoyed by the noise and angrily shouted, "Why can't you be quiet? I can't get a wink of sleep!"

The son, vexed at the landlord's protest, cried out, "How dare you shout at my father? Pay no attention to him, father! Cough as much as you want; even all night long. You have the perfect right to do so. We've paid for the night's lodging, so just keep on coughing."

## NATURE'S RELATIVITY

A shepherd reclining in the shade of an apple tree gazed about his surroundings and meditated, "Nature is often so ridiculous in some of the things she does. Pumpkins which are so heavy grow on the ground and the small apple grows on such a strong tree. That is entirely be-yond my sense of reasoning."

While the shepherd was deep in thought, a gust of wind shook the branches of the tree and an apple fell on his nose.

"Dear Lord," the shepherd cried out, "now you have explained it all to me! If a pumpkin grew on such a tree and fell on my head, I'd never get up again."

## INTRUDERS

A wealthy Jew received a letter of appeal from a Home For The Aged. He appointed his secretary to visit the building and bring him a report, to know whether his money would be given for a worthy cause. The super-intendent of the Home led the secretary through the entire building, showing him how content the inmates were and the cleanliness and orderliness of the place. The secretary was well pleased with what he saw, but there was just one thing wrong.

"Everything is fine," he said. "The place is beautiful and the surroundings are very pleasant, but pray tell me why do you need all these old people here?"

## PECCADILLOES

A shadchan discussed a certain girl with a young man.

"But she is lame," the fellow complained.

"That is an asset," the shadchan smiled, "for she won't be able to run after you."

"She is blind," the young chap protested.

"That is just fine," the other exclaimed. "She will not see you when you go out with other women."

"But she is mute!"

"So what?" the shadchan retorted. "I wish that my wife would lose her togue."

"People whisper that her mother is a wicked woman."

"Do you intend to marry her mother?"

"But she is very ugly."

"That is good," the shadchan replied. "You'll have no fear that another will snatch her."

"But she is a hunchback," the chap groaned.

"You amaze me, young man," the shadchan ejaculated, jumping from his chair. "Did you want her to be altogether perfect?"

## ALMSGIVER

A wealthy man, passing a beggar on the street, reached into his pocket for some change. The smallest he could find was a two dollar bill. "Here is two dollars, my good fellow," the passerby spoke, "and you may give me $1.50 in change."

The beggar did not have the difference.

"All right then," the rich man suggested, "take the two, and if I walk by again you will return the change to me."

"May you be well and happy," the beggar cheerfully assented, "and may you never know of misfortune until I return your change."

## ON GIVING

When Professor Mandelstam returned from the first Zionist Congress, he undertook to interest the wealthy men of Kiev in giving contributions for Palestine. He called a meeting of all the prominent men of the city, including the tremendously rich Brodsky. Mandelstam enthused his audience with the Zionist ideal, telling how urgent it was for each to assist in building up the Holy Land.

"Do you mean, Herr Professor, that I should sell all my land and real estate and settle in Palestine?" Brodsky asked.

"God forbid," Mandelstam rejoined. "Are you a patient in all the hospitals to which you contribute?"

## CROSSED WIRES

A Greek conversing with a Jew proudly boasted, "Years ago while digging to develop water power in Greece, engineers found a long wire in the earth."

"What does that signify?" the Jew asked.

"That proves," the Greek haughtily declared, "that we had the telegraph centuries ago."

"That is astonishing news," the Jew agreed. "Engineers dug much deeper than that in Palestine and still did not find a wire."

"What does that denote?" the Greek inquired.

"It shows," the other explained, "that the Jews had wireless centuries ago."

## THE SEEING EYE

Lady (to blind beggar): Here is a ten-cent piece. Give me five cents change.

Blind Beggar: I am sorry, madam, I cannot accept it. It is a Canadian coin.

## CONTEMPT OF COURT

Judge: You must promise me that you will not be found again in the company of rascals.

Defendant: Your Honor, I give you my word that I'll never be seen here again.

## REJECTION

Editor: Why do you annoy me with your poetry?

Poet: My dear editor, I would like to see my name printed just once.

Editor: Print visiting cards.

## RECIDIVIST

Judge: I hope I don't see you here any more.

Thief: Your honor, do you intend to resign from your position?

## WRONG DIAGNOSIS

Customer: This soup smells of soap.

Waiter (tasting it): What are you talking about? The soup smells of kerosene!

## RETORT

Passerby: Lady, I think I've seen you somewhere.
Lady: Possibly. I once worked in an insane asylum.

## CHOICY

A young man was asked why he had married a short woman.

"Because," he replied, "when choosing troubles, one should always choose the smallest."

## NO LEG TO STAND ON

Patient: My legs are weak. What can I take for them?
Doctor: The trolley car.

## GOOD WEIGHT

Yankel: Congratulate me! My wife gave birth to a ten-pound girl.
Butcher: Including the bones?

## CONJUGALITY

Wife: You have a terrible habit, Chaim. You always talk in your sleep.
Husband: You never let me talk while I am awake.

## TIME FOR DINNER

Frequent Visitor: Tell me, Molly, when do they eat dinner here?
Molly: As soon as you leave.

## NAZI KULTUR

German Customer: I don't understand why pork should be more expensive now than before the war.

Jewish Butcher: You can't compare an old time pig with the present pig. Now the pigs have become a great deal more cultured.

## BREAD OF AFFLICTION

German Woman: 3000 marks for a loaf of bread! It is outrageous! Can't you sell it cheaper?

German Baker: If I were to sell it cheaper, the bread would have to be worse. I give you my word of honor that I couldn't make the bread any worse than it is.

## CLEAR ENOUGH

Teacher: If I loaned your father twenty-five dollars, for him to pay back at two dollars a month, how much would he owe me at the end of five months?

Student (quickly): Twenty-four dollars.

Teacher: You don't know your arithmetic.

Student: You don't know my father.

## SICKENING FATE

First Doctor: What makes you so sad, my friend?

Second Doctor: I've had a great misfortune. In four weeks I've lost my entire money.

365

First Doctor: In four weeks? How did that happen?

Second Doctor: I went on vacation for four weeks and left another doctor in my stead. Well, that fool cured each and every patient.

## CONSISTENCY

Judge: How old are you, miss?

Miss: Twenty-five, your honor.

Judge (angrily): You told me the same thing eight years ago.

Miss: Your honor, I am not the kind of a person who gives a different answer every time.

## NIGHT AND DAY

Judge: Where did you get the audacity to break into a house in the middle of the night?

Thief: The last time I was here, you asked how I dared to break into a house during the day. If not during the day, and not during the night, when can I carry on my trade?

## E X C U S E S

Judge: Why didn't you return the wallet to the police station the same evening that you found it?

Defendant: Because the hour was late.

Judge: Why didn't you return it the following morning?

Defendant: Then it was already empty.

## LIKE FATHER

Father: "She has no money, you have no money, yet you both want to get married."

Son: "My mother did not have any money, and neither did you, still you got married."

Father: "Must you copy all our foolish acts?"

## A GOOD BUSINESS

Two tramps stand before a judge.

Judge (addressing the first): What kind of work do you do?

First Tramp: Nothing.

Judge (addressing the second): And what do you do?

Second Tramp: I help him.

## STRIKING RESEMBLANCE

Young Man: Can you tell me why I have no beard?

Barber: I don't know.

Young Man: My grandfather had a beautiful black beard.

Barber: Perhaps you resemble your grandmother.

Young Man: You are right. She didn't have a beard.

## COURT SCENE

Judge: Have you been married?

Witness: Yes, twice.

Judge: How old are you?

Witness: Twenty-five years.

Judge: Also twice?

## COMPARATIVE AROMATICS

Customer: For ten cents, you give me such a small piece of salami, and it has such a bad odor!

Storekeeper: But if I were to give you a larger piece it would have a worse odor!

## TO HER HEALTH

Wife: You're drunk again! I can't stand it any longer! Your drinking will make me sick.

Husband: You won't get sick, my dear wife. I drink to your health eighteen times a day.

## AT THE BAR TOO?

Judge: I've seen you on that bench for the seventeenth time. Aren't you ashamed of yourself?

Defendant: Your honor, I've seen you on your bench for over a year, and I've never criticized you.

## SIMILITUDE

Sonia: How is your husband?

Mania: Like the sun.

Sonia: Is he so handsome?

Mania: No, but just as the sun disappears every evening, so does he.

## DEAR SPOUSE

Wife: Chaim, how do I look in my new dress?

Husband: My wife, I must confess, with every new dress, you become dearer and dearer to me.

## THE MUSE

Editor: What is your business?

Poet: I write poetry, songs, dramas.

Editor: I understand; but what do you do for a living?

## ONLY ONCE

She: You say that you are ready to die for me?

He: What! You still doubt me? Even a thousand times!

She: Then let me ask you to try just once, so that I will see whether you are in earnest or not.

## DISPOSSESSED

Ike: Where have you been?

Mike: At a display.

Ike: What kind of display?

Mike: The landlord displayed all my furniture on the street today.

## NO HANDOUT

Wealthy Man: When a collection is made, I am the first one to put my hand in my pocket.

Neighbor: Yes, and you keep your hand there until the collection is over.

## THE DEBTOR

Magician: And now, ladies and gentlemen, I will hypnotize this man, so that he'll forget his entire past.

One of the Audience: I protest. I don't want him to forget. He owes me some money.

## SEQUENCE

Lawyer: Did you serve your debtor with the injunc-
tion I gave you?
Client: Yes.
Lawyer: What did he have to say?
Client: He told me to go to the devil.
Lawyer: Then what did you do?
Client: I came to you.

## A GOOD PRICE

First Thief: Where did you get such a good overcoat?
Second Thief: From a peddler.
First Thief: How much did it cost you?
Second Thief: Four weeks in jail.

## PROPERTY RIGHTS

Sheriff: I have a warrant to seize all your possessions.
Man: All that I possess is my wife. You may take
her along, with many thanks.

## CLEVER SERVANT

Mistress: Look, Fraidel, we have a great deal of coal
in the basement. How long do you think it will last?
Servant: If you won't use the coal at all, it will last
for many years.

370

## CONDITIONAL SALE

New Customer: I am sure that we will get along well together.

Grocer: Why not? As long as you don't buy on credit.

## KNOW THYSELF

Mother: Before I entrust my daughter to you, I must find out if you are an honest man.

Young man: Please do, and tell me about it, because I too am anxious to know.

## INDUBITABLY

Berel: I tell you that prescriptions and medicines never help.

Schmerel: I know one whom medicines do help

Berel: Who is it?

Schmerel: My uncle, the pharmacist.

## TURNTABLE

Policeman: Why are you standing here? Why don't you go home?

Drunkard: The entire city is turning around me. I am only waiting for my house to pass by, so I can enter.

## AFTERMATH

Wife: You don't bring me candy any more, as you did before we were married.

Husband: Did you ever see anyone continue to feed worms to a fish after it is caught?

## GREATER VALUE

Husband: You aren't even worth that the devil should take you.

Wife: Then I am still worth more than you.

## FOOLISH QUESTION

Landlord: "When do you expect to pay me for the few months rent you owe?"

Tenant: "How should I know? What am I, a fortune teller?"

## TOO SLOW

Sick Wife: "I gave my burial garments to Yankel the tailor, to sew them for me."

Husband: "What! You gave them to Yankel the tailor! Don't you know that fellow keeps a piece of work for weeks!'"

## COMPLIMENTARY

Mohammed, founder of the Islam religion, said the following about woman:

"She is a product of a crooked bone. Do not struggle to straighten her out, because she may break completely."

# VIRTUE

Cast your bread upon the water, and it will come back to you.

*Ecclesiastes* **11**

Three men are praised by God: a pauper who returns what he has found to the owner; a bachelor who lives in a big city and does not sin; a rich man who gives charity in secret.

*Pesachim* **113**

One who preserves one Jewish life is as if he preserved the whole world.

*Baba Batra* **11**

Do not unto others what you would not have others do unto you.

*Sabbath* **31**

Regard the other man's property as important as your own.

*Abot* **2**

The longer and better I know people, the more I love dogs.

While seeking the best, we often lose the good.

*Shakespeare*

Less evil would occur in this world, if it were not committed under the mask of kindness.

The first step towards good is not to do evil.

*Jean Jaques Rousseau*

His face only glows, whose heart is pure.

If a man has begun a righteous deed, let him finish it.

*Yerushalmi Megillah*

A perfectly righteous man does not exist.

*Ecclesiastes 7*

Better a poor man who walks along the righteous path, than a rich man who walks along the evil path.

*Proverbs 28*

Good and evil are two rivers whose waters have inter-mingled so well, that it is often impossible to divide them.

We often stake our honor on a mere semblance of honor.

When two are seated at a table, the superior should be first to partake of the food.

*Derech Eretz Rabbah 7*

The position does not give distinction to man; it is man who gives distinction to the position.

*Taanit 21*

If you want one to love you, demand not too much of him.

Springtime is a kiss that heaven gives earth.

*Berne*

Love, like fire, must be frequently stirred, otherwise it dies out.

*Feuerbach*

Were the cord of life thicker than man, love would know how to turn it into a string, whereon she can play her melodies.

*Mendel*

Woe to him who dies without sharing his love with another. Woe to the cup which is broken without quenching a parched man's throat.

He who feels no love, must learn to smile, or else he'll lag behind.

*Goethe*

Love covers up all faults.

*Proverbs* 10

## BEGGARY

Poverty follows the poor man.

*Erubin* 41

At the threshold of plenty there are brethren and friends, but at the threshold of poverty neither brethren nor friends are seen.

*Sabbath* 32

Man will recognize a wealthy friend and shun a poor one.

*Krituth* 12

Lowliness is an abomination to a haughty man, so is a poor man an abomination to the rich.

*Ben Sira* 13, 20

The poor is despised even by his own neighbor, the wealthy have many friends.

*Proverbs* 14, 20

Blessed is the rich that is found without blemish, and that goeth not after gold.

*Ben Sira* **31, 8**

For the hungry man the bitter tastes sweet. The satiated man loathes even the sweet.

*Proverbs* **27**

It is easier to help a starving man, than one who is overfed.

A poor man is equivalent to a dead man.

*Abodah Zarah* **5**

Poverty is not shameful, only inconvenient.

The poor have few enemies; the rich have fewer friends.

He who scoffs at the poor, blasphemes his Maker.

*Proverbs* **17**

If you have taken a pledge from a poor man, do not go to bed retaining his pledge.

*Deuteronomy* **24**

We should not condemn a thief who steals to satisfy his hunger.

*Proverbs* **6**

When you take your neighbor's garment as a pledge, return it to him before dark; because it is his only covering garment.

*Exodus* **22**

The insignificant needle sustains a large family.

A hungry dog will devour filth.

*Baba Kamma* **92**

To the hungry man every bitter thing tastes sweet.

*Proverbs* 27

All the days of a poor man are sad.

*Proverbs* 16

We should investigate one who begs for a coat, but not one who begs for bread.

*Baba Batra* 9

Better to be a beggar in broad daylight, than a king in constant darkness.

*Homer*

The poor man lacks much, but the miser has nothing.

A spendthrift ruins his heirs; a miser—himself.

A miser acquires enemies, and a spendthrift—friends, who are worse than enemies.

The death of a miser is his only good deed.

"You can't give to everyone," says the miser, and so he gives to no one.

Eat not the bread of him who begrudges giving it.

*Proverbs* 23

The life of a miser is a comedy, which is applauded only when the last act is over.

## THE NATIONS

God was kind in scattering the Jews among other nations. When they are destroyed in one land, there are survivors in another land.

*Pesachim* 87

379

When one Jew is persecuted all Jews feel it.

*Midrash Song of Songs 6*

Tragedy may spring from foreign sources, but a nation will belittle herself only through her own acts. Outsiders may bring harm, but no shame. A nation, like an individual, cannot lose her honor, so long as she remains sincere to herself.

When a nation depends upon the rule of one man, then she is not worthy of existing.

Diplomats are men who are sent on trips to lie for the welfare of their country.

*Watson*

We are living under a government that is set up partly by men, and partly by morning newspapers.

Nations that encourage discoveries have a future for their culture.

*Auerbach*

The life of a city is like a stream, which is beautiful only while it keeps flowing. Should it stand still, it turns either into ice or a swamp.

*Miller*

The smallest country is not too small for you to love it. The greater the hardships you endure in it, the closer it is to your heart.

*Miller*

Each nationality scorns and criticizes the other, and they are all justified.

*Schopenhauer*

380

For countries that are ruled by despots there is no rescue, only ruin.

*Schiller*

## FOLLY AND WISDOM

The friendship of a fool is dangerous.

*Mivchar Hapeninim*

The fool thinks that all people are fools.

*Kohelet Rabbah* 86

A fool belongs to his parents in his childhood, to his beloved in his youth, to his children in his old age, but never to himself.

*Goethe*

The head of a fool never grows gray.

*French Proverb*

The ignorant understand each other best.

He who can hide his stupidity is not ignorant.

One who marries his daughter to an ignoramus is as if he bound her and threw her to a lion.

*Pesachim* 49

The ignoramus thrusts himself forward.

*Megillah* 12

One who replies before he has heard the question appears foolish and disgraced.

*Proverbs* 18

Regret does not mean to add another foolish act to the former.

*Nietzsche*

A whip for a horse, a bridle for a donkey, and a rod for a fool.

*Proverbs* **26**

No one is as poor as the ignorant.

*Nedarim* **44**

Silence is good for the wise man, but more so for the fool.

*Pesachim* **99**

When a fool is silent he is considered wise.

*Proverbs* **17**

It is unfortunate to encounter a deaf man, a fool, and a child. They are not responsible for injuries they commit, but one is responsible for injuring them.

*Baba Kamma* **87**

A fool and a wise man are never harmful. Harmful is only he who is mediocre.

*Goethe*

Some people are similar to a small business, where the entire merchandise is displayed in the show window.

To scoff at the wise man, is nature's privilege to the fool.

Every man posesses a certain amount of foolishness. The art is to conceal it.

He is wise who learns something from every man.

*Abot* **4**

He is wise who anticipates the future.

*Tamid* **32**

He who has much knowledge suffers much pain.

*Ecclesiastes* **1**

A hint to the wise is sufficient.

*Midrash Proverbs* **22**

The words of the wise are listened to with pleasure.

*Ecclesiastes* **9**

The wise man has his eyes in his head, the fool falters in the dark.

*Ecclesiastes* **2**

Better to lose with a wise man, than to win with a fool.

*Proverbs* **29**

The wise man prepares in his youth.

*Proverbs* **10**

The environment of Palestine makes one wise.

*Baba Batra* **157**

Ye wise, be careful of your words.

*Abot* **1**

One mirror is more important than a gallery of our ancestors' portraits.

Nothing shows up a wise man more than his behavior among fools.

Knowledge is power.

*Byron*

The Tree of Knowledge is not the Tree of Life.

*Byron*

It is easier to make a crown, than to find a head worthy of wearing it.

*Goethe*

He who does not become enthused over great things is not capable of creating them.

Genuine intelligence consists in discovering something extraordinary in the ordinary.

*Emerson*

The ink of the scholar and the blood of the martyr are of equal value in the sight of God.

The envy of learned men enriches knowledge.

*Ecclesiastes*

A genius is born, but practice makes him perfect.

*Berne*

Along the road to great things, one should not neglect the small ones.

Clear your garden of its overgrown weeds, and lovely flowers will sprout up.

He who does not think too highly of himself, is often greater than he thinks.

*Goethe*

The wise weigh their words on a golden scale.

For the ignorant, old age is winter time. For the wise, harvest time.

We learn when young, and understand when old.

Do not show the depth of your heart, nor your purse.

He is wise who appears at the proper time. Wiser is he who leaves at the proper hour.

It is as difficult to acquire knowledge as to acquire a vessel of gold, but as easy to forget as to break a vessel of glass.

*Hagigah* 14

Go to the ant, thou sluggard; observe her ways and grow wise.

*Proverbs 6*

One day of a wise man is more valuable than the lifetime of a fool.

There are no inherent ideas. All our knowledge sprouts from experience.

Knowledge is light.

*Proverbs 9*

We do not find learning and wealth in one place.

*Sanhedrin 36*

Not everyone who is wise has bread, and not everyone who is talented has money.

*Ecclesiastes 9*

Doubt is the beginning of wisdom.

He who will not seek knowledge, knowledge certainly will not seek him.

*Midrash Proverbs 2*

Intelligence conquers fate.

It is difficult to discover whether the rich man is wise or dull until he becomes poor.

A man can secure knowledge only by sacrifice.

*Gittin 56*

## BLESSING AND PEACE

Do not esteem lightly the blessing that a simple man gives you.

*Megillah 15*

Balak said to Balaam, If you will not curse them, at least do not bless them.

*Numbers* 23

You shall not curse the deaf.

*Leviticus* 19

It is easier to make peace with a man than with a woman.

*Bereshit Rabbah* 27

Great is peace; it is to the world as yeast is to dough.

*Mesichta Derech Eretz*

## MAN'S LOT

Every bird flocks to its species and every man to his equal.

*Baba Kamma* 92

The great and the small are equal in the grave.

*Job* 3

He who lacks patience to endure dismal days will not see happy days.

He who forces time ahead will be forced back by time.

*Erubin* 13

On this earth one must either die immediately, or live patiently.

*Luther*

## OPPORTUNITY

He who does not desire when he can, cannot when he desires.

*Latin Proverb*

386

All the rivers flow into the sea, yet the sea is never full.

*Kohelet* 1

Man's eye is never satisfied.

*Proverbs* 27

No man dies having attained even half of that which he desired.

*Kohelet Rabbah* 1

If the wishes of all mankind were fulfilled, this world would be unbearable.

In childhood, our crib is too large. As we grow older, the world is too small.

*Schiller*

Every new wish is the beginning of a new disappointment and a new pain.

*Walter*

Man desires that which is beyond his reach.

*German Proverb*

We nonchalantly stroll by an open gate, but fret when it is closed.

*Keller*

The greater the difficulty, the stronger the desire.

*Keller*

Every man has his hour.

*Abot* 3

Granting others an opportunity to do us good, is good in itself.

Auerbach

Strike while the iron is hot.

*Yosef Lekach on Esther*

## NATURE AND DESTINY

I believe that a world order which man conceives, would be as unbearable for him as the one he does not.

Man is influenced by his environment.
*Abodah Zarah 8*

A wolf changes his hair, but not his nature.
*Mivchar Hapeninim*

Children and animals delight us with their innocence. An upright, natural individual is difficult to find.
*Walter*

The passing of day into night occurs in the twinkling of an eye.
*Berachot 3*

God created all men in the image of Adam, yet not one resembles the other.
*Sanhedrin 37*

Nature is the only book where every page contains a colorful content.
*Goethe*

There is nothing new under the sun.
*Kohelet 1*

If Nature were controlled by as many laws as the state, then I believe that even God would not be capable of governing her.
*Berne*

Water is the most powerful liquid. It turns windmills.

Both the fool and the wise man are not remembered. With the passing of time all are forgotten.
*Ecclesiastes 2*

388

The more pleasure we derive from nature, the more we depend upon her.

Generations come and generations go, but the world moves on eternally.

Kohelet 1

Man's soul is likened to the water, his fate to the wind.

Goethe

It is how one meets his fate that counts, not fate itself.

Humboldt

When circumstances turn against one it is difficult to escape them.

Baba Kamma 80

The world is a prison, where a few are executed daily.

The world is a large circle, whose center is everywhere, without a beginning.

Throw a rod up in the air and it will fall toward its root.

Bereshit Rabbah 87

## TRUTH, PHILOSOPHY, HISTORY

Keep thee far from a false matter.

Exodus 23:7

Truth will even sprout forth from the earth.

Psalms 78

Truthful speech is easily recognized.

Sotah 9

389

The truth is heavy, therefore there are few people who can bear it.

*Midrash*

One should not speak with his mouth what he does not mean with his heart.

*Baba Metzia 49*

Sometimes one may deviate from the truth for the sake of peace.

*Yebamot 65*

How can a living man dare to deny his words, when the man to whom he said them is still alive?

*Berachot 27*

The goal of science is truth. The goal of art is joy.

Seeing is better than hearing.

False witnesses are despised even by those who hire them.

*Sanhedrin 29*

That which you promise, you must keep.

*Deuteronomy 23*

One who does not keep his promise is like one who worships idols.

*Sanhedrin 92*

A person does not dare deny a debt to his creditor's face.

*Shebuot 42*

Silence is confession.

*Baba Metzia 37*

390

A lie is like a snowball. The longer it is rolled, the larger it grows.

*Schopenhauer*

Truth is the simplest role to play. Visualize yourself as you really are, and you will never be in fear of losing your part.

Truth loves peace, but not with fools.

*Schopenhauer*

Truth is a fruit that should be plucked when ripe.

*Walter*

In their youth philosophers readily drink from the cup of life. When they grow older they become pessimists.

*Berne*

Philosophy is the sweet child of tragedy.

*Shakespeare*

We wander about mysteriously surrounded by an atmosphere of which we know nothing, nor how it is united with our spirit.

*Goethe*

When man wants to know that which no other man knows, and acts as if he knows, then he is a philosopher.

*Jordan*

The history of the world is the court of the world.

*Schiller*

The history of every civilized country is the story of its spiritual development.

391

## GOODNESS AND GREATNESS

Whether you are good or bad, you are still God's children.

*Kiddushin* **35**

A saloon will not spoil a good man, and a synagogue will not help a corrupt one.

*Succot* **52**

The good learn from the evil more than the evil learn from the good.

Eat and drink to your heart's content, for the world from which we depart is like a wedding feast.

*Erubin* **54**

We are all jesters; we make the sad merry.

*Taanit* **22**

The higher we elevate ourselves, the smaller we appear to those who cannot fly.

*Nietzsche*

Great men have great faults.

## HEALTH, BEAUTY, FORTUNE

Healthy bodies possess healthy minds.

A healthy pauper is happier than an ailing king.

*Schopenhauer*

A learned man should not live in a city where there is no doctor.

*Sanhedrin* **17**

Cure with understanding, not with medicine.

Don't ask the doctor, ask the patient.

*Kiddushin* **71**

The voice is more enchanting than beauty. Beauty adorns the body, the voice adorns the soul.

A beautiful woman is like a delicate crystal glass, which darkness at the slightest bit of smoke.

*Cervantes*

Raphael's painting requires no praise.

*Italian Proverb*

Beautiful women have the privilege to be foolish.

The world is like a revolving wheel, where one is up today, and down tomorrow.

*Sabbath* **151**

The world is like the wheel on the well. The full pail is emptied, and the empty one is filled.

*Vayikra Rabbah* **34**

People can be compared to grass in the field. Some sprout forth, others wither.

*Erubin* **54**

The greatest hindrance to good fortune, is a bubbling fantasy.

*Lambert*

## POWER AND LAW

For a man who desires, nothing is impossible.

*Mirabeau*

One does not fall because he is weak, but because he thinks he is strong.

393

One may rest in his grave, and still rule this world,
Another will sleep, even while he is a ruler.

*Miller*

To conquer one's self is the greatest victory.

Ants feel stronger than the lion when they stand on
his back.

Some people are like zeros.  They must always have
a number before them.

*Balzac*

When a weak man speaks to himself, he often uses
strong expressions.

*Turgeniev*

The powerful man is always right.

Two are better than one.

*Ecclesiastes 4*

In battle he only wins who is set on winning.

*Tolstoy*

Man was given power to protect his own fortune, but
not to seize the fortune of another.

Power is stronger than justice.

*Bismarck*

Strong is he who has a strong will.

*Jean Jaques Rousseau*

United, the weak become strong.

*Schiller*

Man does not lack strength.  He lacks will.

*Hugo*

Law is mighty, but necessity is mightier.

*Goethe*

It is easy to make laws, but difficult to enforce them.

Hate lordship.

*Abot* 1

The wine belongs to the master, but the servant receives the thanks.

*Baba Kamma* 82

## KINDNESS AND JUSTICE

Let no man eat before his cattle have been fed.

*Berachot* 40

In a year of famine Rabbi opened his storehouse of food and announced, "Let all those who are learned in Scripture, Mishnah and Talmud enter; but the ignorant stay out."

Rabbi Jonathan Ben Amram also pushed his way in with the crowd of people.

"My child," Rabbi asked, "do you study the Mishnah?"

"No," Rabbi Jonathan replied.

"Do you study Talmud?"

"No," was the reply.

"Then why should I feed you?" Rabbi asked.

"Feed me as you would feed a dog or a crow," Rabbi Jonathan pleaded, and he was fed.

When Rabbi Jonathan left, Rabbi was worried.

"Woe is me," he moaned. "I've given food to an ig-norant man."

"Perhaps he was your pupil, Rabbi Jonathan," Rabbi

Simeon explained, "and he did not wish to be fed only because he was learned."

The matter was investigated, and it was discovered that Rabbi Simeon was right. Rabbi immediately announced, "All may enter!"

*Baba Batra* 8

Pity not the unfortunate, help them.

Laugh not a man to scorn when he is in the bitterness of his soul.

*Ben Sira* 32, 11

Thou shalt not afflict any widow or fatherless child.

*Exodus* 23:8

In all the land of your possession you shall grant a redemption for the ground.

*Leviticus* 25:24

Better to suffer an injustice than commit one.

There are people who think they have kind hearts, when in reality they only have weak nerves.

Thou shalt not give thy money upon interest, nor give thy victuals for increase.

*Leviticus* 25:37

Withold not good from them to whom it is due, when it is in your power to do it.

*Proverbs* 3, 27

Nothing influences a child more than praise.

Be slow to chastise, but quick to reward.

Good deeds are best remembered when renewed.

*Plato*

If your enemy is hungry give him bread to eat; if he is thirsty, give him water to drink.

*Proverbs* 25

To perform good deeds requires understanding. Fools are not equipped for it.

*Madame de Pompadour*

A noble deed is its own reward.

One should not drink from one cup, and cast his eyes on another.

*Nedarim* 20

Drink water from your own well.

*Proverbs* 5

Thou shalt not covet thy neighbor's wife.

*Exodus* 20

Too much justice is injustice.

*Cicero*

The greatness of man is found in his heart, not in his head.

Man finds a prison not a very sad place, when justice sits with him.

*Latin Proverb*

He who exercises his rights harms no one.

*Cromwell*

Mankind can tolerate a great deal, but not man.

*Berne*

He that pleads his cause first seems just, but when you've heard the second side re-examine the first.

*Proverbs* 18

397

Blame not before you have examined, understand first and then reprimand.

*Ben Sira*, 11, 7

## RELIGION AND FREEDOM

If I obey God, I am tormented by my evil inclination. If I obey my evil inclination I am tormented by God.

*Berachot* 61

It is more important to be hospitable to strangers than to welcome God.

*Sabbath* 127

We receive our religion from God. Its teachings come from man.

Religion grows from the heart, not from the head.

A woman who is disdaintful of religion is like a flower without an odor.

*Heine*

There is only one religion, but various beliefs.

*Heine*

Many individuals ply their religion like a trade.

*Goethe*

The world is a living reflection of God.

He who possesses science and art, possesses also religion. One who does not have both, should have religion.

"I am the first and I am the last," saith the Lord.

*Isaiah* 44

God created man in the image of God.

*Genesis* 1

398

Man should praise God for misfortune as well as good fortune.

*Berachot* 33

A repentant sinner is greater before God than a righteous man.

*Berachot* 37

Correct yourself first, then correct others.

*Sanhedrin* 19

To be God's servant does not necessarily imply visiting the House of God. It means to do Godly deeds.

Fear God, and all those who do not fear him.

We seek God with our intelligence, but find him only with our heart.

God forsakes no people, until they forsake themselves.

Freedom is bread, which a nation must earn by the sweat of her brow.

Freedom is the eternal youth of the races.

Freedom consists in being permitted to do all that will not harm another.

*Schiller*

That government which suppresses free speech, because it cannot tolerate the truth, is like a child who closes his eyes so as not to be seen.

*Berne*

Man is as free as a bird in a cage. He can do things only to a certain degree.

## LIFE, HOPE, HAPPINESS

He who loathes gifts will live.

*Proverbs* 15

Life is a deliciously concocted wine, which must be sipped slowly. If consumed like water, in one gulp, it loses its flavor, and its value remains unknown.

Time changes, and we change along with it.

The greatest loss is the loss of time.

You die against your will.

*Abot* 4

To risk one's life to save another is a noble deed, but we must not forget that our own life comes first.

Your own life takes precedence over the life of your fellow-man.

*Baba Metzia* 62

Regardless of how ugly old age may be, everyone yearns for it.

Hope is the oversoul of the unfortunate.

*Goethe*

Only the hopeful live.

*Holmes*

Hope is the last resort in life.

*Diogenes*

Money lost, nothing lost. Time lost, much lost. Hope lost, all lost.

Brevity is the soul of wit.

*Shakespeare*

Joy is appraised by the memory it leaves.

Happy are only those who are ignorant.

Necessity led to invention, invention to comfort, and comfort to joy.

He who can rejoice today, should not put it off for tomorrow.

*Goethe*

The greatest joy is to give joy to others.

*Byron*

Happy is that country whose rich are not too rich, nor whose poor too poor.

A wise man does not pursue happiness, but that which staves off unhappiness.

Man's happiness consists of successful deeds.

*Aristotle*

Happiness cannot be appreciated when possessed, only when it is lost.

There is no harbor for a boat that sails on the ocean of fantasy. Happy are those who drift on it and reach no shore.

Wine gladdens the sad heart.

*Proverbs* 31

They who sow with tears will reap with joy.

*Psalms* 126

In quest of happiness for others we often find our own happiness.

*Plato*

The happy are rich, but not all the rich are happy.

*Holmes*

Fortune and misfortune depend upon one's character as well as on fate.

Often we travel in search of that which we have near at hand.

*Walter*

It is not difficult to be happy. The difficulty lies in wanting to be happier than another.

Better a dry piece of bread in peaceful surroundings, than much food in a quarrelsome atmosphere.

*Proverbs 17*

Better a small pumpkin today, than a large pumpkin tomorrow.

*Temurah 9*

Happy is not he who has that which he desires, but he who desires not that which he has not.

How can everyone be happy when each one wants to be greater than the other?

*Gorki*

## WORK AND IDLENESS

The virtues of having an occupation ranks higher than the advantage of inheriting riches.

*Tanchuma*

Man is happy when he supports himself from his own earnings.

*Abot 31*

What benefit has man from his toil under the sun?

*Ecclesiastes 1*

402

Skin a carcass in the marketplace and earn your living,
and do not say, I am a great man and it does not befit me.

*Baba Batra* 110

Man slaves for his stomach.

*Kohelet* 6

He who earns his livelihood by his own toil is greater
in the eyes of God than the man of piety.

*Berachot* 80

If a father does not teach his son a trade it is as if he
taught him to be a thief.

*Kiddushin* 28

By the sweat of your brow shall you eat your bread.

*Genesis* 3

The people of Israel said to King David, "Noble king,
the children of Israel need sustenance." King David replied, "Go and earn your living from one another."

*Berachot* 3

He who will not work, shall not eat.

He who tends the fig tree shall eat its fruits.

*Proverbs* 27

Those who eat much and sleep long, possess no aptitude
for great things.

Idleness is more fatiguing than work.

## SPEECH AND SLANDER

Greater is the crime when you have deceived man
verbally than when you've swindled him of money.

*Baba Batra* 58

Weigh thy words before thou hast uttered them.

Beware, lest thou be taken by thine own words.

The tongue is the pen of the heart.

Scholars, be careful with your speech; one harsh word may bring much harm.

*Abot 1*

Speak not your thoughts to others, for if you cannot fulfill them you will be regarded as a fabricator.

The tongue is a sabre that never grows rusty.

Make a balance and weigh for your words and make a a door and a bar for your mouth.

*Ben Sira 28, 25*

A word spoken at the right time is good.

*Proverbs 15*

The tongue is the deadliest weapon in the world.

A sharp tongue is the most cutting instrument, which becomes sharper with use.
Excess talk leads to sinful talk.

*Proverbs 10*

Talk less and do more.

*Abot 2*

A soft word yields a soft reply.

*Proverbs 15*

He who speaks so that others understand, speaks well.

Man uses speech to conceal his thoughts.

Sometimes one speaks and his words pierce like a sword.

*Proverbs 12*

Two things are detrimental to the man who wants to reach his goal: silence when it is time for speech; speech when it is time to be silent.

Walls have ears.

*Midrash Tehillim* 7

It is difficult to speak when one is ashamed to be silent.

He who listens to slander, is as guilty as he who spreads it.

One who speaks slander, one who listens to it, and a false witness, deserve to be cast to the dogs.

*Pesachim* 111

You shall not be a talebearer.

*Leviticus* 19

People eat and drink with one another, and stab each other with their tongues.

*Yoma* 9

## GENERAL

Do not investigate that which is hidden from thee.

*Hagigah* 13

To sail against the current is to invite trouble.

*Berashith Rabbah*

Be not angry when you are humiliated for a trivial act, because often you are praised for a foolish one.

Let another man praise thee and not thine own mouth; a stranger—and not thine own lips.

*Proverbs* 27, 2

A man's character is determined by his purse, his cup, and his temper.

*Erubin 65*

Heaven's gates are never locked to tears.

*Baba Metzia 59*

People resemble their era more strongly than their parents.

*Fleischer*

Courage is the strength of the weak.

A man does not commit a sin when he derives no personal benefit from it.

*Shebuot 42*

Habit is man's second nature.

*Cicero*

Do not throw dirt into the well from which you drink.

*Baba Kamma 92*

All religious groups are liberal and tolerant, as long as they are suppressed, and in the minority. As soon as they come into power, they become even less tolerant than their predecessors.

*Hartman*

Superstition is a natural weakness of man.

*Goethe*

He who marries a woman for money will have unseemly children.

*Kiddushin 114*

Wine and women make the wise foolish.

God has given more understanding to woman than to man.

*Niddah* 48

There is a time for everything.

*Ecclesiastes* 3

If you are not concerned about yourself, who will be concerned about you?

*Abót* 1:14

One who buys a Jewish slave acquires a master over himself.

*Arachin* 30

Efficient lawyers live well, work hard and die poor.

*Webster*

Two kings cannot wear one crown.

*Hullin* 60

A golden hammer can break iron doors.

There is no prosperity in anything that is weighed, measured, or counted.

*Taanit* 8

Before a man eats and drinks, he has two hearts. After he eats and drinks he has but one heart.

*Baba Batra* 12

Women are most powerful when they display their weaknesses.

The last is the most precious.

*Midrash*

Let reason be the beginning of every work, and let counsel go before every action.

*Ben Sira* 37, 16

You shall have one law both for the stranger and for him that was born in the land.

*Numbers* 9:10

One shakes the tree while the other catches the fruit.

Lame legs can hobble along a straight path; but lame heads can not.

In marriage, the wife takes the husband's name; in bankruptcy, the husband take the wife's.

A learned man may attain wealth through his wisdom; a fool will never become wise through his riches.

People make false money; money makes false people.

Very few women will accept the hand of a man when it is empty.

Men would shun one another if they could see through each other.

Diamonds are last to be bought and first to be sold.

Think always before attempting something, but attempt not always what you think.

Bad habits are easier to break today than tomorrow.

The roots of education are bitter, the fruits are sweet.

As cold waters to a thirsty soul, so is good news from a far country.

*Proverbs* 25:25

Understand the pledge before thou hast made it.

***Tanchuma***

Show no kindness to the wicked and the wicked will never come to thee.

*Berashit Rabbah*

If the peasant should become even a king he would not remove the basket from his neck.

*Megillah 7*

If thou hast begun upon a good deed, work it out to the end.

*Tanchuma 80*

One penny in a bottle makes a loud noise.

*Baba Metzia 85*

He is honored who honors others, as it is said: For them that honor me I will honor, and they that despise me shall be held in scorn.

*Abot*

He is wise who learns from all men, as it is said: From all my teachers I have gotten understanding.

*Abot*

Give much or give little, but let thy heart be turned heavenward.

*Berachot 5*

Be moderate in praising a man when he is present, but give him full credit when he is absent.

*Erubin 18*

This nation is compared to the dust and is compared to the stars, because if they descend it is to the dust, and if they ascend it is to the stars.

*Megillah 16*

Woe to the age that has lost its leader; woe to the boat that has lost its oarsman.

*Baba Batra* 81

Love depending upon a thing ceases when the thing is no more.

*Abot* 5

Love him who upbraids thee on account of thy faults; and despise thy flatterer; for the former brings thee to the life of the world to come and the latter causes thee to depart from the world.

*Abot d'Rab Nathan*

The reward of knowledge is understanding.

*Berachot* 6

The stones and the beams of one's house will testify against him.

*Taanit* 11

If a vineyard is plucked of its grapes before they are ripe, not even vinegar can be made of them.

An ignorant man will always be the first to be heard.

*Megillah* 12

The hunchback does not see his hunch.

*Minchah Hadashah*

Truth is heavy, therefore very few can bear the burden of it.

*Abot*

A quarrel is like the burst of water from a small leak —as the water continues to flow the leak increases in size.

*Sanhedrin* 7

410

A proud man is detested even by the people of his own house.

*Baba Batra* 88

He who is proud is a man with a blemish.

*Megillah* 29

If the dog follows his master, it is only for the sake of the bread.

*Abodah Zarah*

Do not do unto thy neighbor that which is disagreable to you.

*Sabbath* 31

The sins a man commits in his youth, will blacken his face when old age approaches.

*Sabbath* 152

The Torah speaks in the language of the people.

*Ketubot* 68

Let the man who has failed in one place, try elsewhere.

*Zohar Vayeshev*

A man can protect himself from his enemies but not from his friends.

*Rashi, Psalm* 58

If a man will not seek knowledge, it will not seek him.

*Yalkut Mishle* 132

Disclose thy secret to one in a thousand.

*Yebamot* 63

The man who causes the deed is greater than he who performs it.

*Baba Batra* 9

A man in whom I had faith raised his fist against me.

*Sanhedrin* 7

411

While the wine is new it must be mixed with the old wine, but when the wine becomes old it can stand by itself.

*Yerushalmi Betzah* 81

In this world a wheel is constantly moving around.

*Sabbath* 151

When in the presence of a convert, even one of ten generations ago, do not abuse a member of the nation to which he formerly belonged.

*Sanhedrin* 84

He who robbed a stranger and died cannot be forgiven, for he has profaned the name of God.

*Tosephta Baba Kamma* 86

The soldiers do the fighting, and the generals are heroes.

*Berachot* 53

Greater is he who has shown hospitality to strangers than he who has accepted the Divine Presence.

*Sabbath* 127

Greater are the righteous after death than during their life-time.

*Hullin* 7

He who has been recalled from sin is greater than he who has never sinned.

*Yoma* 27

Great is labor; it brings honor to him who indulges in it.

*Nedarim* 49

Often a rose is found among thorns.

*Zohar*

The provisions are scanty and the road is long.

*Ketubot* 67

Circumstances determine the cause.

*Sotah* 45

The weaver will take off the spindle the same kind of material he has put on it.

*Kohelet Rabbah*

Woe to him who does not know how to distinguish between good and evil.

*Sanhedrin* 103

Impudence is a kingdom without a crown.

*Sanhedrin* 28

The heart carries the feet.

*Yalkut Vayetze*

Even if a donkey is laden with gold, he will seek his food among thorns.

The camel went and begged for horns, and his ears were cut off.

*Sanhedrin* 100

Between the shepherd and the wolf, the lamb is torn to pieces.

*Tanchuma*

Whisper no secrets in fields where there are hills.

*Midrash*

If a man endeavors to lead an upright life, God will help him in his efforts; if he is inclined to evil, the path is open to him.

*Sabbath* 104

An accuser can be no defender.

*Rosh Hashanah* 26

413

Be not sweet, lest you be swallowed.

*Mivchar Hapeninim*

Compare not the man who is without bread to the man who has bread in his bag.

*Yoma* 18

Do not take an example from simpletons.

*Niddah* 30

If the leaves are bitter, the vinegar made thereof is very sharp.

*Echah Rabbati* 120

Seek a teacher, acquire a friend and judge all kindly.

*Abot*

## CONSCIENCE, FALSEHOOD, PUNISHMENT

There is a difference between him who does no misdeeds because of his own conscience and him who is kept from wrong-doing because of the presence of others.

*Taanit* 15

Conscience is a courthouse, where man is his own plaintiff, witness, judge, and executioner.

Conscience is the voice of the soul; passion, the voice of the body.

*Jean Jaques Rousseau*

Man must be the master of his will, and the slave of his conscience.

Witnesses were created only because of the liars.

*Kiddushin* 65

The penalty of the liar is that even when he speaks the truth people do not believe him.

*Sanhedrin* 89

**414**

Hillel the Elder saw a head floating on the water, and he addressed it, "Because you have drowned others, you were drowned, and those who have drowned you will be drowned themselves."

*Sukkah* 53

## LIFE, DEATH, SUSTENANCE

People are like the herbs of the field—while some are growing up others are withering.

*Erubin* 54

Man is like the shadow; here today, gone tomorrow.

*Berachot* 28

Life is likened to a child's game where the infant plays all day with his toys, grows weary towards evening, leaves everything behind and goes to sleep.

Those who are long dead, are better off than those who are still alive. But better than both are those not yet born.

*Ecclesiastes* 4

As long as there is life, there is hope.

*Yerushalmi Berachot* 9

Better a living dog than a dead lion.

*Ecclesiastes*

After one is dead he is called holy.

*Emanuel* 167

Man comes in vanity and departs in darkness.

*Ecclesiastes* 6

The secret of long life is not to shorten it.

Saving a man's life supersedes the observance of the Sabbath.

*Sabbath 132*

The pigeon said to God, "Let my food be as bitter as the olive, as long as it come from Your hand, rather than sweet as honey and come from the hand of man."

*Sanhedrin 108*

## EXPERIENCE AND MISFORTUNE

One who does not prepare food on the eve of the Sabbath will not have food for the Sabbath.

*Abodah Zarah 3*

He who rents one garden will feed on poultry, but he who rents many gardens will be consumed by the poultry.

*Yalkut Kohelet*

He who eats the pulp of the date tree will be struck by its branches.

*Yalkut Tazria*

If misfortune is destined to strike, it will strike even along the straight path.

Man should not speak of evil, as it gives Satan his opportunity.

*Berachot 19*

Woe to the ship that has lost her captain!

*Baba Batra 91*

Experience is a beneficial school but the study is expensive.

Experience is a gold mine, from whose depths many dig up treasures of life.

## THIEVES AND ENEMIES

Even the thief prays to God when he is about to commit a crime.

*Berachot* 23

Thieves adhere to the laws of honesty when dividing their loot.

*Dostoyevsky*

He who steals from a poor man blasphemes his Creator.

*Proverbs* 14

The broken lock invites the thief.

*Sukkah* 26

Seven friends cannot contribute as much joy, as one enemy can contribute harm.

We say to the bee: We want neither your honey nor your sting.

*Bemidbar Rabbah* 20

Man's enemies are often the people of his own house.

*Micah* 7

He who cannot tolerate his enemies, is not worthy of his friends.

Beware of your friend's enemy, as you would of your enemy's friend.

## ART AND FAME

The flute which affords sweet music to kings, is not appreciated by cobblers.

*Yoma* 20

417

Music speaks to the deaf, heals the sick, and inspires the aged.  Music penetrates the clouds and reaches the heart of our Creator.

Music is the language of passion.

*Wagner*

The human voice is the oldest and most beautiful organ of music.  Music must be thankful to it for its very existence.

*Wagner*

Music is an international language in which one soul converses with the other.

Art is not the bread, but the wine of life.

The artist must serve his guests golden apples on silver platters.

*Goethe*

An artist's duty is to bring light into the depths of man's soul.

*Schumann*

Some people are famous, and some deserve to be famous.

*Lessing*

Some achieve fame for what they've attained; others, for what they've ignored.

*Grimm*

## THE SELF

Envy and wrath shorten a man's days and care brings old·age before its time.

*Ben Sira* **30:24**

418

Envy not the glory of a sinner, for thou knowest not what shall be his defeat.

*Ben Sira* 9, 11

To envy, is to feel inferior.

We are often envied by those who are less fortunate than we.

People are prone to throw mud on those who are superior to themselves.

*Cervantes*

When you portray your own egotism, remember the egotism of your listeners.

*Fiermon*

We are all egotists in our most sorrowful and painful moments.

Many love those qualities in themselves which they detest in others.

We usually consider a person wise who agrees with our opinion.

Judge not a pitcher by its exterior but by its interior.

*Abot* 4

A man sees everybody's faults but his own.

*Negaim* 2

A man is judged in the manner in which he judges others.

*Sanhedrin* 100

Self-depreciation is more distasteful than self-appreciation.

*Shakespeare*

419

That which we laud in the morning, we criticize at night.

*Frederick the Great*

Do not point out in another a defect which your possess yourself.

*Baba Metzia 59*

Judge your friend favorably.

*Shevuot 30*

Man observes everyone's faults but his own.

*Negaim 2*

A man should not speak of his friend's good qualities, for in speaking of the good qualities he may mention the bad ones.

*Baba Batra 165*

If we had no faults, we would not search for them in others.

*Fenelon*

Better is the criticism of a wise man, than the praise of a fool.

*Ecclesiastes 7*

Before passing judgment examine thyself.

*Ben Sira, 18:20*

Blame not others for thy faults.

*Baba Metziah 59*

Man is measured as he measures others.

*Sotah 8*

## PRIDE AND DOUBT

The glory of God is man, and the glory of man is his dress.

*Derech Eretz*

420

If we were not proud ourselves, we would never complain about the pride of others.

Doubt destroys everything, even one's self.

*Walter*

Doubt is the school of truth.

*Bacon*

Doubt is more contagious than belief.

He who disobeys his parents in his youth, will obey the executioner when mature.

*German Proverb*

He who has self-confidence, wins the confidence of others.

*Goethe*

Man understands life only when he has self confidence.

*Goethe*

Do nothing without counsel, and when thou hast once done, repent not.

*Ben Sira 32, 19*

## SUCCESS AND HONOR

This world is like the buckets of the well: while the full bucket is being emptied of its water, the empty one, at the bottom of the well, becomes filled.

*Yalkut Behar*

This world is like a ladder: While one climbs up, the other goes down.

If you strive for too much, you may obtain nothing. If you strive for little, you may obtain something.

*Hagigah 17*

421

Successful is he who hides his faults, not he who flaunts his talents.

Have self-respect, if you want others to respect you.

*Latin Proverb*

We pay our greatest respect to people when we listen to their speech.

*Goethe*

It is more shameful to lose honor, than not to possess it.

He who seeks honor—honor will flee from him. He who flees from honor—honor will seek him.

*Erubin* 13

A worthy man must not feel inferior.

*Taanit* 15

The honor bestowed upon prominent individuals must be appraised by the methods they utilized in obtaining it.

Not all that is permitted, is honorable.

## FAMILY AND OLD AGE

'Tis a wise father who knows his own child.

*Shakespeare*

Only one thing on earth is more beautiful and sacred than a wife—a mother.

The heart of a mother is the school of her child.

Henry Ward

A mother, when toiling for her child, is toiling for herself. Every accomplishment for her child beautifies and adorns her own being.

422

Children are God's blessing.

*Psalms*

Childhood knows no past or future, only the present.

The child repeats words which his parents utter.

*Succoth* 56

As the fingers of the hand are unlike so are often children of the same parents.

*Pesachim* 112

Everyone desires long life, no one old age.

*Swift*

Old age hurries upon him who commits adultery.

*Sabbath* 152

## FEAR AND SUFFERING

No one is free from suffering.

*Bereshith Rabbah*

Better a fearful end, than an endless fear.

*Schiller*

An elephant fears the fly.

*Sabbath* 77

Fear only him who fears you.

*Persian Proverb*

Worry not for the morrow, for you know not what the morrow may bring.

*Ben Sira*

There is time enough for worry when the worry comes.

*Berachot* 9

When I speak of my troubles, I feel easier.

*Job* 32

423

Ever since the temple was destroyed God has not been happy.

*Abodah Zarah* 4

The latter troubles makes us forget the former.

*Berachot* 3

No misfortune is as great as its anticipation.

You can run away from your country, but not from yourself.

He who interferes makes things worse.

*Sanhedrin* 29

There are three classes of people whose lives are miserable: the good-natured, the ill-tempered, and the melancholy.

*Kallah* 10

Weep not for the dead; weep for the living who suffer.

*Jeremiah* 22

Man is born to suffer.

*Job* 5

Even at the point of the sword one should pray for mercy.

*Berachot* 10

Trouble shared by many is half a consolation.

*Sifre Debarim* 2

There is not a man who does not suffer.

*Midrash*

If it were not for the dark, one would never appreciate the light.

*Zohar*

A small pain is cured by means of a larger one.

*Shakespeare*

There is no pain or suffering, either physical or spiritual, that time does not weaken, or death heal.

*Cervantes*

He who desires the sweet, must often taste the bitter.

Man can bear his sorrow quietly, but not his joy.

*Goethe*

Gold is tested with fire; a heart with suffering.

*Schiller*

In all Israel's afflictions, God suffers.

*Isaiah* 63

One should not beget children in years of famine.

*Taanit* 11

Sorrow kills the strongest of the strong.

*Sanhedrin* 100

## RICHES AND SUCCESS

Whether it be good or bad, lick the bone which has fallen to thy lot.

*Ben Sira*

A cucumber at hand is better than a pumpkin in the future.

*Ketubot* 83

It is better to eat garlic and have a peaceful mind than to dine on turkey and be burdened with a troubled conscience.

*Pesachim* 80

He is wealthy who is content with his lot.

*Abot* 4

425

Better is the life of a poor man under a shelter of logs than luxurious fare in another man's house.

*Ben Sira* 29, 22

Better one captured bird than a hundred in the air.

*Kohelet Rabbah* 4

It is difficult to be content with little, but more so with much.

A piece of gold may be found in a heap of refuse.

*Baba Metzia* 17

He is rich who enjoys what he possesses.

*Sabbath* 25

Satiety deprives the rich of sleep.

*Ecclesiastes* 5

It is good to attach ourselves to the rich.

*Baba Kamma* 92

There are many who despise wealth, but few who are willing to part with it.

He that loveth silver shall not be satisfied with silver.

*Ecclesiastes* 5, 10

Wealth obtained by vanity shall be diminished, but he that gathereth by labor shall have increase.

*Proverbs* 13, 11

Money will proclaim an ignorant man leader of a community.

Money is a cruel master, but a very obedient servant.

*Bacon*

Animals betray their nature when they see blood; men, when they see money.

*Schopenhauer*

426

The rich are overfed, but not well fed.

More pleasant is a man without riches, than riches without a man.

*Boccaccio*

Money is ideal, if only people knew how to utilize it.

The tears of an heir mask his laughter.

One cannot acquire riches without doing others injustice.

Much wealth, much worry.

*Abot 2*

A belated good fortune is like a beautiful autumn. It yields great joy.

Money is a tool to the rich, and a goal to the poor.

When a man is wealthy, he is an Israelite. When poor, a Jew.

*Heine*

Wealth is like water. The more one drinks, the thirstier he becomes.

*Schopenhauer*

Genuine wealth does not consist in earning much, but in spending it wisely.

*Napoleon*

When the end is good, all is good.

*Lekach Tov Bereshit*

. Drop by drop the bucket is filled.

*Bemidbar Rabbah 17*

## WICKEDNESS

The maker of the arrow will be killed by it; he will be paid by the work of his own hands.

*Pesachim* 28

Woe to the wicked and woe to his followers.

*Ben Sira*

Four kinds of men are repulsive: a poor man who is proud, a rich man who pleads poverty, an old man who is licentious, a leader who is abusive.

*Pesachim* 113

The bread of the needy is the life of the poor; he that depriveth him thereof is a man of blood.

*Ben Sira* 34, 21

He that constructs his house with other men's money is like one that gathers himself stones against winter.

*Ben Sira* 21, 8

One is righteous and lives in misery; another is wicked and lives in prosperity.

*Berachot* 7

To plan an evil deed is worse than the deed itself.

*Yoma* 29

One who deceives his fellowman deceives his Maker.

*Kallah* 10

He who destroys life is as if he had destroyed the whole world.

*Sanhedrin* 37

Even before one is dead, another gets ready to take over his house.

*Baba Batra* 91

A man who has no conscience deserves no pity.

*Sanhedrin* 92

Woe to the wicked, and woe to his neighbor!

*Sukkah* 56

When the stomach is full one seeks bad company.

*Berachot* 37

The path of modern learning leads from humanity, to nationality, to bestiality.

The greater the man, the greater are his evil inclinations.

*Sukkah* 52

Four classes of men will not be accepted by God: the scoffers, the liars, the flatterers, and the slanderers.

*Sanhedrin* 103

One who associates with the unclean becomes unclean himself.

*Baba Kamma* 92

Do not say: "As he has done to me so shall I do to him."

*Proverbs* 24

When one spits upwards it falls down on his own face.

*Kohelet Rabbah* 7

Do not try to pacify a person when his anger is still burning.

*Berachot* 7

Anger is the weapon of the weak.

The end of anger is the beginning of regret.

When man is enraged he has no respect even for God.

*Nedarim* 22

## CHARITY AND FRIENDSHIP

He who gives a small contribution of his own is better than he who robs the people and gives a large contribution.

*Kohelet Rabbah* **84**

Even he who is dependent upon charity should give charity.

*Gittin* **7**

Man has two hands, so that he may give with one what he obtains with the other.

Let not thine hand be stretched out to receive, and closed when thou shouldst repay.

*Ben Sira* **4, 31**

In giving charity, let not your left hand know what your right hand is doing.

It is better not to promise, than to promise and not pay.

*Ecclesiastes* **5**

Who gives charity after death, gives not his own, but that of his heirs.

*Eschenbach*

To have and not to give is in some instances worse than stealing.

*Eschenbach*

It matters not whether one gives much or little, so long as it is given wholeheartedly.

*Shebuot* **14**

Prepare your Sabbath in a week-day fashion, rather than beg of a fellowman.

*Sabbath* **118**

430

He who accepts charity, though not in need of it, will eventually need it.

*Ketubot 68*

Friendship can grow strong only with age and deep understanding.

*Cicero*

Loneliness is beautiful, but we always need someone with whom to discuss its beauty.

Friendship frequently meanders off into love. Love never into friendship.

*Byron*

A friend is one soul existing in two bodies.

*Aristotle*

A false friend is deadlier than an honest enemy.

*Ben Sira*

Love appears to be most delicate of all human instincts, which even the blind and the mute can sense. Sincere friendship is more beautiful and tender than love.

God, protect me from my friends. From my enemies I will protect myself.

To make peace with an enemy is like patching a broken mirror.

He who seeks a faultless friend remains friendless.

*Turkish Proverb*

False friends are like wandering birds. They appear in fair weather, and disappear in bad.

*Ben Sira*

431

.Friendly people are blessed at birth by nature with the key to strange hearts.

You may quarrel with your friend, but never reveal what he has confided to you.

*Proverbs* **25**

One should rather hurl himself into a burning furnace than insult another in public.

*Ketubot* **68**

Do not visit your friend too often, because he may grow tired of you and detest you.

*Proverbs* **25**

Love thy neighbor as thyself.

*Leviticus* **19**

Receive every man with a smile.

*Abot* **1**

Be not joyful among the sorrowing; be not sorrowful among the joyous.

*Kallah* **10**

As water reflects the face, so does one heart reflect the other.

*Proverbs* **27**

A friend is often more attached than a brother.

*Proverbs* **18**

It is easy to gain an enemy, but it is difficult to gain a good friend.

*Yalkut Vaethanan*

He who prays to God for a friend who is in need, when himself in need, God will help him first.

*Baba Kamma* **92**

When you are in your friend's orchard you may eat to your heart's content, but put nothing in your pocket.

*Deuteronomy* **23**

On the threshold of wealth there are always brothers and friends. On the threshold of poverty there are neither brothers nor friends.

*Sabbath* **32**

Not without cause did the raven join the crow, for they are one of a kind.

*Baba Kamma* **92**

Better a close neighbor, than a distant brother.

*Proverbs* **27**

A man should not segregate himself from society.

*Berachot* **47**

A sincere friend is a strong defense; and he that has found him has found a treasure.

*Ben Sira* **18:15**

He who disgraces his friend in the presence of others, is as if he sheds blood.

*Baba Metzia* **58**

# BIOGRAPHIES

## JACOB DAVID AMSHINOVER

Rabbi Jacob Amshinover (Amshinover Rabbi) was a pupil of Reb Shloime Laib Lentshner and a grandson of Reb Isaac Worker and Reb Ezekiel Kozenizer. He died in Warsaw, December 3, 1864.

## ARIEH LAIB

Rabbi Arieh Laib (Shaagas Arieh) was born in Lithuania in 1695. He was a brilliant and intellectual man, author of the book "Shaagas Arieh." He served as rabbi and headmaster of the yeshivah in the city of Minsk. He died in the French city of Metz on June 23, 1785.

## ISRAEL BAAL SHEM TOV

Rabbi Israel Baal Shem Tov was founder of modern hassidism, which originated in the Ukraine and then spread throughout the world.

The Baal Shem Tov died on the 2nd day of Shavuoth in the year 1760.

## LEVI ISAAC BERDITCHEVER

Rabbi Levi Isaac Berditchever was noted for his benevolence and his defence of the Jews. He suffered because

**434**

of his public interpretations of hassidism though his book "Kedushoth Levi" was accepted by Jews throughout the world. Reb Levi Isaac Berditchever died October 22, 1810.

## NAFTALI ZEVI YEHUDAH BERLIN

Rabbi Naftali Zevi Yehudah Berlin, known as Reb Hirsh Laib, was born in Meer in 1817. He was headmaster of the yeshivah of Wolozin. Hundreds of prominent scholars were his students. His art of teaching was similar to that of the Vilner Gaon. Reb Hirsh Laib died in Warsaw, August 10, 1873.

## SIMCHA BUNIM OF PSYCHA

Rabbi Simcha Bunim was known as the Holy Jew of Psycha. He studied hassidism under most promient teachers, among them the Lubliner Chozeh, the Kozinitzer Maggid, Reb Moishe Laib Sossover, and Reb Isaac Vorker. Among his disciples were Isaac Meyer of Ger. He wrote "Kol Simcha," a commentary on the Torah. He died in 1726.

## ELIAHU (ELIJAH)

Rabbi Eliahu (Vilner Gaon) was born in Seltz, April 23, 1720. He was considered the greatest genius of modern Jewry. His one purpose in life was study of the Torah and all related knowledge. Hassidism arose during his era; and he proved one of its strongest opponents. Reb Eliahu died in Vilna, October 9, 1797.

# CHAIM HALBERSTAM

Rabbi Chaim Halberstam is known as the founder, of the Sandzer Dynasty. He was an idealist who believed that the purpose of every rabbi was to study and to divide the earnings of his rabbinate among the poor. He died April 19, 1876.

# YOM TOV LIPMAN HALPERN

Rabbi Yom Tov Lipman Halpern was known as Lipele Bialystoker. He is the author of the famous book "Oneg Yom Tov." He died in 1882.

# ISRAEL MEYER KAGAN

Rabbi Israel Meyer Kagan, known as "Hafetz Hayyim," is the author of numerous books on Jewish laws and customs. He was born in 1837 and died in 1933.

# JACOB KRANZ

Reb Jacob Kranz (Dubner Maggid) was born in a city near Vilna in the year 1741. He is famous throughout the world for his sharp parables. His many books were sold in tremendous quantities. He is best known for the "Ohel Jacob," a commentary on the Torah. Jacob Kranz was a preacher in Dubno for eighteen years, where he was given the name "Dubner Maggid." He died in Zamosht, December 19, 1804.

# ELIMELECH LIZENSKER

Rabbi Elimelech Lizensker (Rabbi Elimelech) was author of "Noam Elimelech," a book on the Torah. He was a pupil of Reb Ber Mezritscher, who was one of the first followers of Reb Israel Baal Shem Tov, first hassidic leader. Reb Elimelech, together with his brother Reb Zusha of Hanipola, were refugees for a long time, until he decided to settle in the Galician city of Lizensk, where he died in 1786.

# MEYER LAIBISH MALBIM

Rabbi Laibish Malbim (The Malbim) was born in Volotschinsk, Poland. He was an outstanding genius of his era, but endured much hardship due to his enemies, wandering about and serving as rabbi in various communities. He wrote "Ha'Torah Ve'Hamitzvah," which was sold in many editions. Reb Meyer Laibish Malbim died at 65 in Koenigsberg, September 18, 1879, the first day of Rosh Hashanah. He had become ill while on his way to take the position of rabbi of Kiev, Russia.

# BERISH MEISELS

Rabbi Berish Meisels was born in 1800 to a very wealthy family. He served as Rabbi of Krakow for many years, and when he lost his fortune, became Rabbi of Warsaw, where he remained until his death. An ardent patriot of the Polish government, he helped spread propaganda during the Polish revolution of 1863. The Poles still mention his name with reverence. He died February 16, 1870.

## ELIAHU CHAIM MEISEL

Rabbi Eliahu Chaim Meisel was born in Horodok, Vil-na, in 1791. He was for many years Rabbi of Lodz, where he devoted much time and energy in influencing others to aid the Jews. He died in 1912.

## MENACHEM MENDEL

Rabbi Menachem Mendel (Mendele Kotzker) was founder of the famous hassidic dynasty marked by indi-vidual ideas of hassidism. He was always concerned with the tragic fate of the Jewish people, and his attempts to alleviate their misfortunes brought him to such a state of disappointment that he became a recluse during the latter part of his life and refused to see his followers. Rabbi Menachem Mendel died on January 27, 1859.

## ISAAC MEYER

Rabbi Isaac Meyer of Ger was a pupil of Reb Mendele Kotzker and a follower of his hassidic teachings. He was author of "Chidushe Harim," a commentary on the Talmud, and founder of the Gerer dynasty. Reb Isaac Meyer died March 10, 1866.

## BER MEZRITCHER

Rabbi Ber Mezritscher was a student of the Baal Shem Tov. After the latter's death the Mezritscher replaced him in hassidism. He died at 61 in the year 1771.

438

## SAMUEL MOHILEVER

Rabbi Samuel Mohilever was born in Halubaki, 1824. During the latter part of his life he was Rabbi of Bialystok. He was one of the first rabbis to devote his entire life to the upbuilding of Palestine. Rabbi Samuel Mohilever died in Bialystok in 1898.

## MOSES ISAAC

Reb Moses Isaac (Kelmer Maggid) was born in the city of Slonim, Poland, in 1828. In 1850 he became the preacher of Kelm, from where he derived his name. He preached in the city of Zager in 1853 and in Ashmino in 1858. In his sermons the Kelmer Maggid always fright- ened his audience with horrible legends and pictures of the next world. Modern scholars ridiculed his stories, which were filled with folklore and devout ecstasy. He died in Lida, Poland, in 1900.

## ISRAEL PIKEVER

Rabbi Israel Pikever (Pikever Rabbi) was the son of Rabbi Levi Isaac Berditchever. He studied hassidism un- der all the great rabbis of his era. Walking in the foot- steps of his father, he continually strove to encourage and aid the Jewish people.

## ISRAEL REZHINER

Rabbi Israel Rezhiner was born on September 23, 1797. He was founder of the Sadigurer hassidic dynasty, which later spread to various Galician and Romanian cities, situated near the Russian border. His conception of hassidism was that the rabbi should assume the role of one who is worthy and entitled to luxuries. Due to these beliefs, heated controversies arose after his death with the dynasty of the Sandzer Zaddik, who regarded material comforts as utter foolishness. Rabbi Israel Razhiner was a grandson of Reb Ber Mezeritsch. He died October 9, 1850.

## SHALOM ROKEACH

Rabbi Shalom Rokeach of Beltz (Beltzer Rabbi) was a pupil of Uriel Strelisker and the Lubliner Rabbi Chozeh. He learned his hassidism from them. He was the first of a rabbinical family which was to remain in Beltz until the first World War. He died September 10, 1855

## ISRAEL SALANTER

Rabbi Israel Salanter was born in 1810 in the city of Kovno. He was the greatest Jewish moralist of the 19th century. He became leader of Rameiles' yeshivah in Vilna, where he later resigned to found his own yeshivah. He died in Koenigsberg in 1883.

## JOSHUA ISAAC SHAPIRO

Rabbi Joshua Isaac Shapiro (Eisel Chariff) was rabbi of the city of Slonim in Poland. He was the author of several important books. Eisel Chariff died in the year 1873.

# JACOB DAVID SLUTZKER

Rabbi Jacob David Slutzker was a prominent rabbi in the city of Slutzk. He wrote the well known commentary on the Jerusalem Talmud. Later he arrived in America, where he served as rabbi in Chicago. Several years thereafter he left for Palestine, where he died at Safed in 1910.

## MOISHE SOIFER

Rabbi Moishe Soifer (Chasam Soifer) was born in Frankfurt in 1763. He was rabbi and headmaster of the yeshivah of Pressburg, Hungary, where thousands of students from all parts of the world studied; many became famous rabbis. At that time religion took a turn towards Reform, and Rabbi Moishe Soifer was always on guard to strengthen the orthodox belief. The Chasam Soifer died in Pressburg, October 3, 1839.

## SIMON SOIFER

Rabbi Simon Soifer was born in Hungary in 1821, son of the Chasam Soifer. He was Rabbi of Krakow for twenty-three years. He was an adviser to the Austrian Parliament in 1879. He also organized Jewish Orthodoxy under the name "Machzike Hadas." Rabbi Simon Soifer died in Krakow, March 26, 1883.

## JOSEPH BER SOLOVEITCHIK

Rabbi Joseph Ber Soloveitchik was born in Niesveszh in 1828. He was headmaster of the yeshivah of Wolozin for many years. In 1858 he resigned from his position so that Rabbi Hirsh Laib Berlin could take his place. He was Rabbi of Brisk in 1878, and was a devoted Zionist. In 1889 he organized a pioneer group for Palestine, dying in Brisk in 1892.

## CHAIM SOLOVEITCHIK

Rabbi Chaim Soloveitchik was born in Brisk in 1853. He later became headmaster in Wolozin. In 1892 he took the place of his father as Rabbi of Brisk, where he remained until his death in 1919.

## MOSHE TEITELBAUM

Rabbi Moshe Teitelbaum was born in Primishla, Galicia, in the year 1759. He was the author of several outstanding works, including "Yismach Moshe," a commentary on the Torah, and "Tefillah L' Moshe," a commentary on the Psalms. He died in Satoralyauhely, Hungary in 1841, after serving as rabbi there for three years.

RABBENU SHLOIME YITZHAKI
(Rashi)

RABBI ISRAEL BAAL SHEM TOV

RABBI CHAIM SOLOVEITCHIK

MOSHE BEN MAIMON (Rambam)

RABBI ELIAHU (Elijah Vilna)

RABBI MOSHE SOIFER

RABBI JOSEPH BER SOLOVEITCHIK

RABBI ISRAEL MEYER KAGAN
(Hafetz Hayyim)

RABBI ABRAHAM ISAAC COOK    RABBI BER MEZRITSCHER

DON ISAAC ABARBANEL

RABBI SAMUEL MOHILEVER

RABBI SIMON SOIFER

RABBI JACOB DAVID SLUTZKER

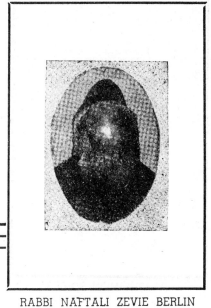

RABBI NAFTALI ZEVIE BERLIN

RABBI BERISH MEISELS

RABBI MEYER LAIBUSH MALBIM

# GLOSSARY

BAAL TAKSE—Supervisor to collect slaughtering tax

BARECHU—"Bless ye"

BAR MITZVAH—Confirmand

BETH DIN—Religious court

BETH MIDRASH—House of study

BIMAH—Pulpit

COHEN—Priest

ERETZ YISRAEL—Palestine

ESROG—Citron, ritual

FAST OF GEDALIAH—Day after Jewish New Year commemorating assassination of Gedaliah

GABBAI—Synagogue official

GAON—"Excellency," noted scholar

GEFILLTE FISH—S t u f f ed fish

GEHENNA—Hell

GEMARA—Talmud

GOLEM—Mechanical man

GOY, GOYISHE—Gentile

GULDEN—Coin

HAD GADYA—"One Kid"— Passover song

HAGGADAH—Passover ritual

HAMAN—Villain in Book of Esther

HASKALAH MOVEMENT — "Enlightenment"

HASSID—Member of pious sect

HEVRA KADDISHA—Burial society

KADDISH—Holy prayer for the dead

KOHEN—Priest (Cohen)

KOHANIM—Plural of above

KOL NIDRE—Famed Yom Kippur chant

KOPEKS—Small coins

KOSHER—Ritually edible

KITTEL—Praying cloak

KUZARI—Philosophical work by Judah Halevi

LEVITE—Descendant of Levi, Temple servant

LITVAK—Lithuanian

LULAV—Palm branch, ritually used

MACHZOR—Holiday prayer-book

451

MAGGID—Preacher

MELAMED—Teacher

MATZOTH—Unleavened bread

MAZAL TOV—Good luck

MECHUTAN—Relation or associate by marriage

MIDRASH—Homiletic literature

MILCHIGE—Dairy food

MINYAN—Prayer quorum

MITZVOTH—D i v i n e commands

MIZRACH—East

NEILAH—Final Yom Kippur prayer

NISSAN—Month in which Passover occurs

PORITZ—Wealthy farmer

POTATO KUGEL—Pudding

PURIM—Feast of Esther

RABBENU—"Our master"

RAMBAM—Maimonides

RASHI—Great commentator

REB—Mister

REBBITZIN—Rabbi's wife

REMA—Famed scholar

ROSH HASHANAH — N e w Year

RUBLE—Russian coin

SEDER—Passover ritual feast

SHABESSDIGE—Sabbath

SHADCHAN—Marriage broker

SHALOM ALECHEM—greeting

SHAVUOTH—Pentecost

SHEMONEH ESRE—M o s t important portion of prayer

SHIDDUCH—Match

SCHNORR—Beg

SCHNORRER—Beggar

SHULCHAN ARUCH—Legal code

TALMUD—Great post-biblical literature

TALLIS, TALLEISIM— prayer shawl

TASHLICH—New Year sin-cleansing ceremony

TEFILLIN—Phylacteries

TISHAH B'AB—Day of destruction of Temple

TREFAH—Ritually unclean

YOM KIPPUR—Day of Atonement

TORAH—Pentateuch

ZADDIK—Righteous man

ZADDIKIM—Plural of above

ZLOTYS—Coins

452

# CONTENTS

# CONTENTS

454

# CONTENTS

457

# ANECDOTES

458

# CONTENTS

459

# CONTENTS

CONTENTS

461

## CONTENTS

### PROVERBS

462